Teaching Social Studies Through Art

by

Sharon Jeffus

I would like to thank Josh and Cindy Wigers for all their help and encouragement. Their book Teaching Geography Through Art is highly recommended for use with this text. Go to this website to order: http://www.geomatters.com/ or call (606) 636-4678.

The picture below is of the Belgicus, done in the early 1600's. It was a map of the Low Countries or Netherlands. The map itself is of a beautiful lion in the shape of the country. It is a magnificent work of art. Students can begin this book by drawing a picture of their state or country and turning it into an animal. Make sure the basic shape stays intact. You can add a tongue, teeth, etc, as long as the state is still recognizable. Today we are very practical when we make a map. We don't care about the artistic beauty of the finished product, but about how well it tells us directions. Go to this website to see wonderful examples of map history:
http://en.wikipedia.org/wiki/Ancient_world_maps#Babylonian_world_map

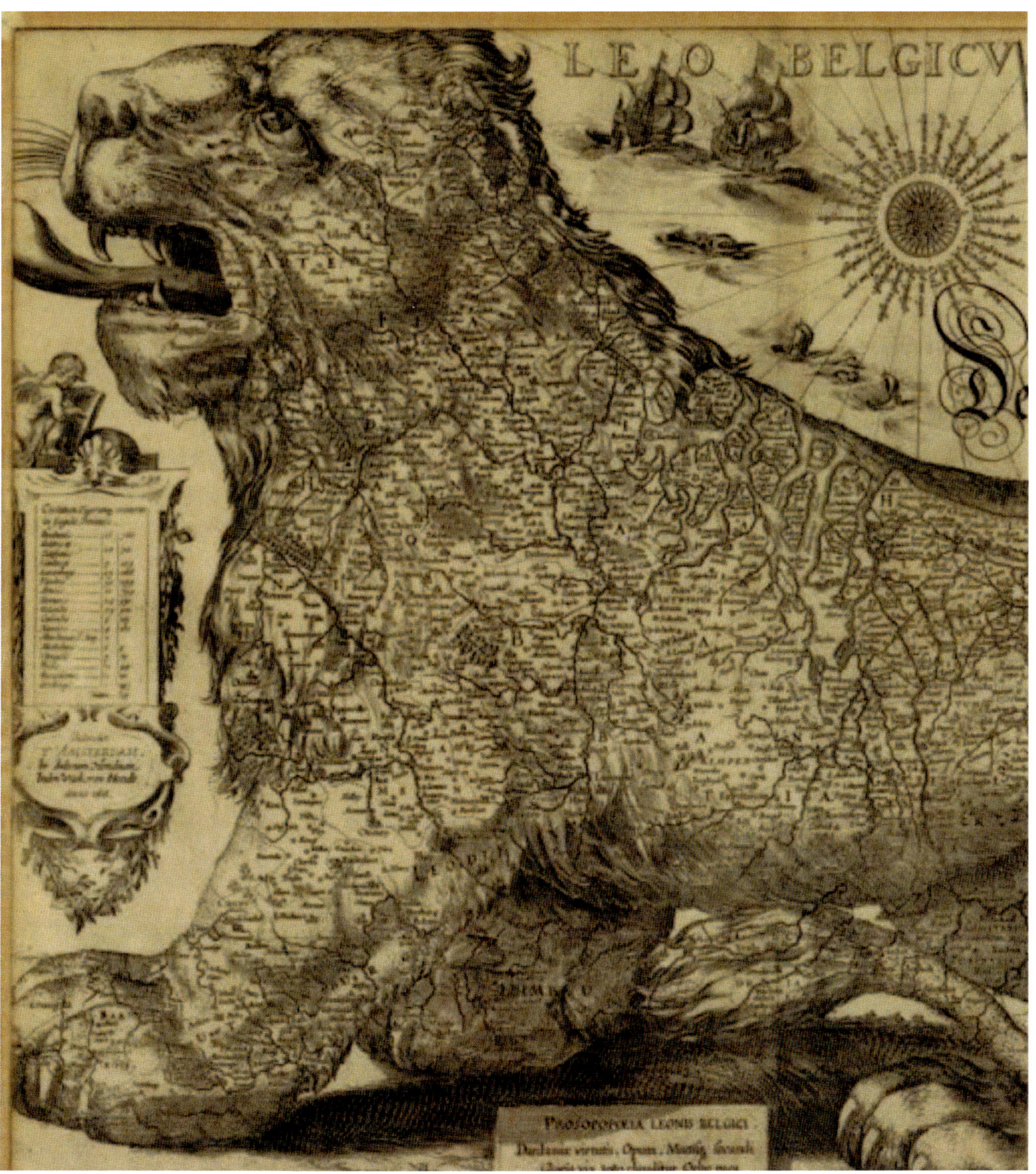

Table of Contents

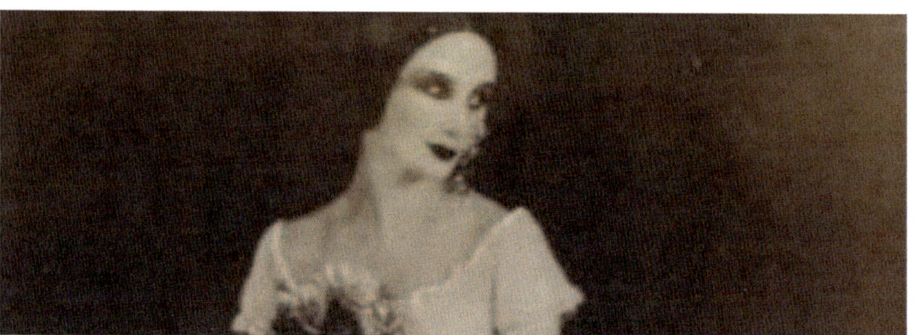

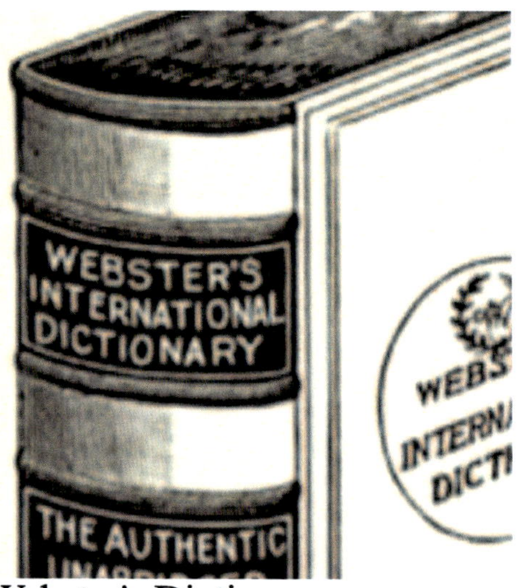

Webster's Dictionary says "that social studies is a part of a school (or college) curriculum concerned with the study of social relationships and the functioning of society and usually made up of courses in history, government, economics, civics, sociology, geography, and anthropology." This book is a supplement to this study with hands on activities and visual images for students to reinforce learning. Children remember more of what they see and do according to research. Go to this website for more information on this: http://www.cals.ncsu.edu/agexed/sae/ppt1/sld012.htm

The picture on the left is of a famous Russian ballerina, Anna Pavlova. She was called "The Swan." Ballet originated with the Italian Renaissance and was futher developed by Russia and France. Go to this website to see an animated ballerina: http://upload.wikimedia.org/wikipedia/commons/2/2d/CF4661

INTRODUCTION

This book will give activities and lessons for visual and kinesthetic learners in the study of the arts, culture and architecture of the world. Teaching Geography Through Art by Sharon Jeffus and Cindy Wiggers is carried by Geography Matters and is a recommended text to complement this study. This book is part of our art through the core package. We pray God will bless your time doing these projects and that students will be inspired and encouraged to use creativity and problem solving in the projects. Our goals in this book are as follows:

1. To develop questions and ideas to initiate and refine research.

2. To show students how to conduct research and to answer questions and evaluate information and ideas.

3. To use technological tools and other resources to locate, select and organize information.

4. To comprehend and evaluate written and visual works.

5. To discover and evaluate patterns and relationships in information, ideas and structures.

6.To identify, analyze and compare the institutions, traditions and art forms of past and present societies.

7. To process and techniques for the production, exhibition or performance of one or more of the visual or performed arts.

8. To know the principles and elements of different art forms

9. To know the vocabulary to explain perceptions about and evaluations of works in dance, music, theater and visual arts.

10. To understand visual and performing arts in historical and cultural contexts.

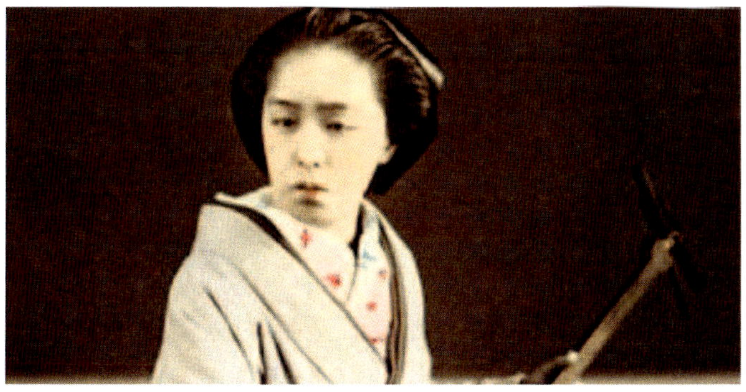

Costume and dancc are a part of the culture of a country. Geisha's are traditional female Japanese entertainers. They perform various Japanese arts, such as classical music and dance. They are an important part of the culture of Japan. The picture on the left shows how they traditionally dress.

Maps

The picture on the left shows planets to scale with other planets. We live on earth and showing other planets gives us an idea of how big the place we live really is in relation to the universe. A cartographer is someone who makes maps for a living. Do you believe there are people who make moon maps today? Go to this website to see a wonderful picture of the moon: http://en.wikipedia.org/wiki/Image:Lunar_libration_with_phase_Oct_2007.gif

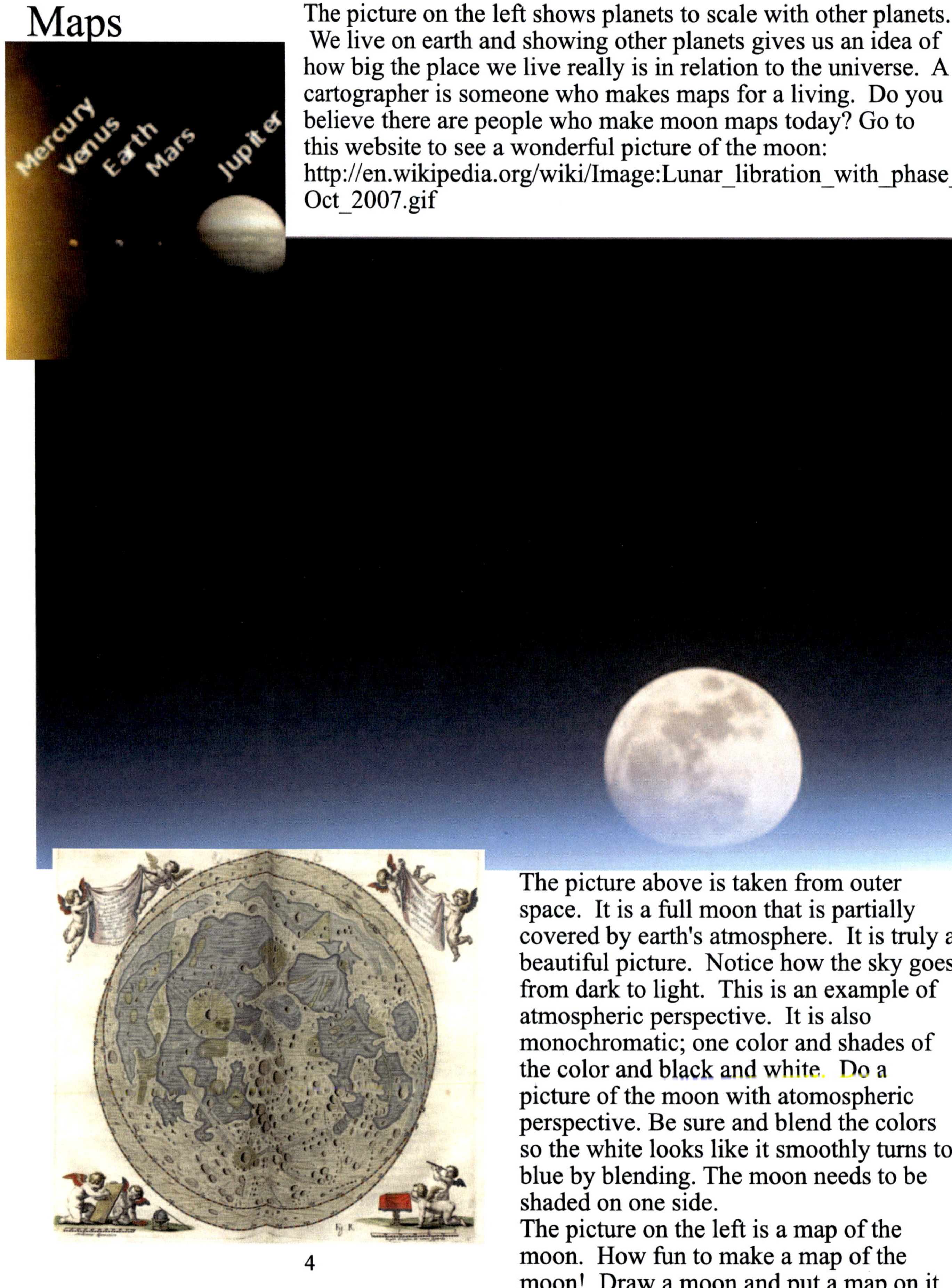

The picture above is taken from outer space. It is a full moon that is partially covered by earth's atmosphere. It is truly a beautiful picture. Notice how the sky goes from dark to light. This is an example of atmospheric perspective. It is also monochromatic; one color and shades of the color and black and white. Do a picture of the moon with atomospheric perspective. Be sure and blend the colors so the white looks like it smoothly turns to blue by blending. The moon needs to be shaded on one side.

The picture on the left is a map of the moon. How fun to make a map of the moon! Draw a moon and put a map on it just like Hevelius did in the 1600's.

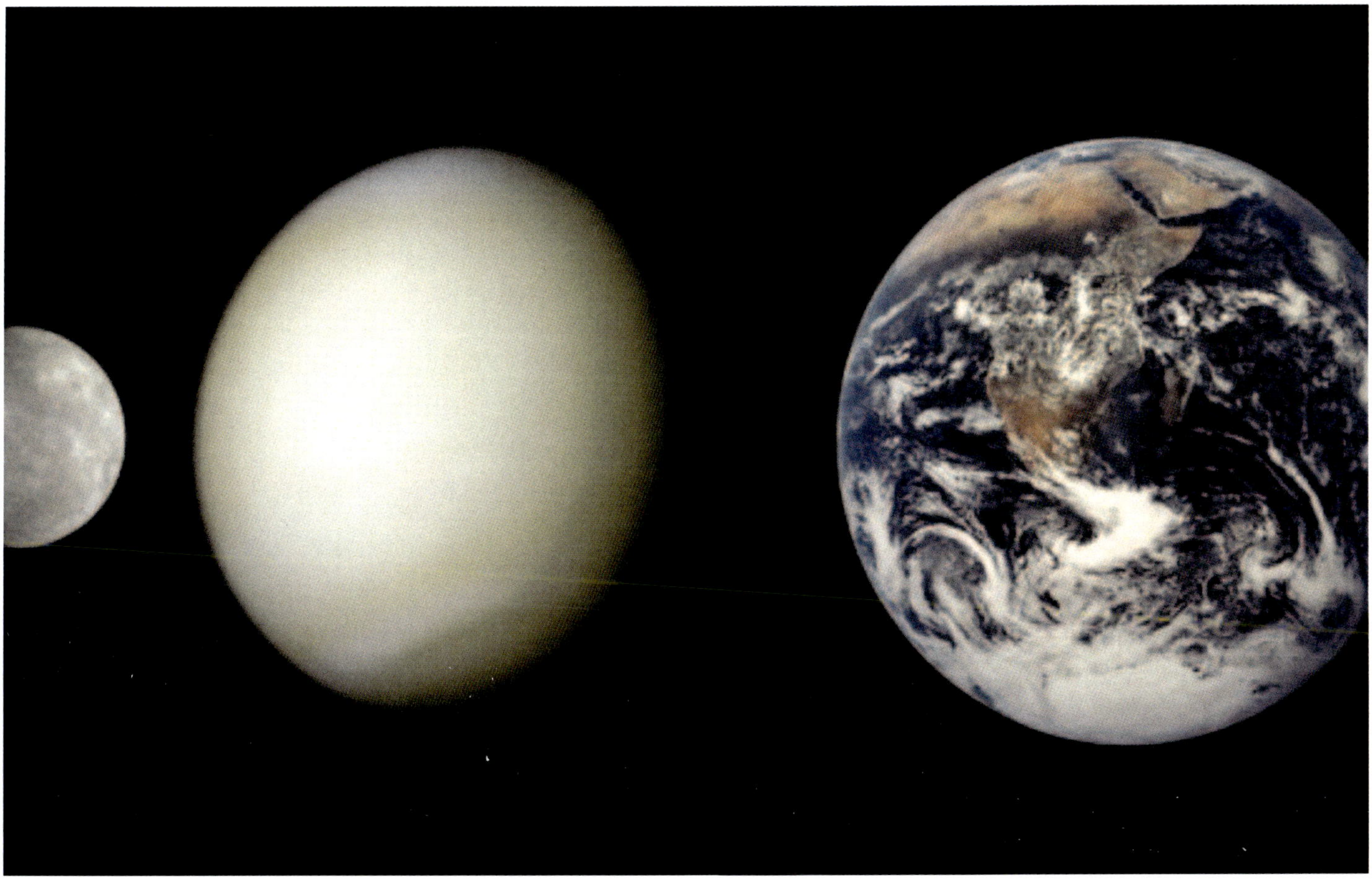

The Blue Marble is the most famous photograph of the earth, taken by the crew of the Apollo 17 Spacecraft at a distance of 45,000 kilometers. A wonderful art project is to take black paper and oil pastels and make a picture of outer space. If you mix and blend the colors well, you can use shading to make your planets look three dimensional.

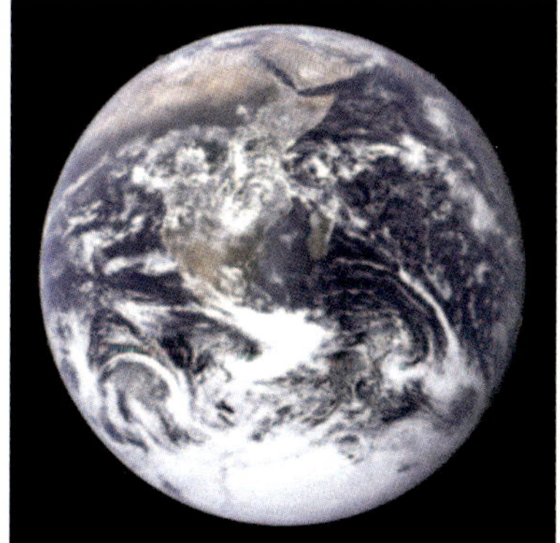

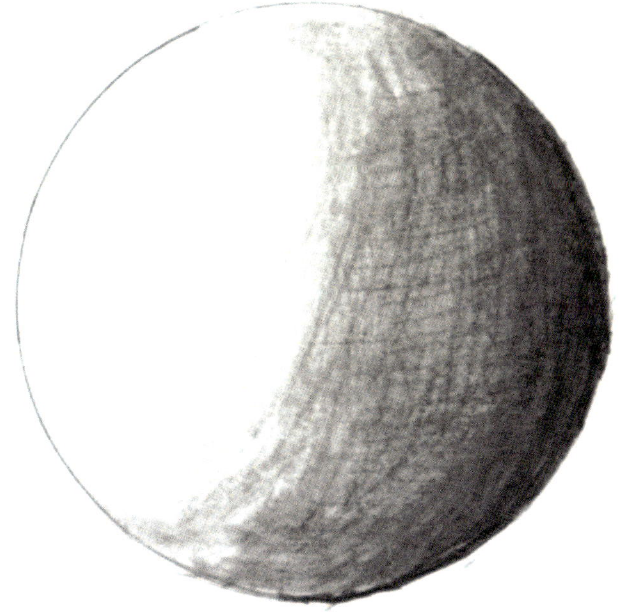

Culture is manifested in music, literature, lifestyle, painting and sculpture, theater and film and similar things.The folk art of a country is a part of their culture. Minhwa (folk painting) style is a part of the culture of Korea. In the same way, Wycinanki (pronounced Vee-chee-non-key) is Polish folk art paper cutouts that are symbolic of the culture of Poland.
Bridges of the world, lighthouses of the world, deserts of the world, mountains of the world, cities of the world, oceans of the world, and waterways of the world are all part of our human culture. In Austria, a large part of the culture of one of its greatest cities is the opera. Vienna is famous for its many opera houses. The three pictures below are of opera houses in Vienna.

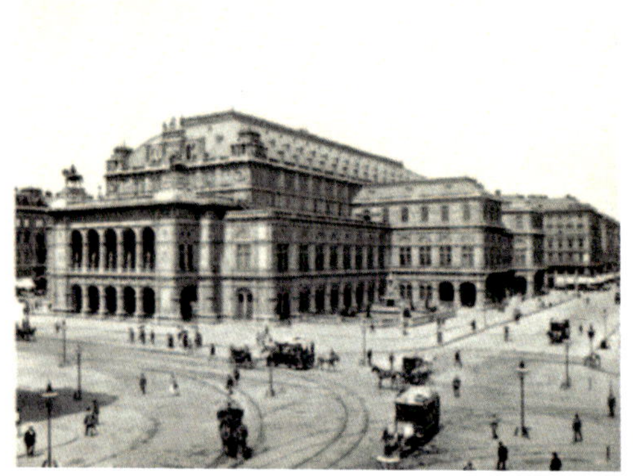

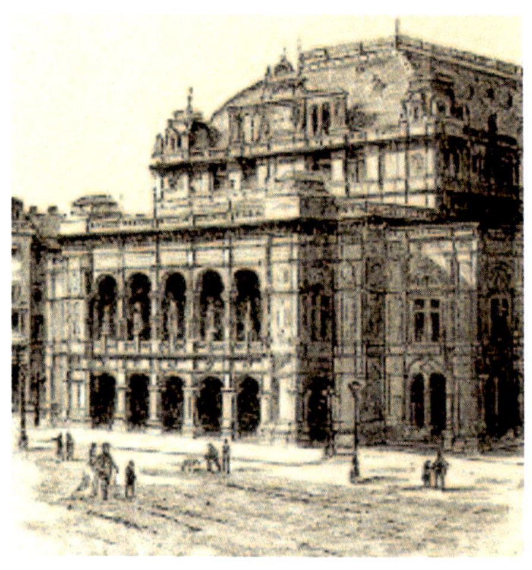

The drawing above is of the building in the picture below. The building was the first major building on the Wiener Ringstrae commissioned by the controversial Viennese "city expansion fund" in 1861 and was completed in 1869. Drawings like the above left were done before the invention of the camera. Draw the picture below using a grid. Go the end of the book to see how to do and use a grid.

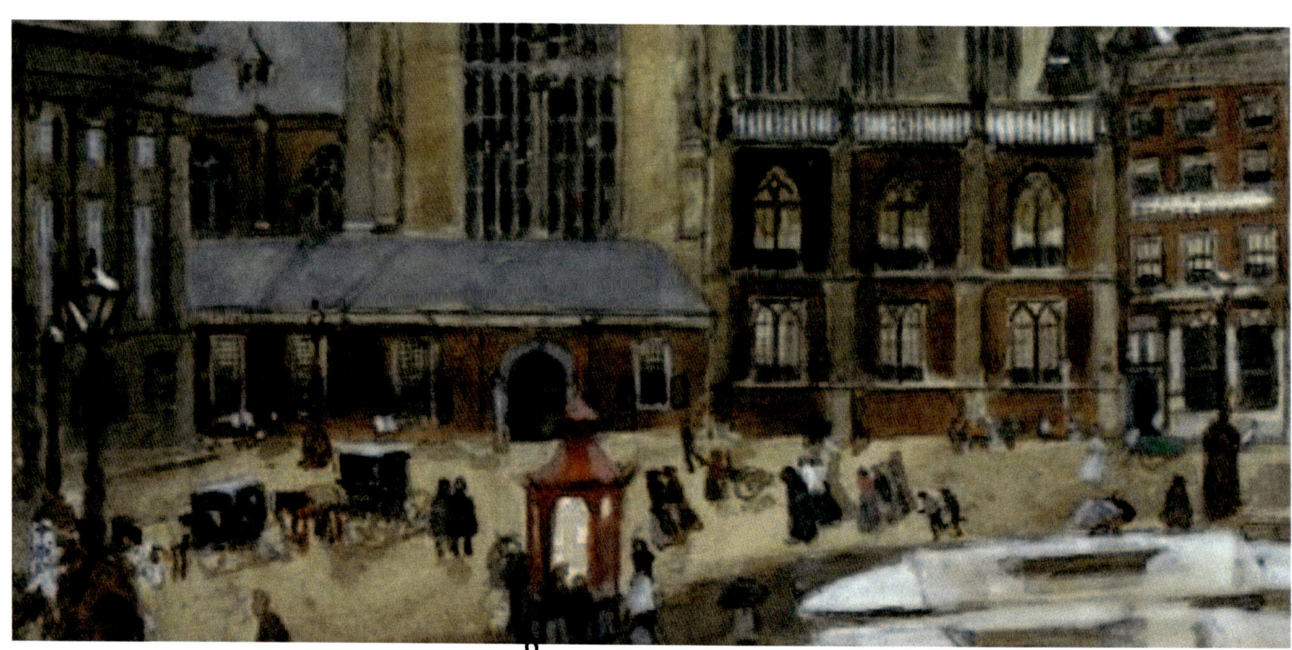

Lighthouses of the World

Most countries on the coast of the oceans have lighthouses. A lighthouse is powered by a light on the top to show ships where the coast is during storms. Practically every large country with a sea coastal area had a lighthouse. There are some people in life who are also a "lighthouse" to those around them. Many people believe that light is Jesus. Then spake Jesus again unto them, saying, I am the light of the world: he that followeth me shall not walk in darkness, but shall have the light of life. (John 8:12)

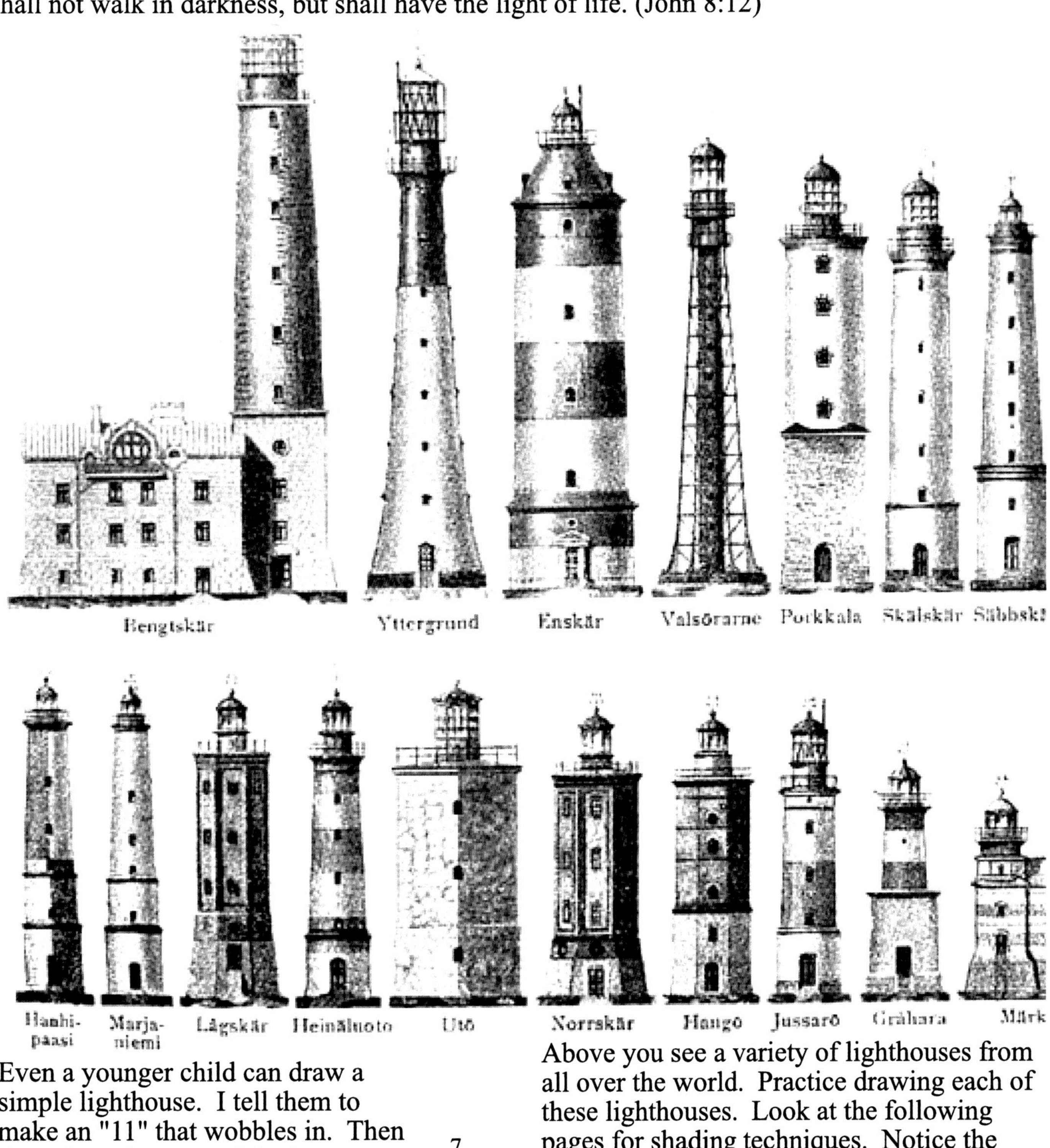

Above you see a variety of lighthouses from all over the world. Practice drawing each of these lighthouses. Look at the following pages for shading techniques. Notice the variety of shading, shadow and texture you see on each one of them.

Even a younger child can draw a simple lighthouse. I tell them to make an "11" that wobbles in. Then they close the top and the bottom.

Drawing a lighthouse:

Most lighthouses are cylinders. The lighthouse on the right can be drawn using a variety of cylinders. Notice the reflection in the water. You can squint your eyes and see different values. Notice the details. Drawing requires observation and practice. Be sure and put the details you see in the picture.

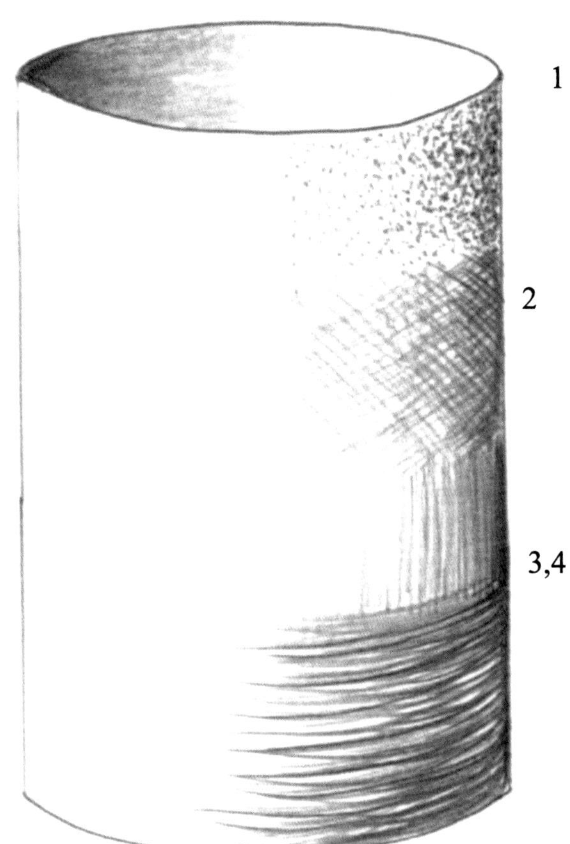

Shading:

#5 This type of shading is called smudging. You color with your pencil and use your finger or a smudge stick to make the cylinder look three dimensional.

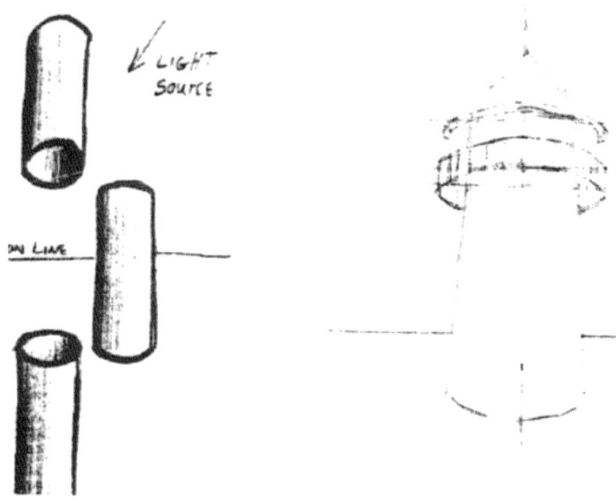

#1 Stipling is shading using smaill dots.

#2 This type of shading is called crosshatching. You cross lines to show variations in value.

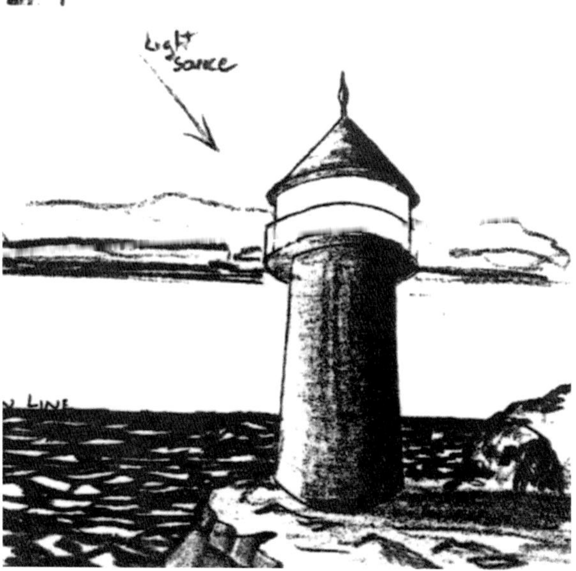

#3, 4 These kinds of shading are made by stroking your pencil with lines. It is called stroking.

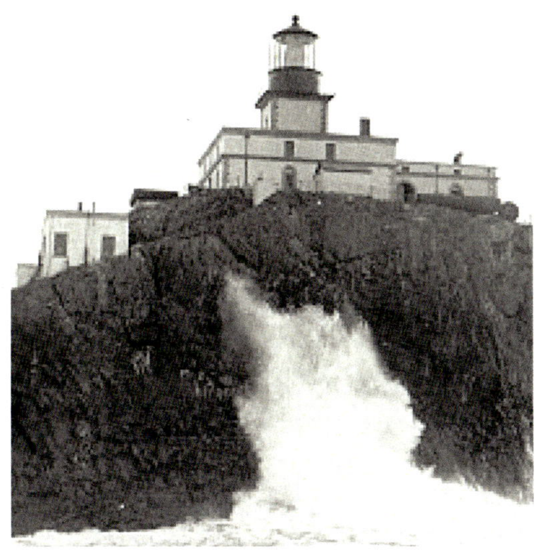

The beauty of this lighthouse in Wales is that the seascape in front of it is so wonderful.

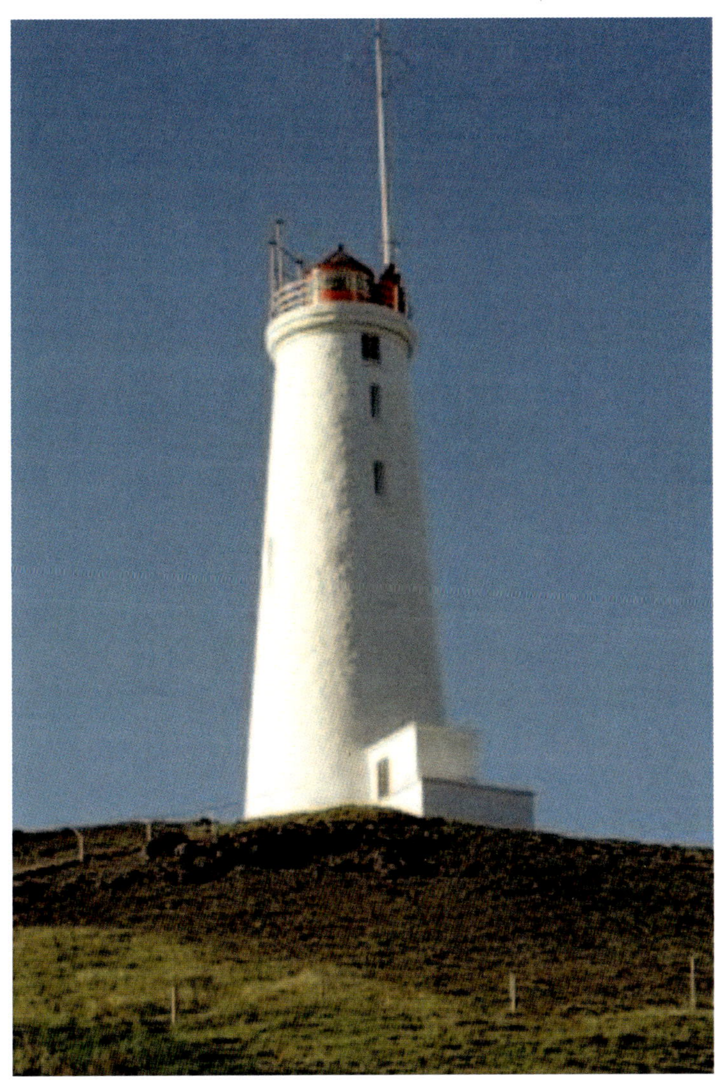

This lighthouse in Poland has a building on the bottom.

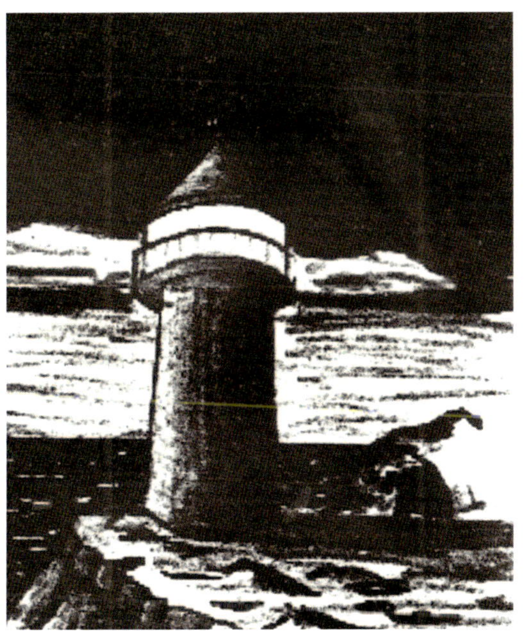

This lighthouse in Brazil is red and white striped. You can still see the shading. Draw this lighthouse and make it striped.

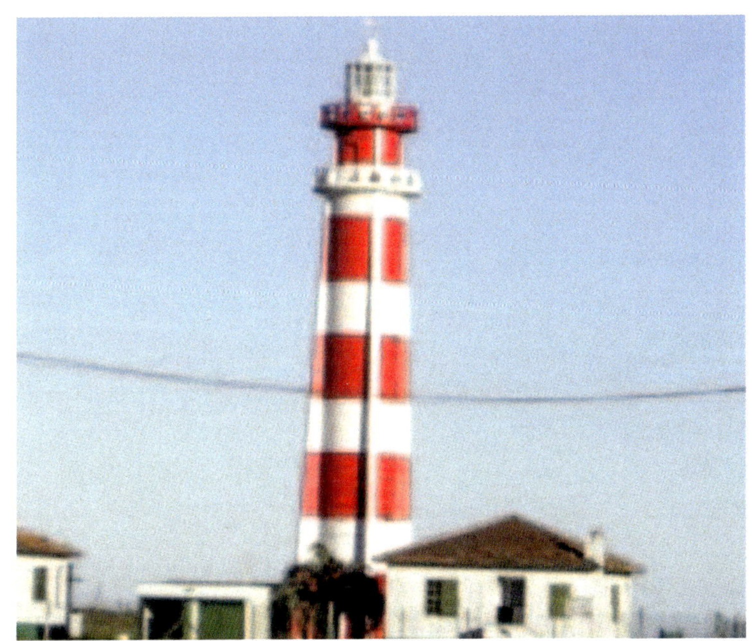

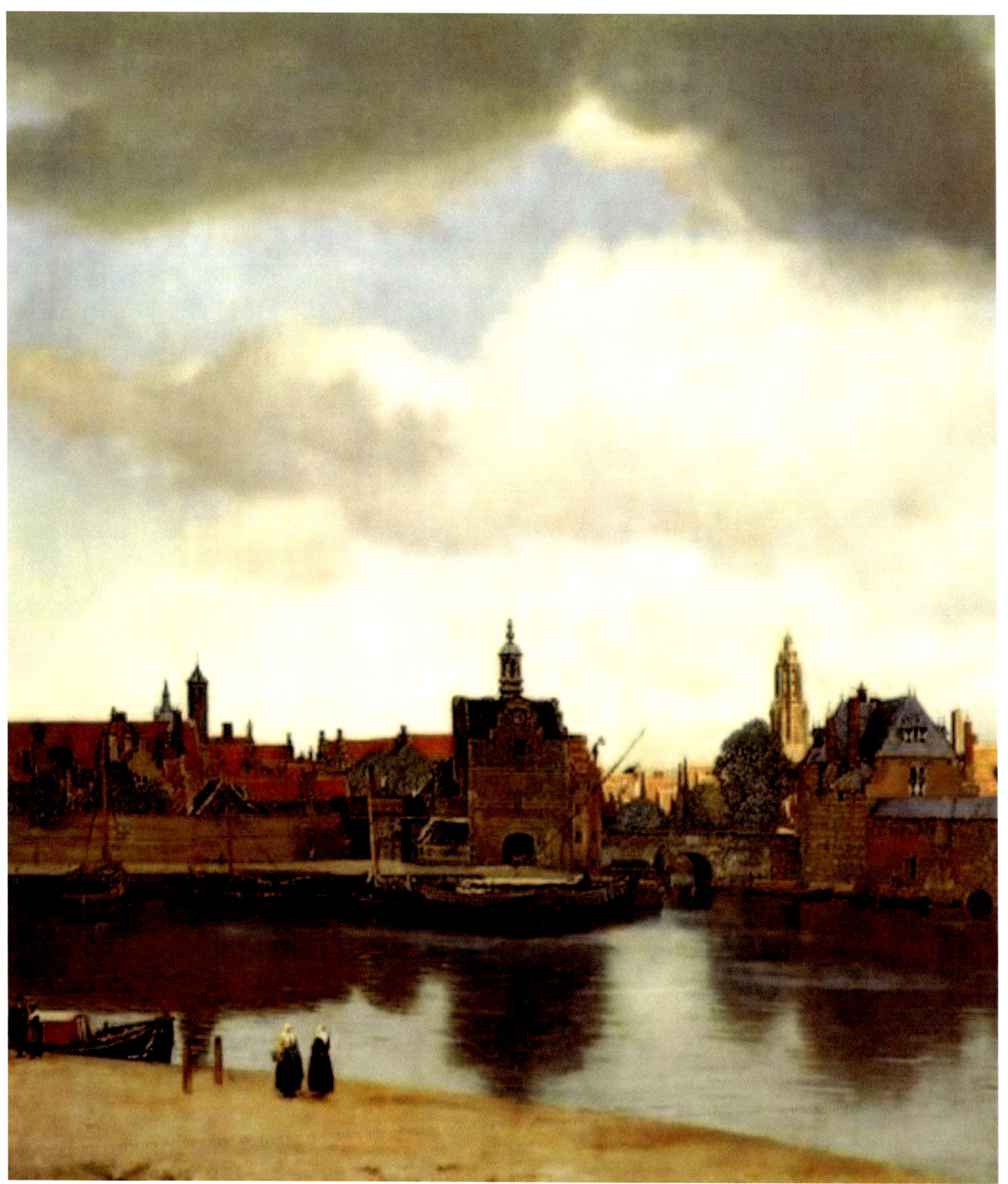

Artists paint many beautiful locations in a variety of countries. Vermeer's "View of Delft" shows us what a town in Holland was like in the early 1600's. Today we could take a picture with a camera. Artists pictured history, culture, and geography before the invention of the camera. When portraits were done, sometimes people would pose for hours. Try to stay perfectly still for one minute. It is not easy.

A **harbor** is an area of water that is deep enough that boats can be protected from winds, waves, etc. and can safely anchor.

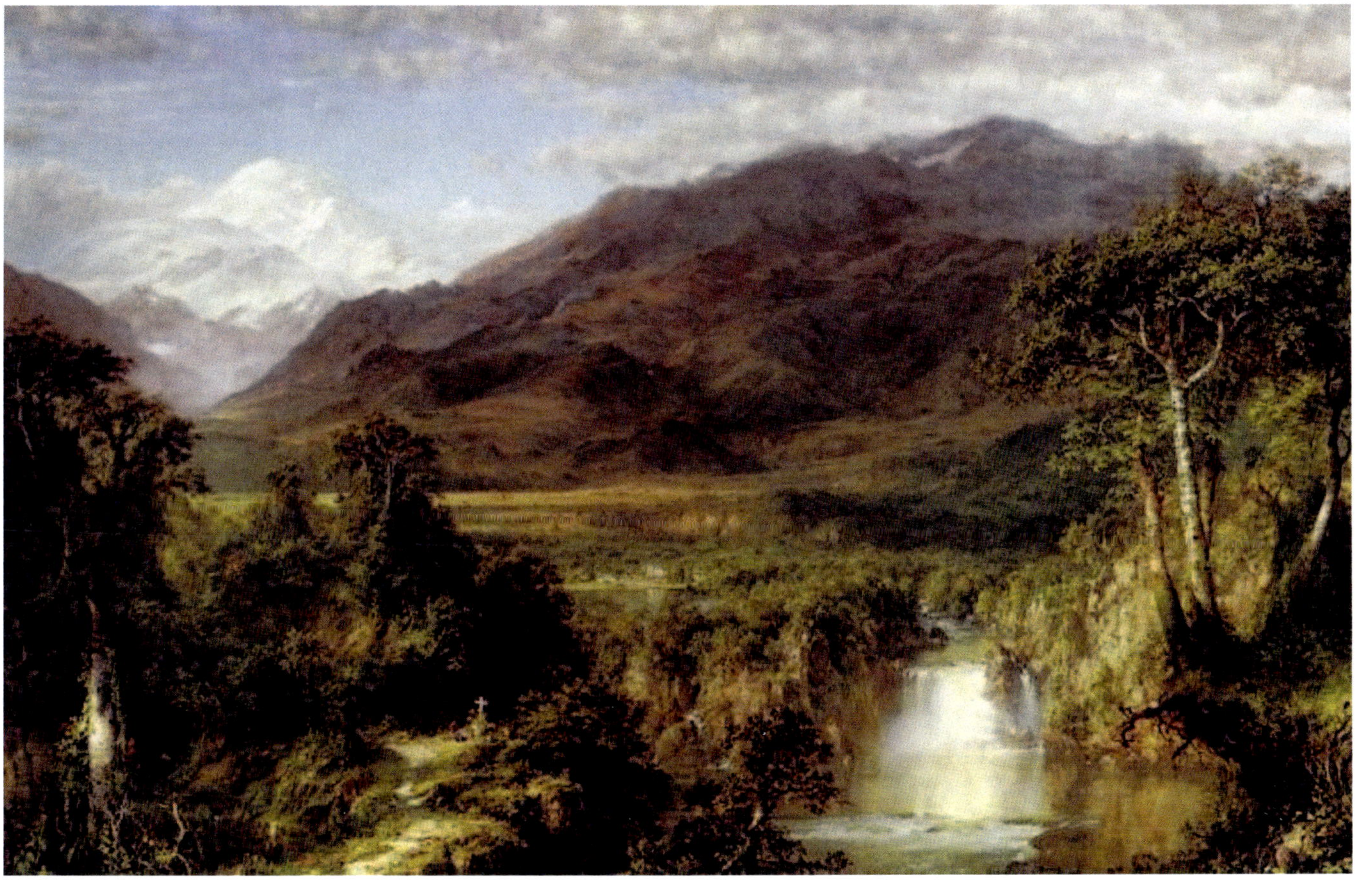

"Heart of the Andes" in South America is a very famous picture. Heart of the Andes, oil on canvas, 167.9 × 302.9 cm is by the artist Frederic Church. It depicts the beautiful scenery of the mountains in the Andes. Notice the mountains in the background are lighter. The mountains in the foreground are darker. Do a painting of this and use a sponge for the trees. Go to this website for great tips on landscape paintings: http://painting.about.com/od/landscapes/a/landscapetips.htm and practice paintings.

Below is an oil-painting, by Adrien Lavieille (1848-1920), a french landscape painter, representing Moret-sur-Loing, a small town near Fontainebleau, in south-east of Paris. Do you have a favorite place near you that you would like others to appreciate and enjoy? Get busy and paint it.

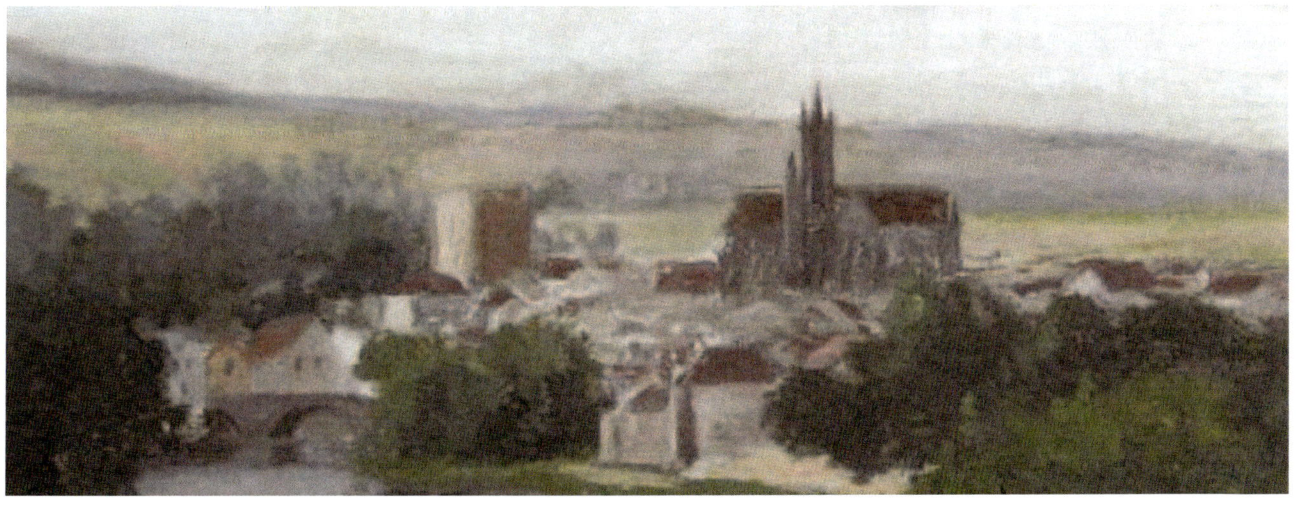

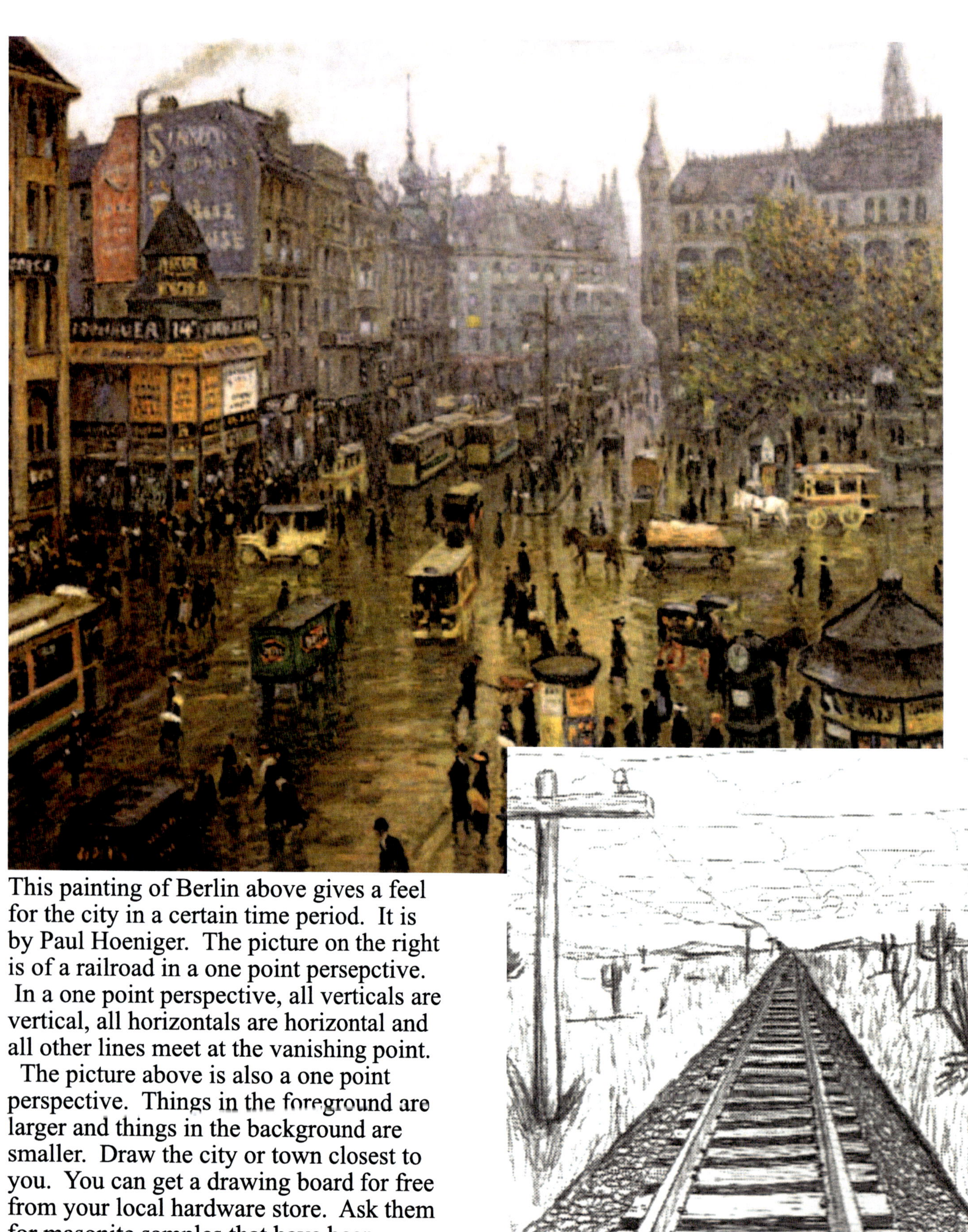

This painting of Berlin above gives a feel for the city in a certain time period. It is by Paul Hoeniger. The picture on the right is of a railroad in a one point persepctive. In a one point perspective, all verticals are vertical, all horizontals are horizontal and all other lines meet at the vanishing point.

The picture above is also a one point perspective. Things in the foreground are larger and things in the background are smaller. Draw the city or town closest to you. You can get a drawing board for free from your local hardware store. Ask them for masonite samples that have been discontinued. You will get a very smooth board of the perfect size to sit outside and draw your city or town. You can even create a city around your railroad track.

All around the world are buildings by a variety of religions including this one called the Tikal in Central America built sometime around 800 B.C.
Artists draw and paint these places and it becomes part of a country's culture and history.

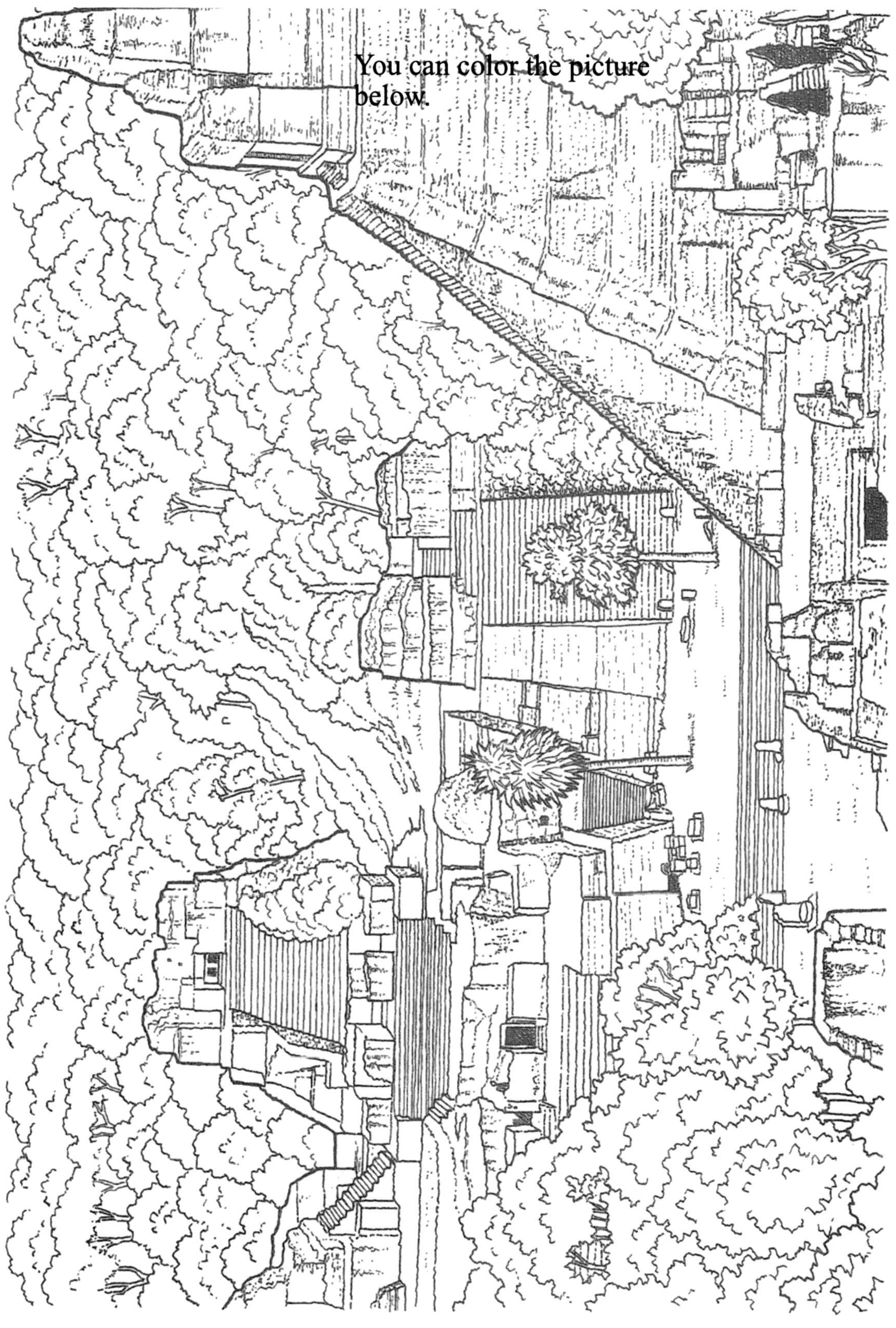

Tikal, which was once a thriving metropolis, is now the most impressive and magnificent Mayan ruin in Central America, located in the steamy jungles of El Peten province, on the Yucatan peninsula of what is now Guatemala. It seems to have been inhabited from 800 B.C. to A.D. 900, with over 100,000 inhabitants at its peak around A.D. 750. The great pyramidal temples that dominated the skyline used to be covered in bright colors—some of them completely red.

Around A.D. 900, Tikal declined as Maya civilization in the re
mysterious collapse—whether because of overpopulation, enviro
dation, drought, or warfare, no one knows. Tikal was abandone
centuries, as its buildings were reclaimed by the jungle, became a
of its structures have now been restored, but most remain by the
etation that is home to howler monkeys and brightly colored bir

Another thing that indicates culture is a country's crafts. According to German legend, nutcrackers were given as keepsakes to bring good luck to your family and protect your home. Every part of the world has similar symbols for protection of the home, from the Mexican God's Eye to the pagoda roofs of the orient, people were always trying to protect their property. The legend says that a nutcracker represents power and serves like a trusty watch dog guarding your family from danger. A nutcracker not only cracks nuts, but bares his teeth and can look very frightening. Children love to draw and color a nutcracker. It is made from basic shapes. They can learn to shade the cylinders and add texture to the hair.
Patterns are formed by buttons. Older students can create designer nutcrackers with a theme. They can create ninja nutcrackers, lion nutcrackers or come up with any number of original themes.

Cuckoo clocks and nutcrackers are examples of crafts from the Black Forest.

Nutcrackers

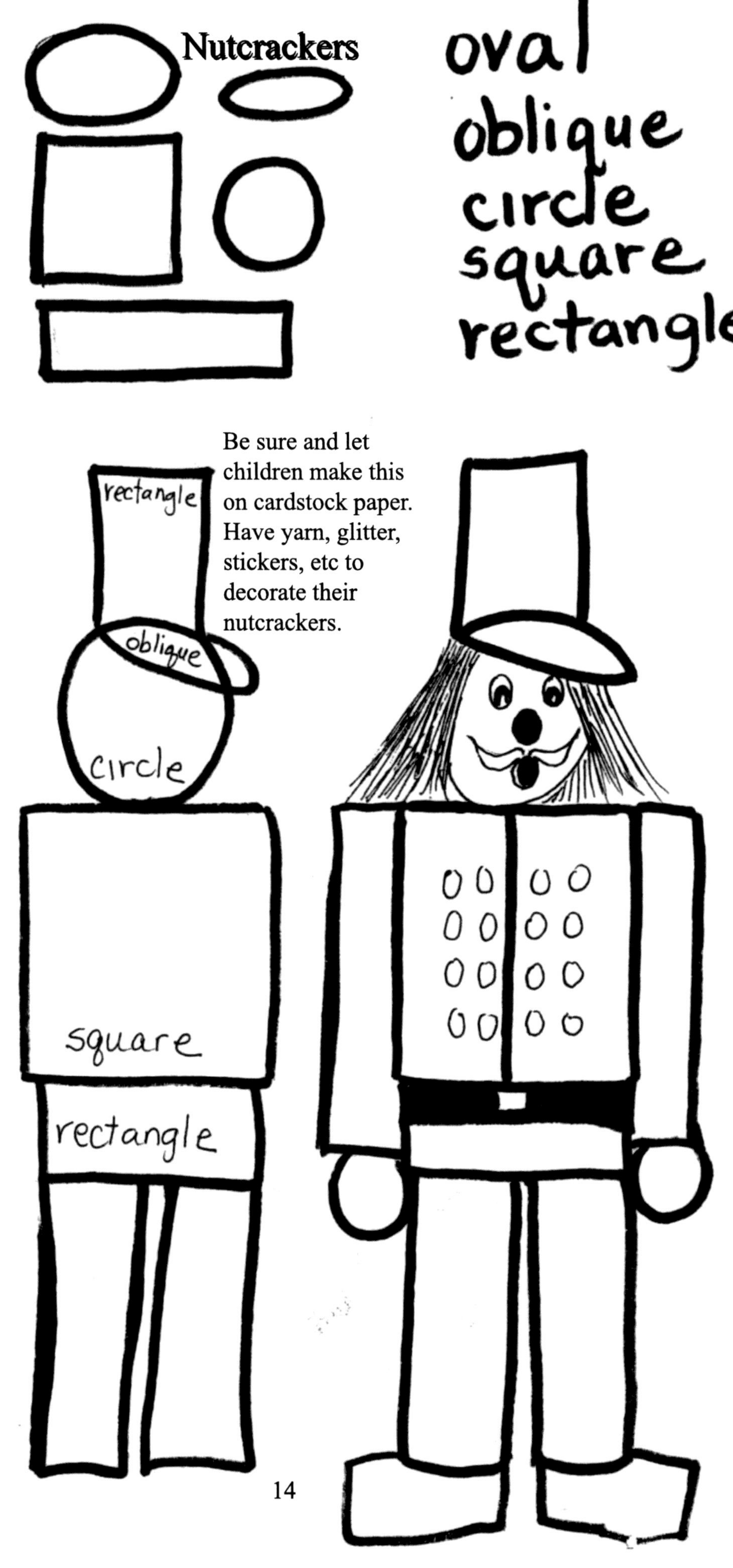

Be sure and let children make this on cardstock paper. Have yarn, glitter, stickers, etc to decorate their nutcrackers.

Cuckoo Clocks

Children can cut out the pattern for the cuckoo clock on this page. The middle os the cuckoo clock can be the colorwhel. If you accordion fold a piece of paper and then glue a bird on it, you can glue it on your cuckoo clock.

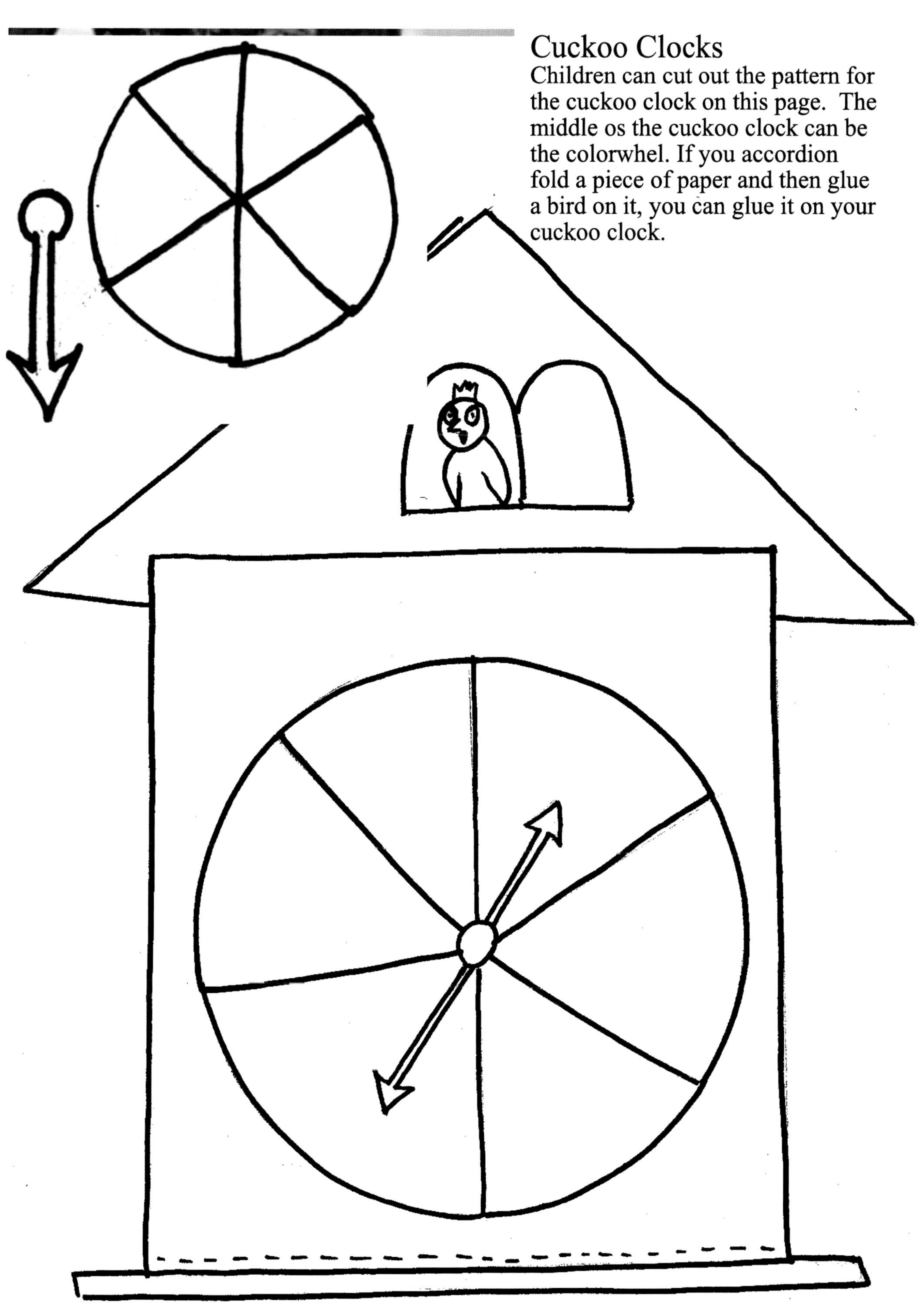

Nutcracker Ballet

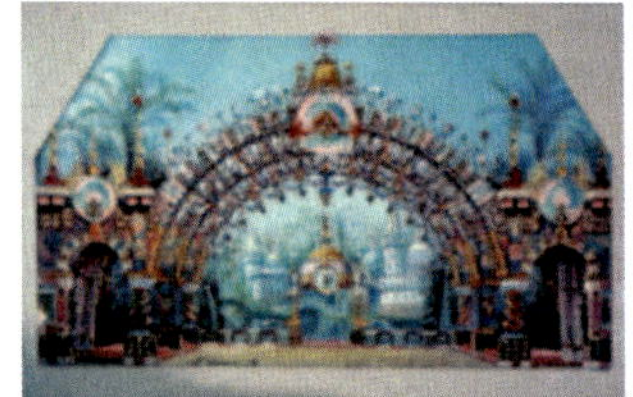

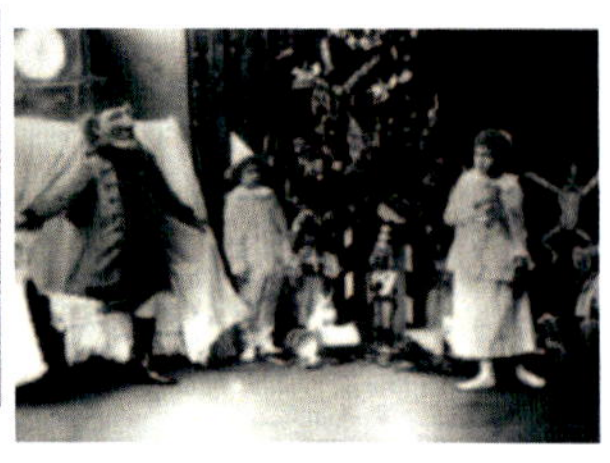

There is a very famous ballet called "The Nutcraker." You can go to this website to read all about it: http://en.wikipedia.org/wiki/The_Nutcracker. It is about toys coming to life and is very popular around the Christmas season. The music of a country is an important part of its culture. Ballet is an important part of dance.

The Cuckoo Clock is also from Germany and the Black Forest. A cuckoo clock is a clock, usually with a pendulum, that strikes the hours using small bellows and pipes and imitates the call of the Common Cuckoo. The cuckoo call was installed in almost every kind of cuckoo clock since the middle of the eighteenth century and has remained almost without variation until the present. One of my favorite projects with children is to make a colorwheel clock and find a bird that is every color in the colorwheel. You can purchase a clock now that makes the sound of the bird of that color when the clock strikes the hour. I like them to call there clock an "It's time to say I LOVE YOU! clock."

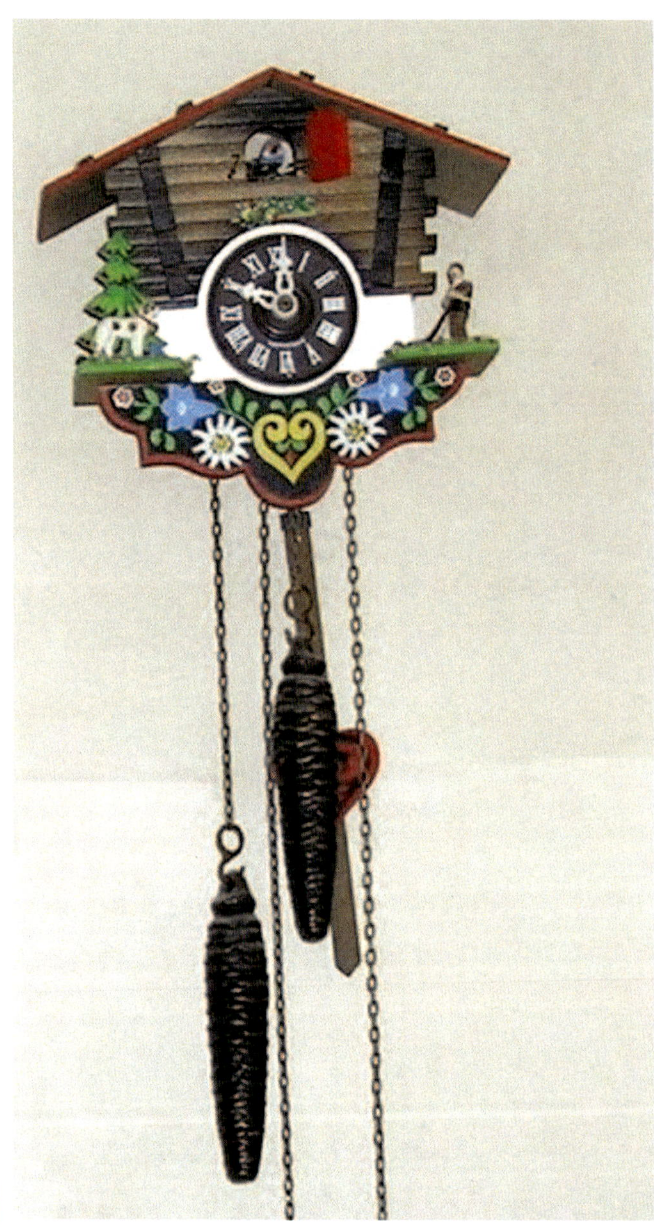

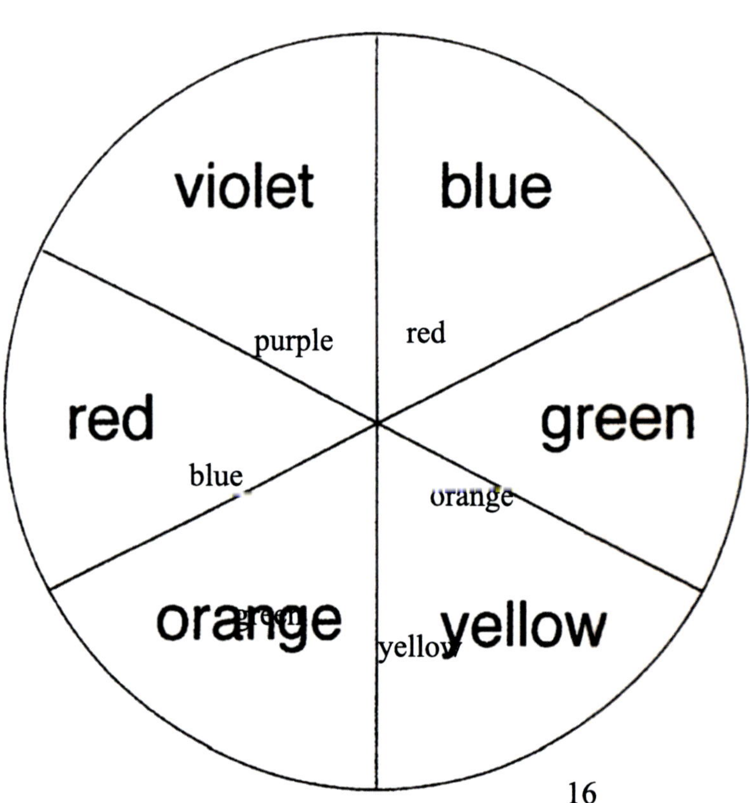

Children can easily make a cuckoo clock that is a colorwheel. They can use a brad and make an arrow that goes round and round. They can decorate their clock with flowers and houses and different patterns.

Flora and Fauna of the World:

Go to this website to hear birds singing from a variety of gardens worldwide:
http://voices.gardenweb.com/birds/

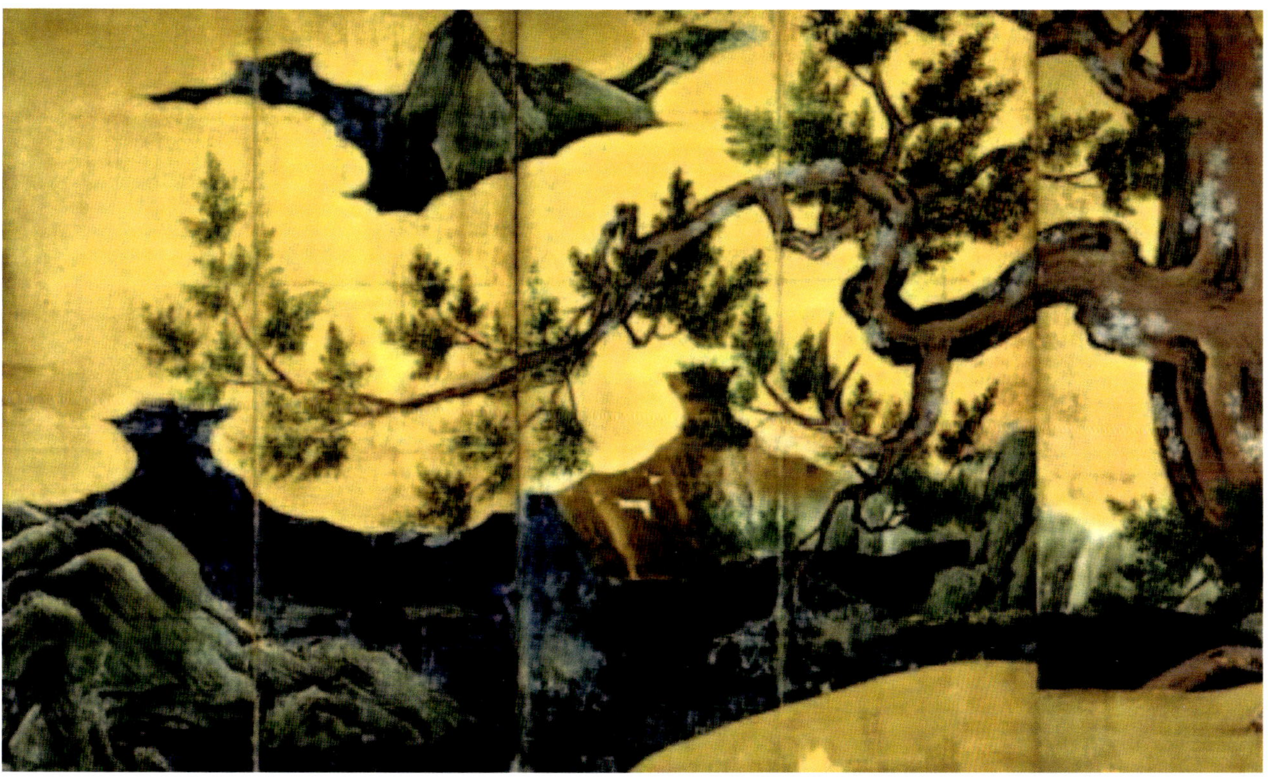

The paintings above and below are Oriental and done in washes. When a stroke is painted, it cannot be changed or erased. When using washes, you always want to go lighter than you think is necessary. You can always get darker, but you can't lighten up the colors. This makes ink and wash painting a technically difficult art. The paper is generally not heavy, but very lightweight. Rice paper is sometimes used.

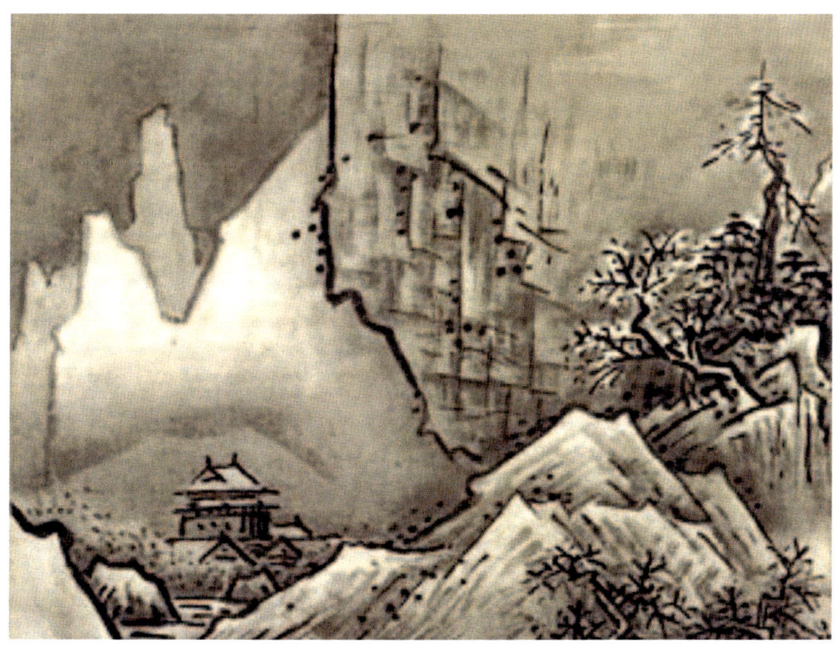

The pictures on the immediate left and bottom are done by the master artist Bierdstadt. Notice the atmospheric perspective in both pictures. The trees get lighter as they go back into the distance. There are less details.

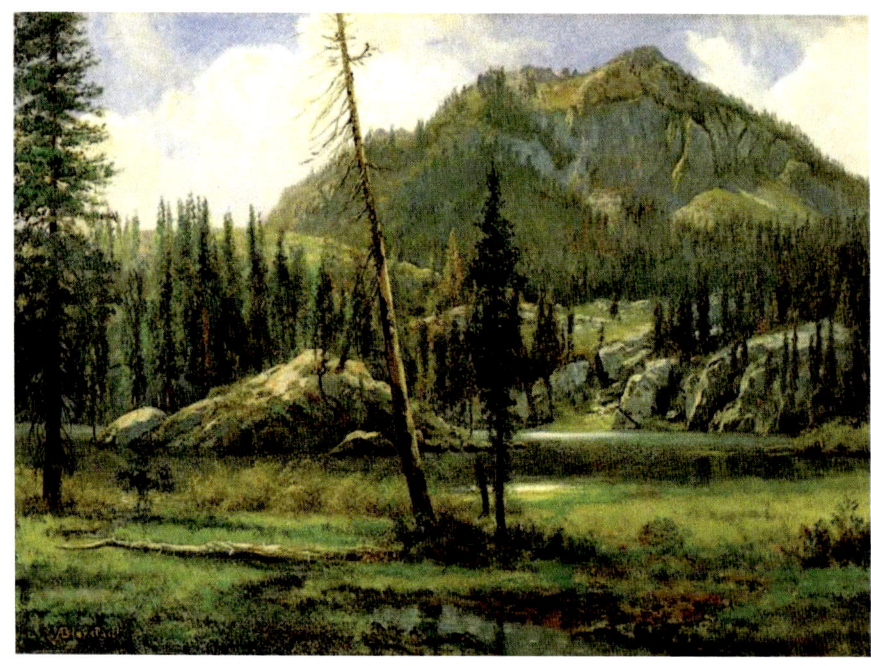

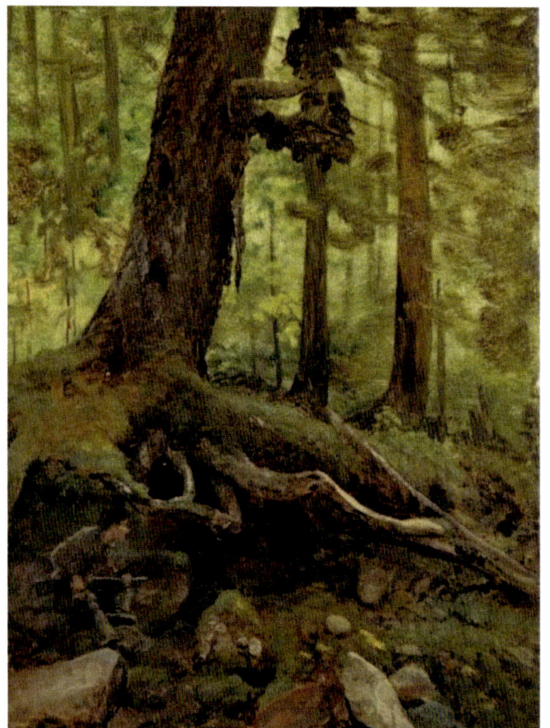

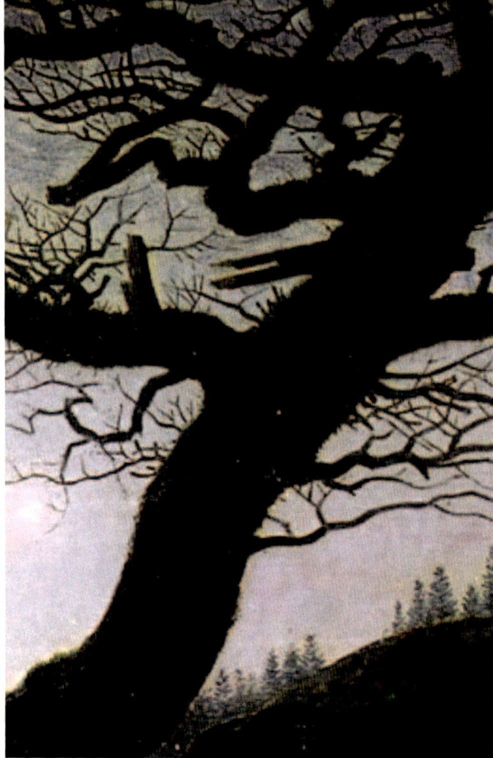

Casper Friedrich did the tree on the immediate left. He was a Romanticist.

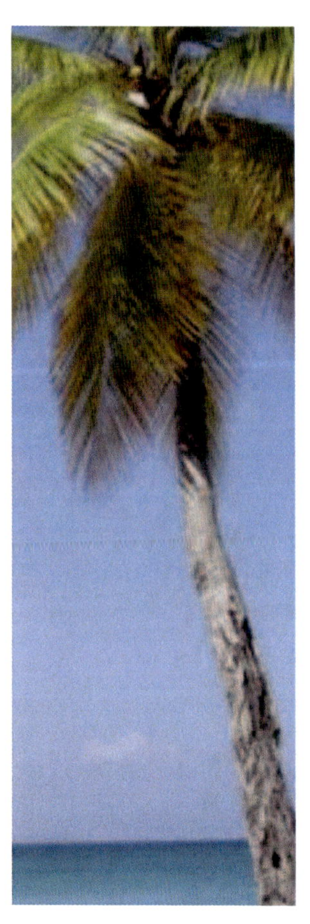

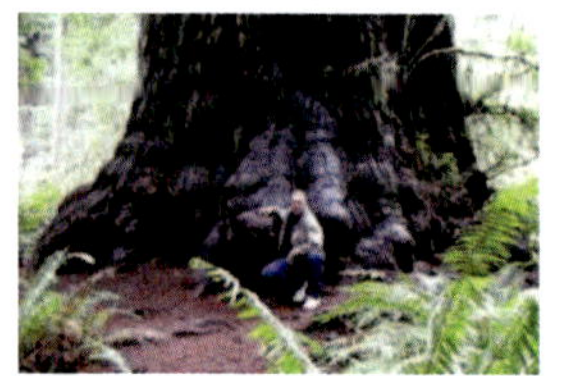

Be creative and make a large tree with a door in the trunk.

Redwood trees are seen in California, such as the one on the left.
The picture on the right is of a Palm tree in Martinique. Kinds of trees sometimes tells us where we are in the world.

I always tell students to start with the letter "Y" and make that the tree trunk. If they keep adding Y's that are smaller and smaller, they have the branches of a tree!

Start by finding an actual tree. This is one near my house next to a meadow.

Now draw individual leaves. Using light and dark leaves to intensify the shadows, give depth to the shading and add highlights. Draw individual leaves apart from the shadows or groups of leaves. These individual leaves can be "not connected" to anything, or you may want to draw fine lines to them to indicate the small twigs. Lastly, draw the ground line.

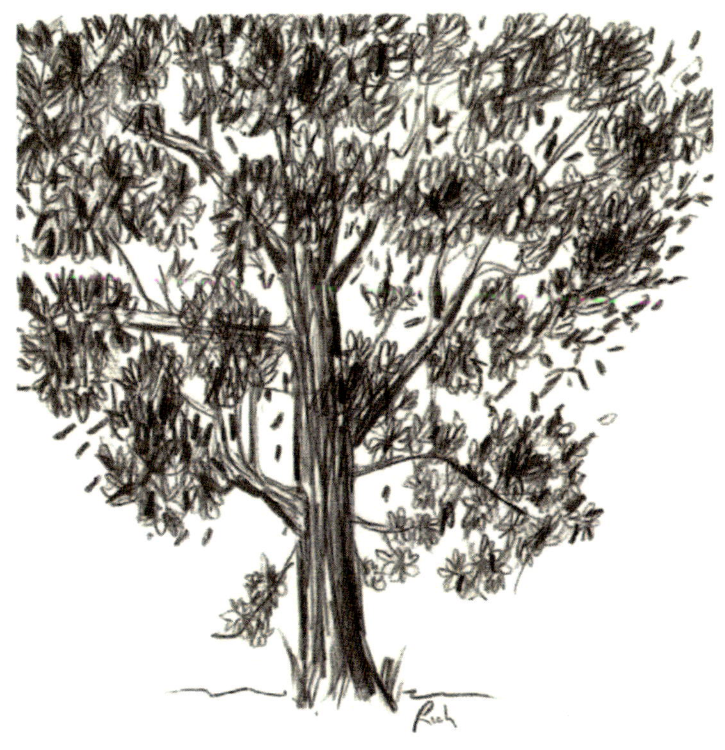

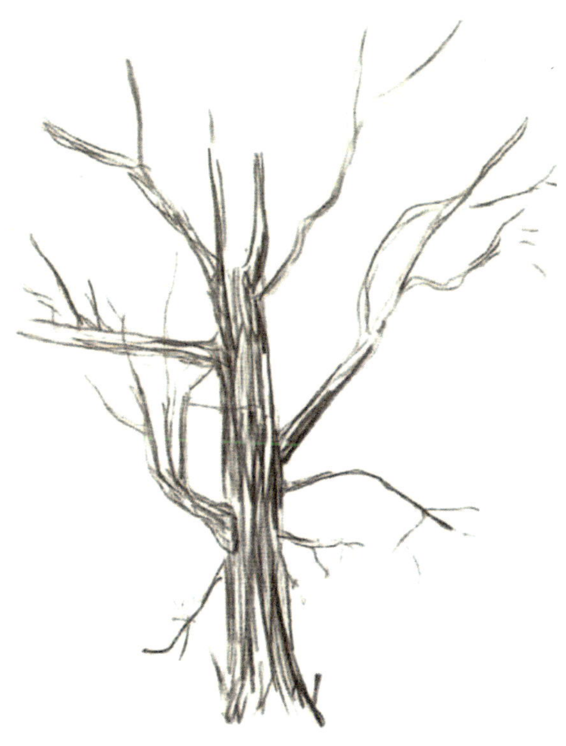

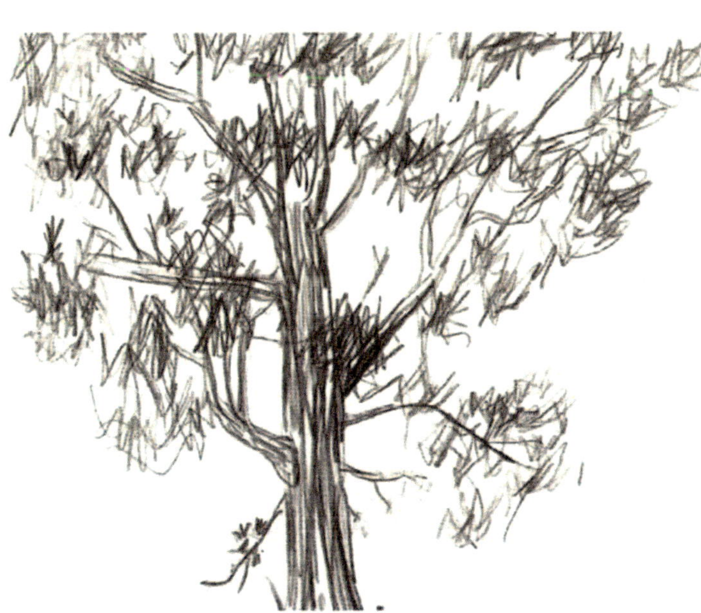

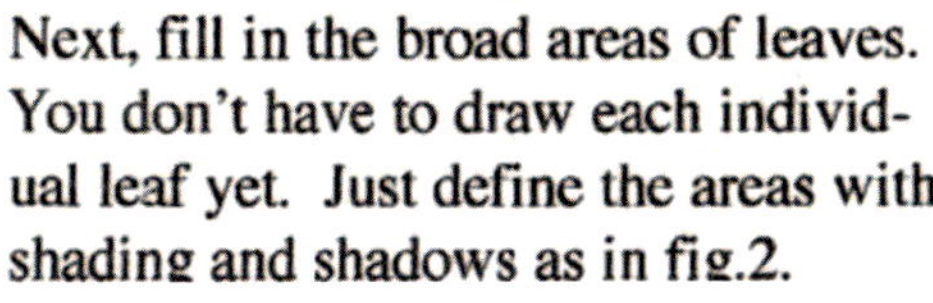

Next, fill in the broad areas of leaves. You don't have to draw each individual leaf yet. Just define the areas with shading and shadows as in fig.2.

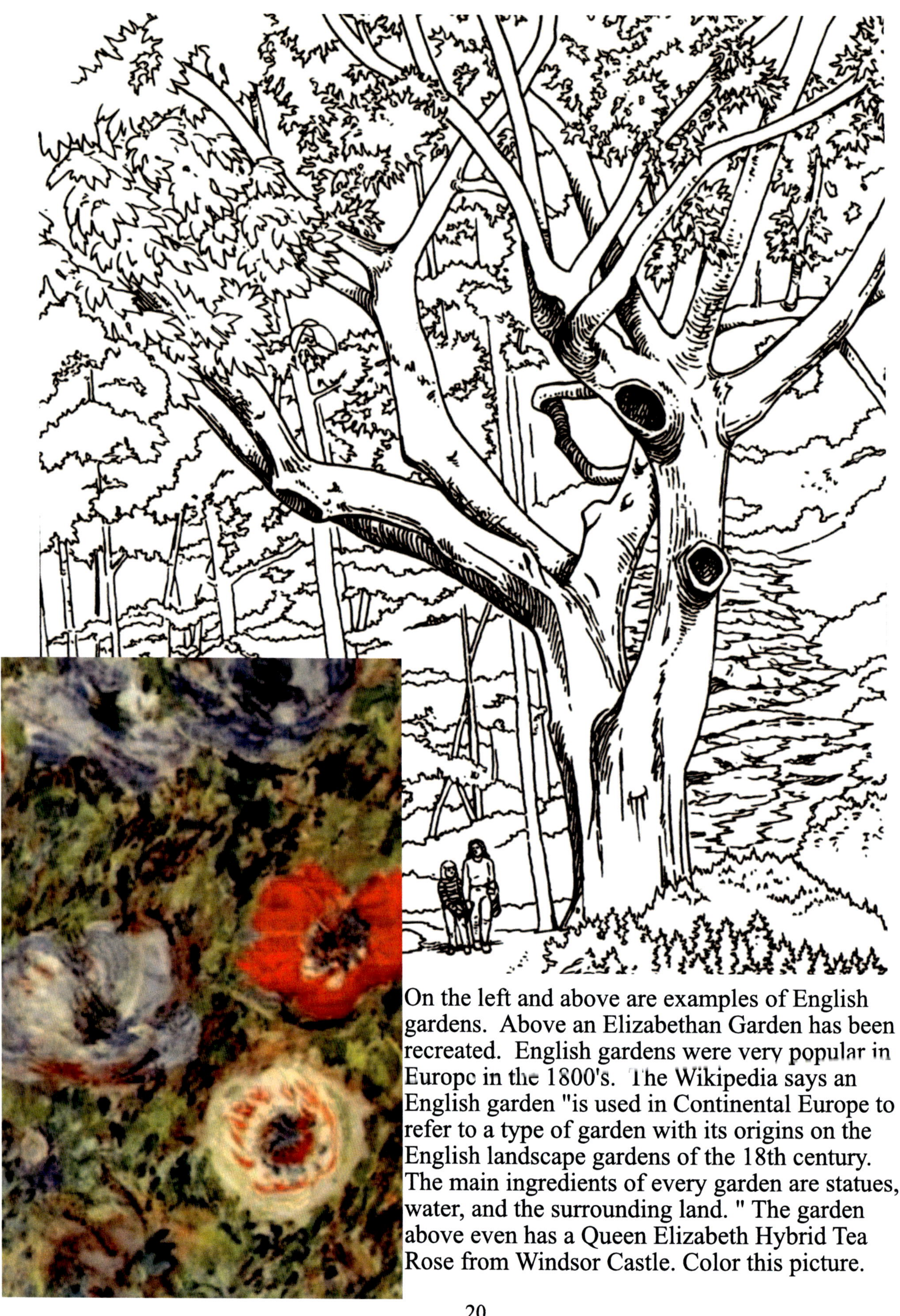

On the left and above are examples of English gardens. Above an Elizabethan Garden has been recreated. English gardens were very popular in Europe in the 1800's. The Wikipedia says an English garden "is used in Continental Europe to refer to a type of garden with its origins on the English landscape gardens of the 18th century. The main ingredients of every garden are statues, water, and the surrounding land. " The garden above even has a Queen Elizabeth Hybrid Tea Rose from Windsor Castle. Color this picture.

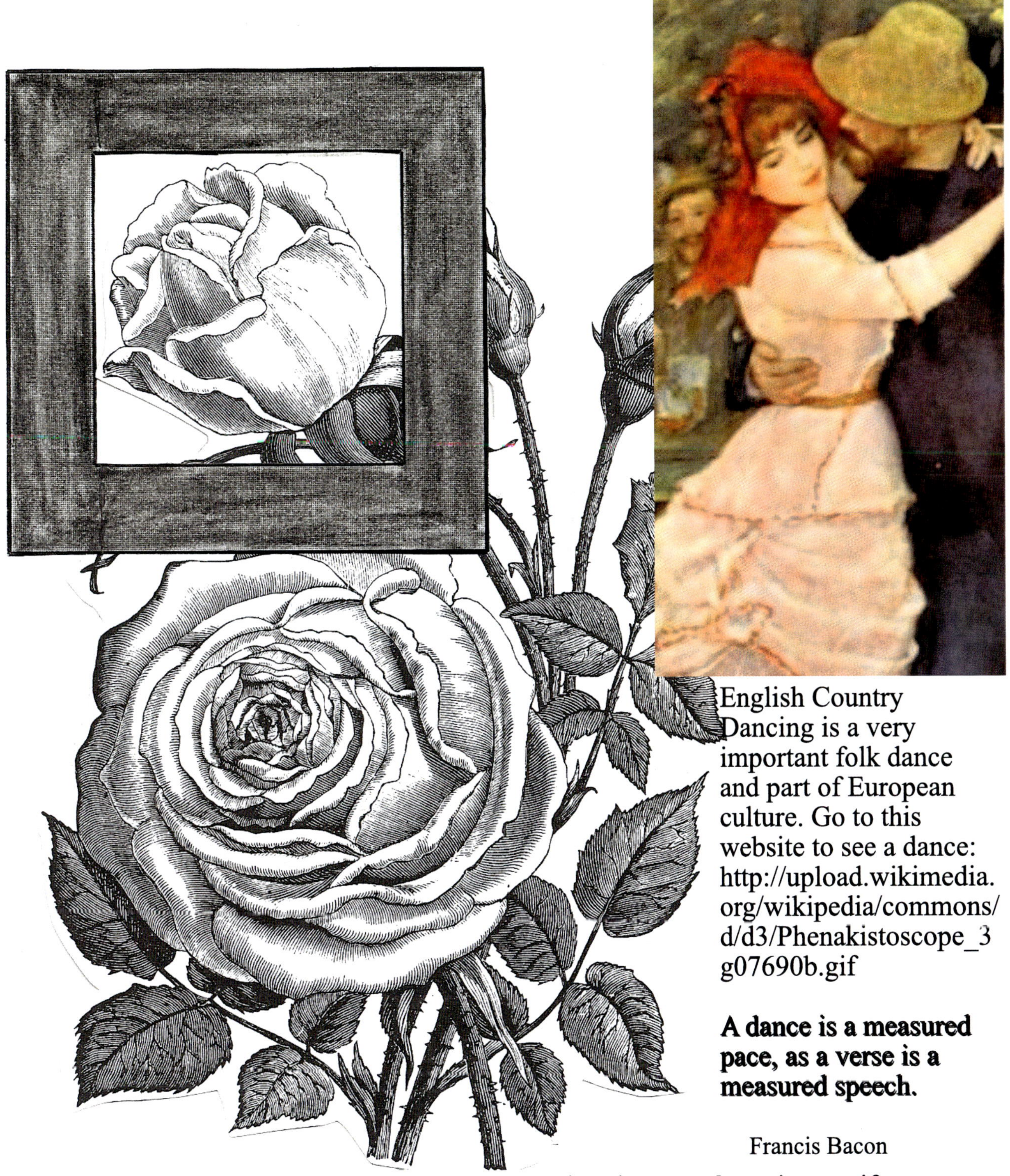

English Country Dancing is a very important folk dance and part of European culture. Go to this website to see a dance: http://upload.wikimedia.org/wikipedia/commons/d/d3/Phenakistoscope_3g07690b.gif

A dance is a measured pace, as a verse is a measured speech.

Francis Bacon

Drawing requires observation and practice. Drawing the rose above is easy if you take a portion of the rose and focus on it. Add shading, shadow and texture to make it look real. **Landscape architecture** is the art of making plans, designing, management, preservation and rehabilitation of the land and garden areas in coordination with human made structures. You can draw and design what flowers and trees you would like planted around your house; this is the job of a landscape architect. You can make a window similar to the one above and use it to draw flowers.

Painting Flowers

When painting watercolor flowers, you can learn excellent techniques in blending. Remember that nothing is just one color because of light. No two petals will look exactly the same. Be sure and just put a small amount of paint on your brush. You can always go darker and remember that you need a paper towel or blotting cloth. Be creative and free when you paint. Notice the variety of values (dark and light in a color) in the Monet picture below.

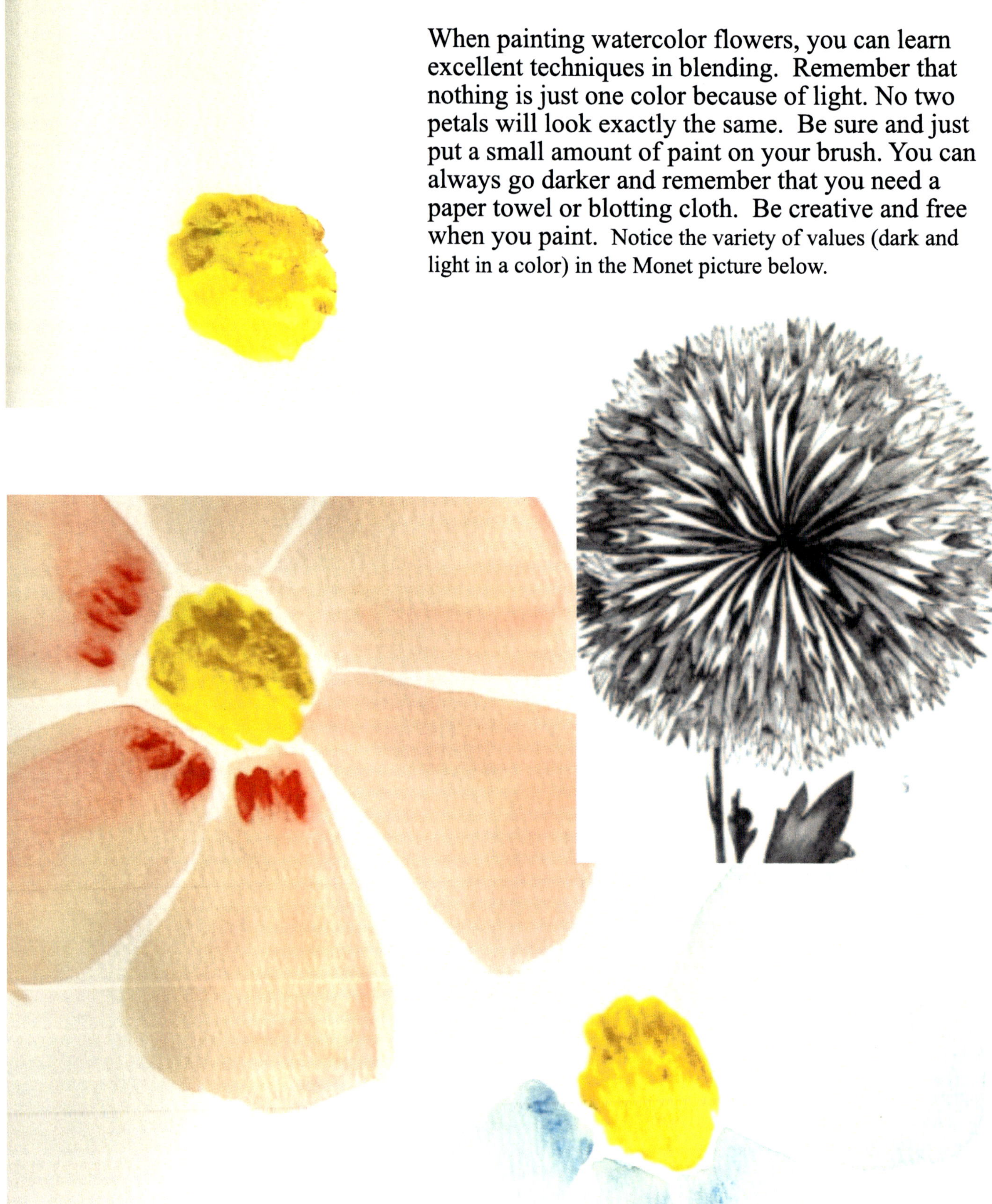

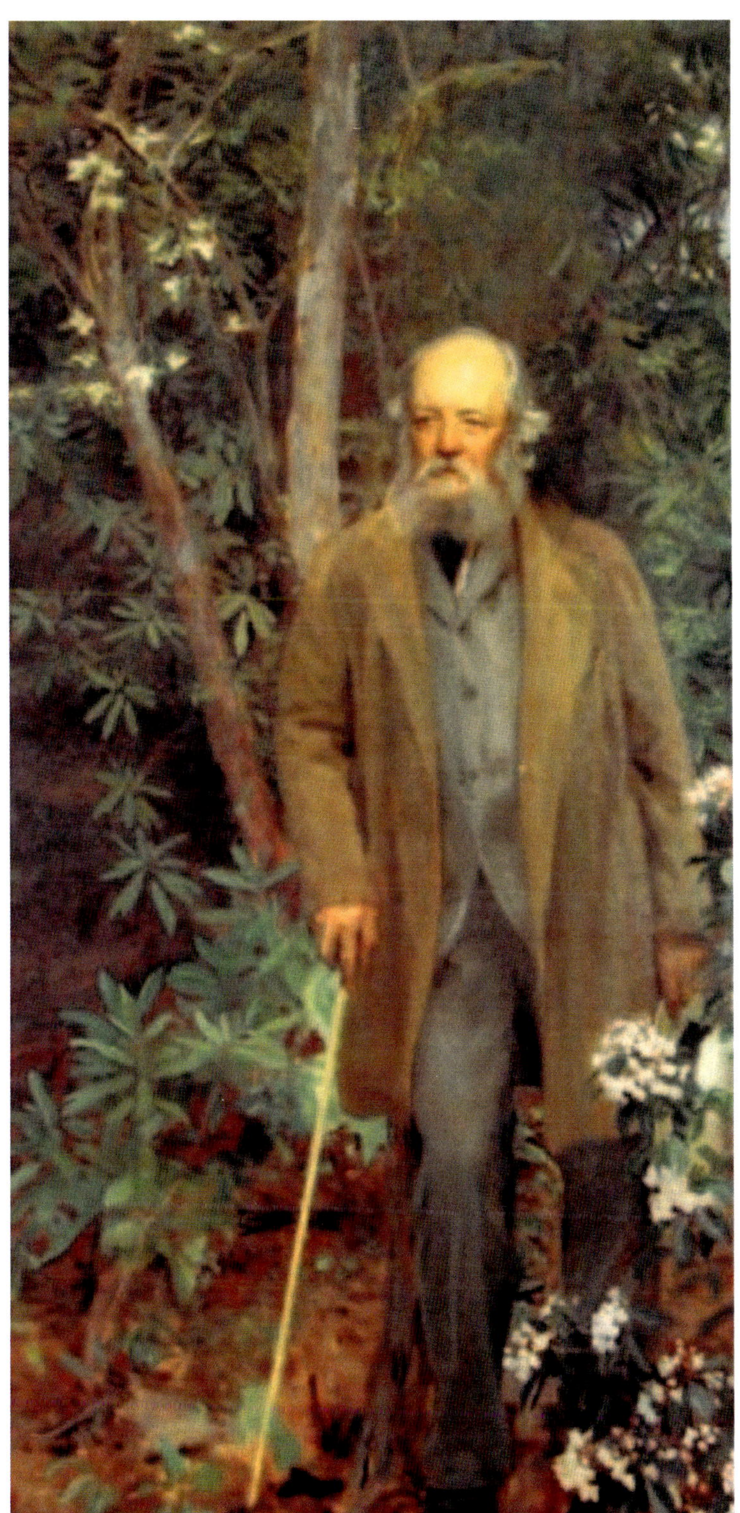

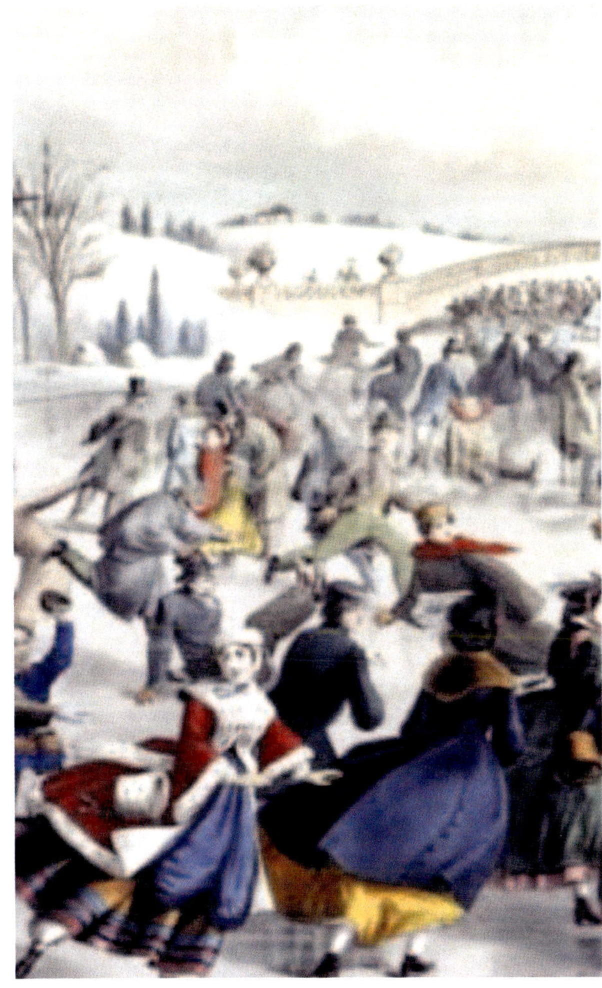

Currier and Ives did the wonderful picture of Central Park seen above.

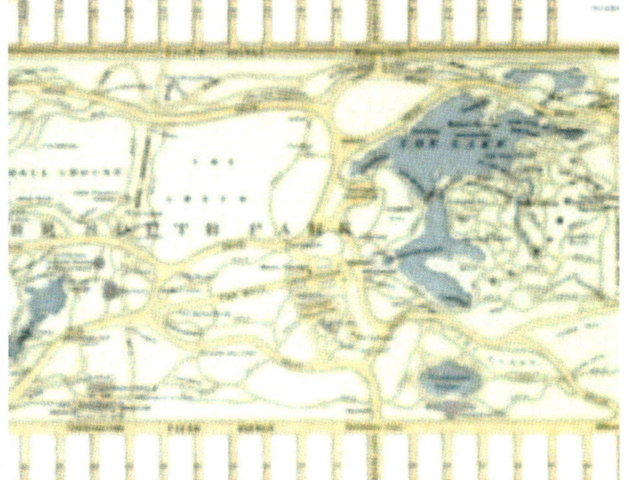

Olmstead, pictured in the painting above by Sargeant was the designer of Central Park in New York City in 1857, one of the greatest feats of **landscape architecture** in history. According to Olmsted, the park was "of great importance as the first real Park made in this century—a democratic development of the highest significance…", a view probably inspired by his stay, and various trips in Europe in 1850 where he visited several parks, and was in particular impressed by Birkenhead Park near Liverpool, England, which opened in 1847 as the first publicly funded park in the world. Use your imagination and design the perfect park. Would there be a skating pond? Would there be horse riding trails, rose bushes?

Spain

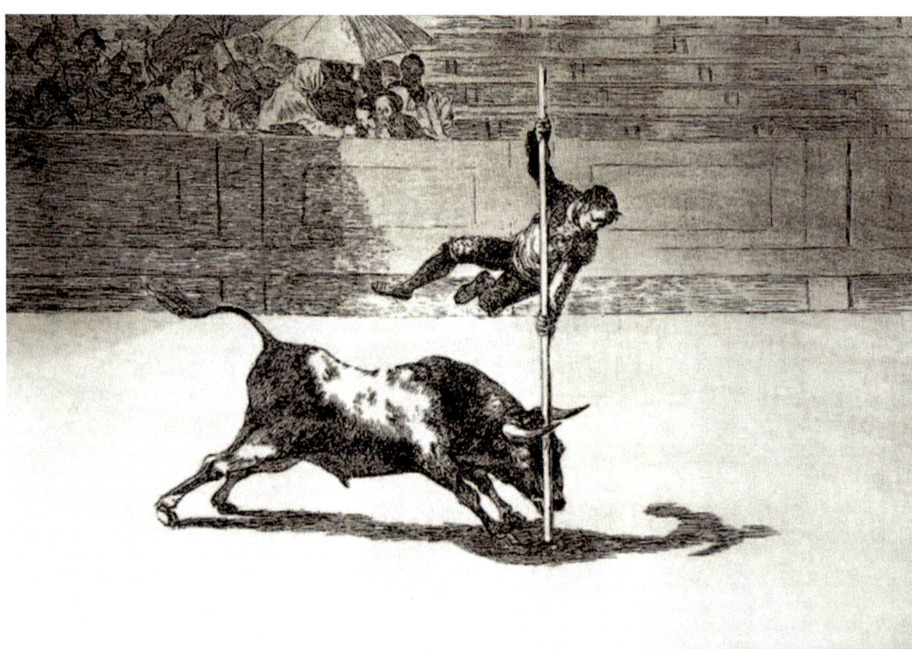

Write a persuasive paragraph on why you believe/or do not believe bullfighting is a good sport.

In Spain, bullfighting is as popular as football in America.
The picture on the left is by the master artist Goya. Below is a painting by the master artist Manet. Manet was a famous Impressionistic artist in the same style as Monet. Below you can see the background of the bullfight. He has suggested a large crowd. The center of interest is the scene of the horse and bull in the middle of the picture. A bullfighter is called a matador. Many people disagree with bullfighting because they believe it hurts the bull.

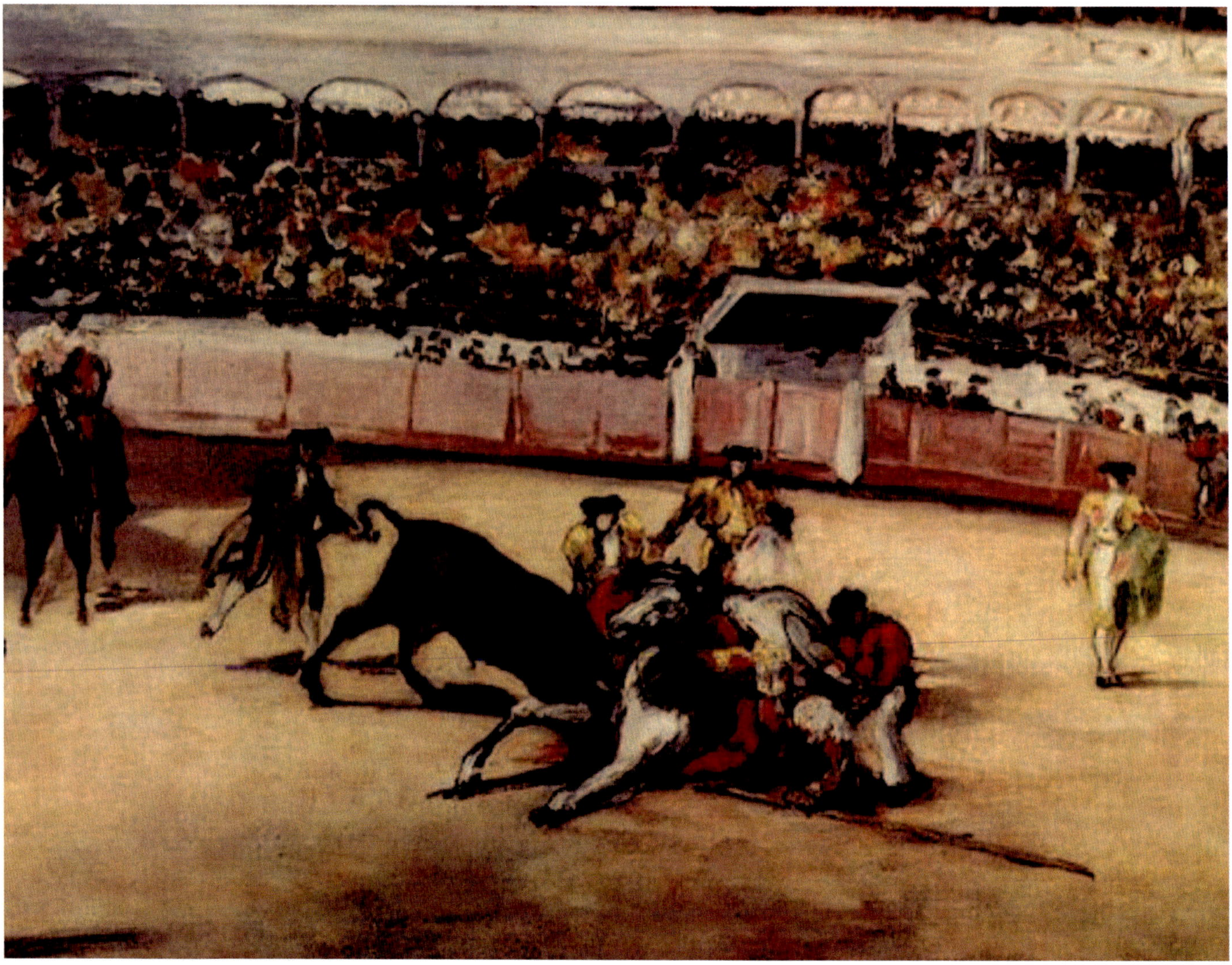

Draw a bull and put him in an arena.
Suggest the faces using bright colors.

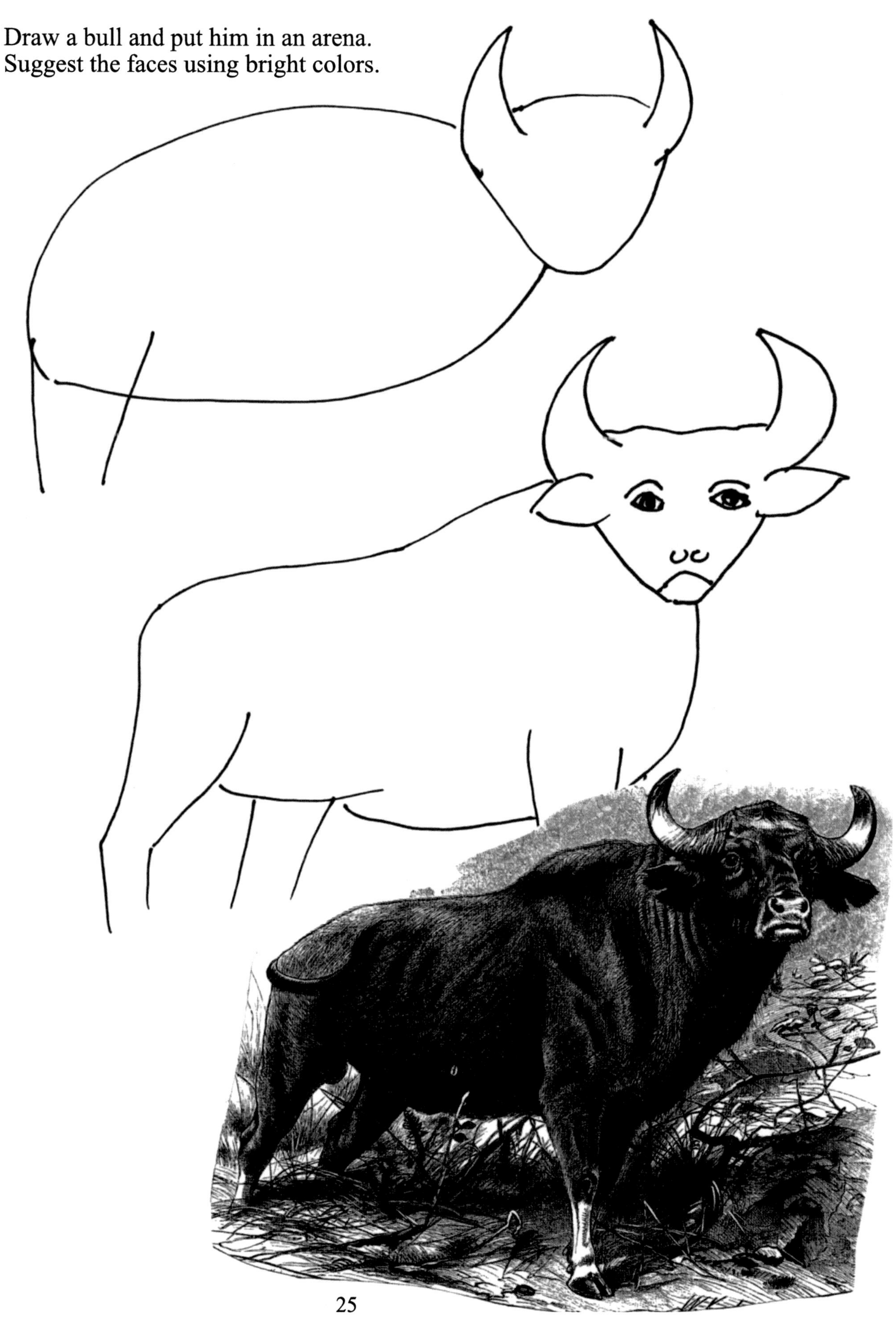

Sculpture

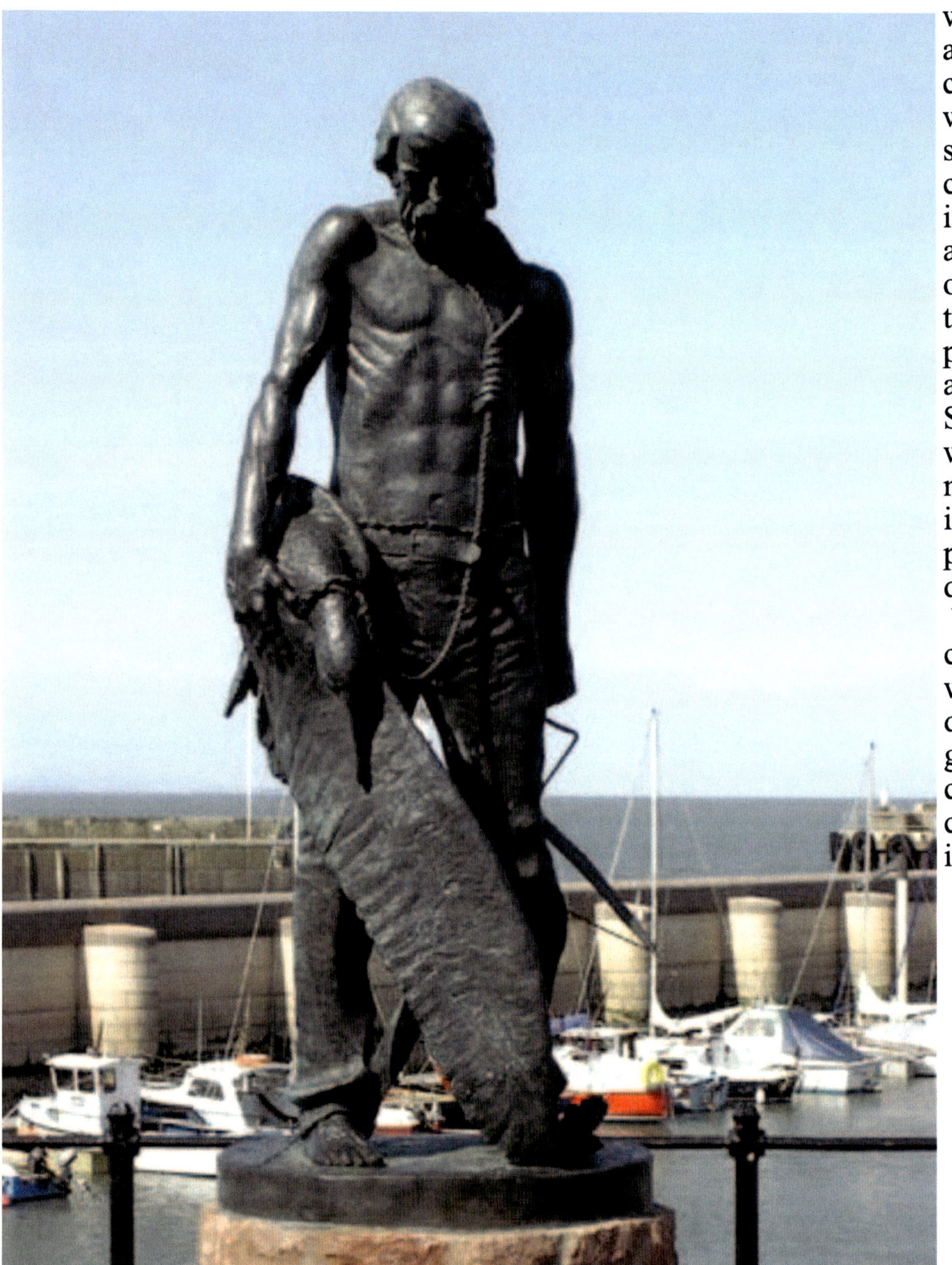

Sculpture is really art that you can walk all the way around. Many countries have well known sculptures. The clay soldier below is found in China, amoung an army of them buried in the ground to protect a ruler after death. Sculpey is a wonderful medium to sculpt in and can be purchased in most discount stores. We use terra cotta clay in our workshops. If you don't fire and glaze it, you can cover it with white craft glue to make it strong.

Part of the study of geography is the study of a nation's culture through its sculpture, painting, architecture, folk art, dance and literature.

Three dimensional art is art that you walk around. Every country has sculpture that somewhat shape their culture. This is a statue of the Ancient Mariner at Watchet Harbour in Somerset, England. It is a tribute to Samuel Taylor Coleridge who wrote the famous poem about the ancient mariner.

Ah ! well a-day! what evil looks
Had I from old and young!
Instead of the cross, the Albatross
About my neck was hung.

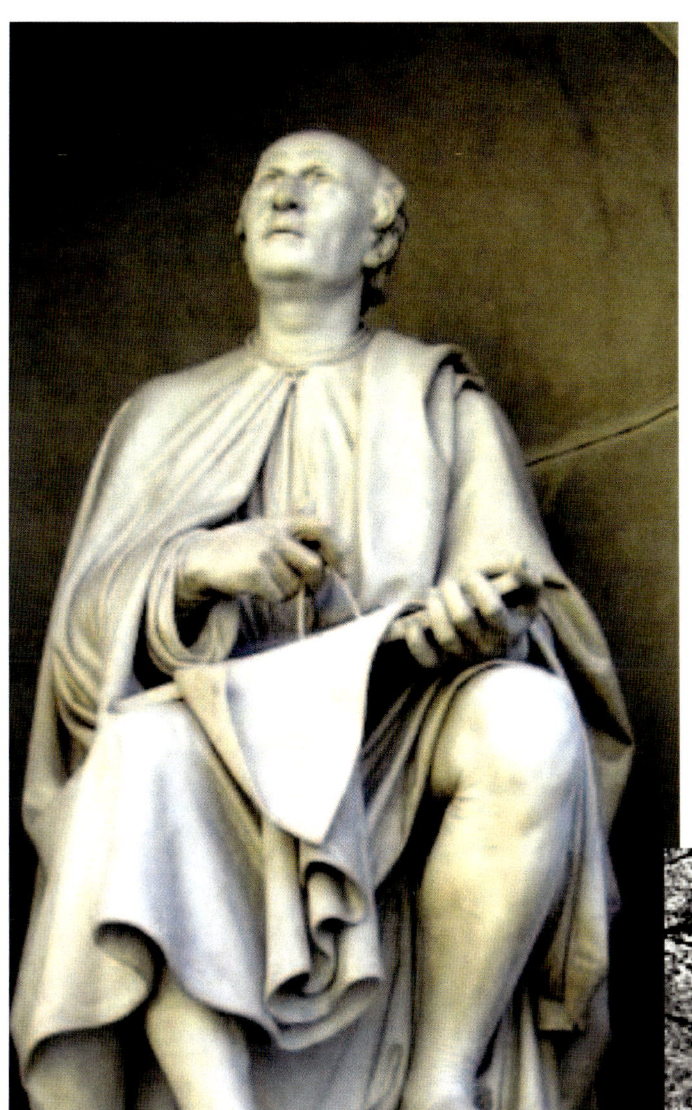

Tow of the greatest architects of all time, Brunelleschi (father of systematic perspective) and Frank Lloyd Wright were innovators and pioneers.

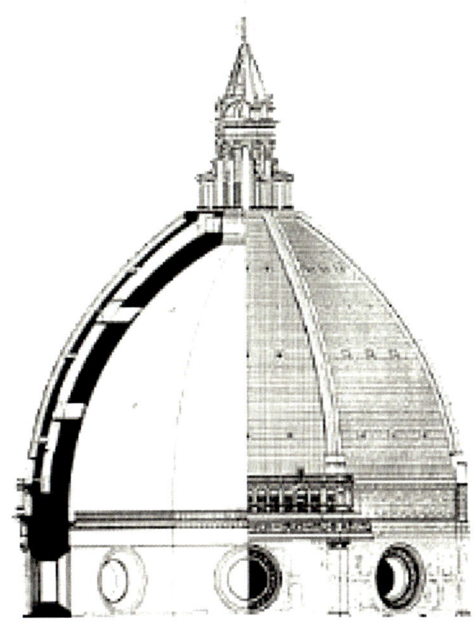

Above you see a sculpture of Brunelleschi. One of the most famous structures in all of architecture is Brunelleschi's famous domc. Because he had to actually figure out how to get it up on the building, he was the first engineer. Architects first draw a building in two dimensions before they build it....you can see that he first drew the building and then he saw it in real completion. This occurred in the 1500's in Italy. On the right is an equally important architectural wonder. It is the Robie House, by Frank Lloyd Wright, master architect of the 20th century. Go to this website to see his preliminary drawings: hhttp://www.delmars.com/wright/flwright.htmttp://www.delmars.com/wright/flwright.htmhttp://www.delmars.com/wright/flwright.htm

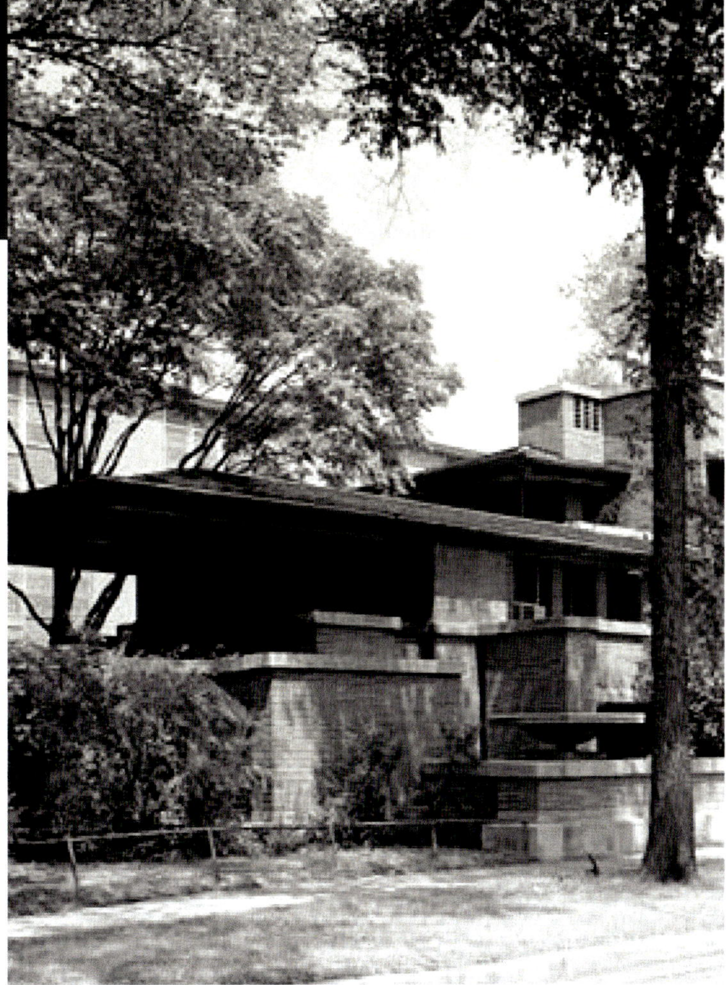

A gondola is a part of the culture of which country? This city has streets that are filled with water. Gondolas are boats that take people from place to place in the water. The small picture below is of a parking lot of Gondolas. Francisco Guardi was the artist who did the paintings of Venice. I love the idea that this famous city is and always has been on the water. Can you point to the gondolas? Imagine that your house is surrounded by water and draw the boat that would be your car. An engineer designs boats, cars and bridges. If your house was surrounded by water, design a boat that you would use instead of a car.

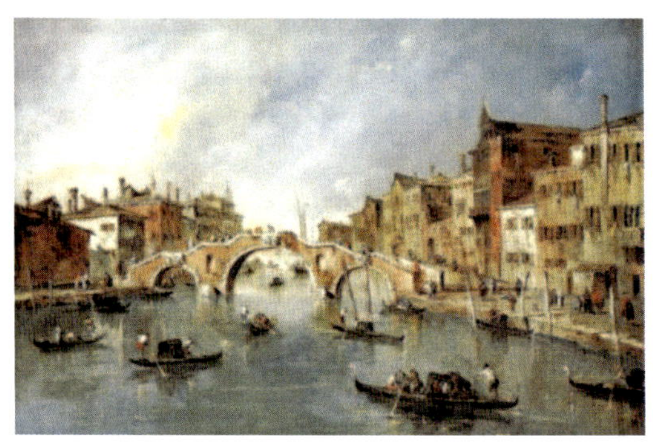

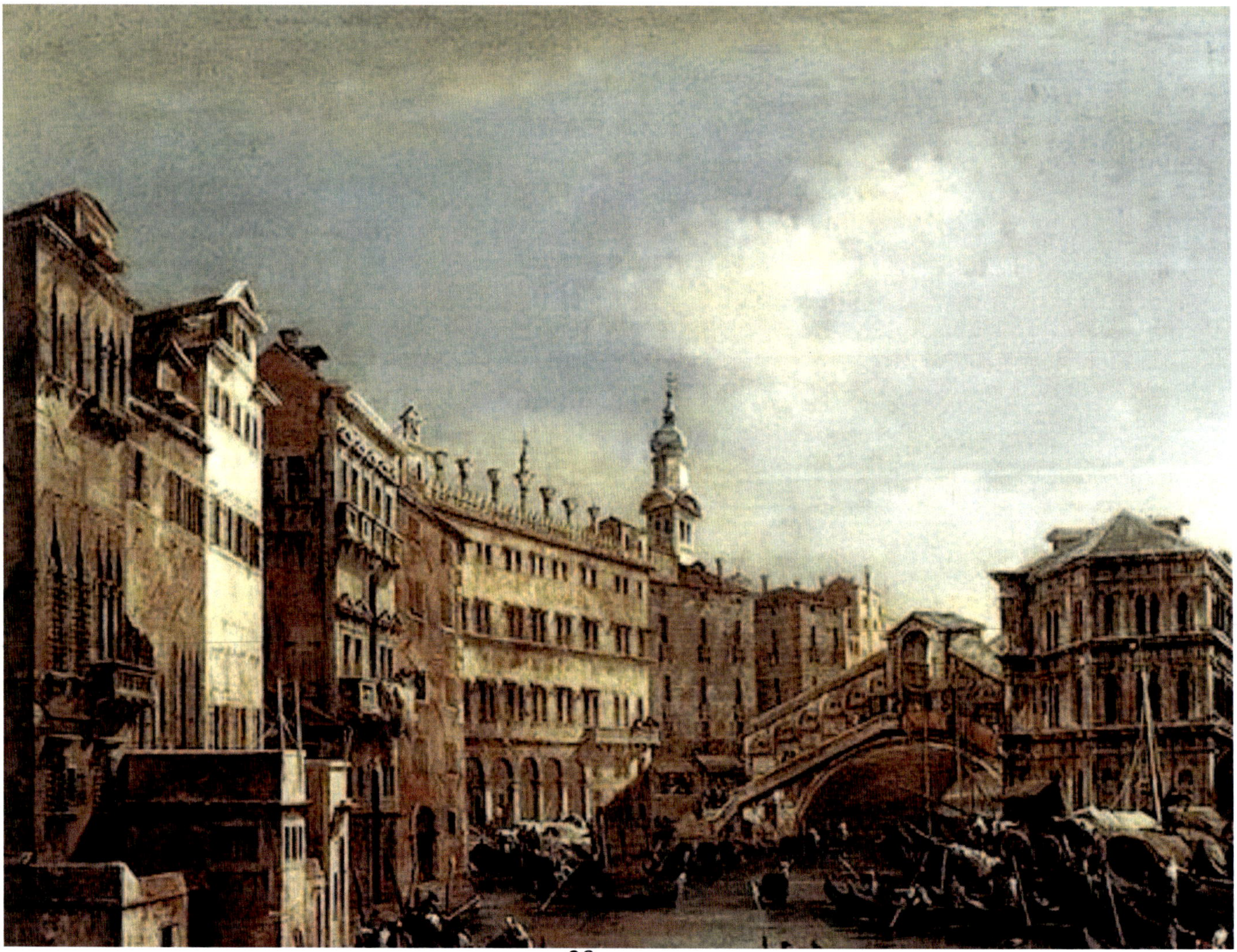

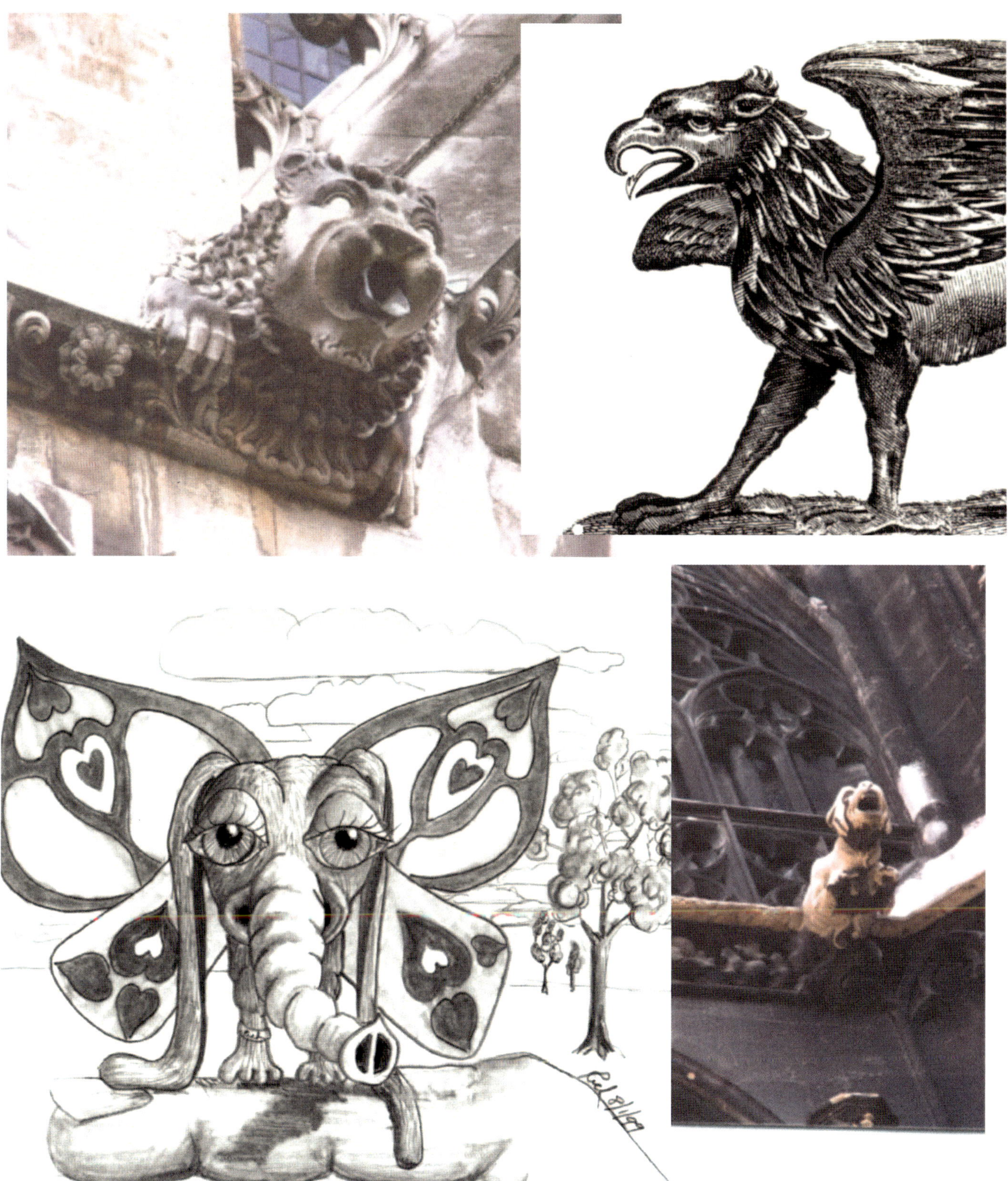

Griffins and Gargoyles to anme a few are made up animals that became part of the architecture in the Gothic era. An enjoyable project is to have children create their own animal from different animals that are put togeher. For an excellent lesson on stone carving go to: http://www.stonecarvingcourses.com/the-geometry-of-gothic-architecture.

St. Mark's Basilica is one of the most perfect examples of Byzantine architecture seen in Italy. Go to this website to hear the bells: http://commons.wikimedia.org/wiki/Image:GlockenSMarco.ogg
You can see griffins and all kinds of freizes on this magnificent structure.

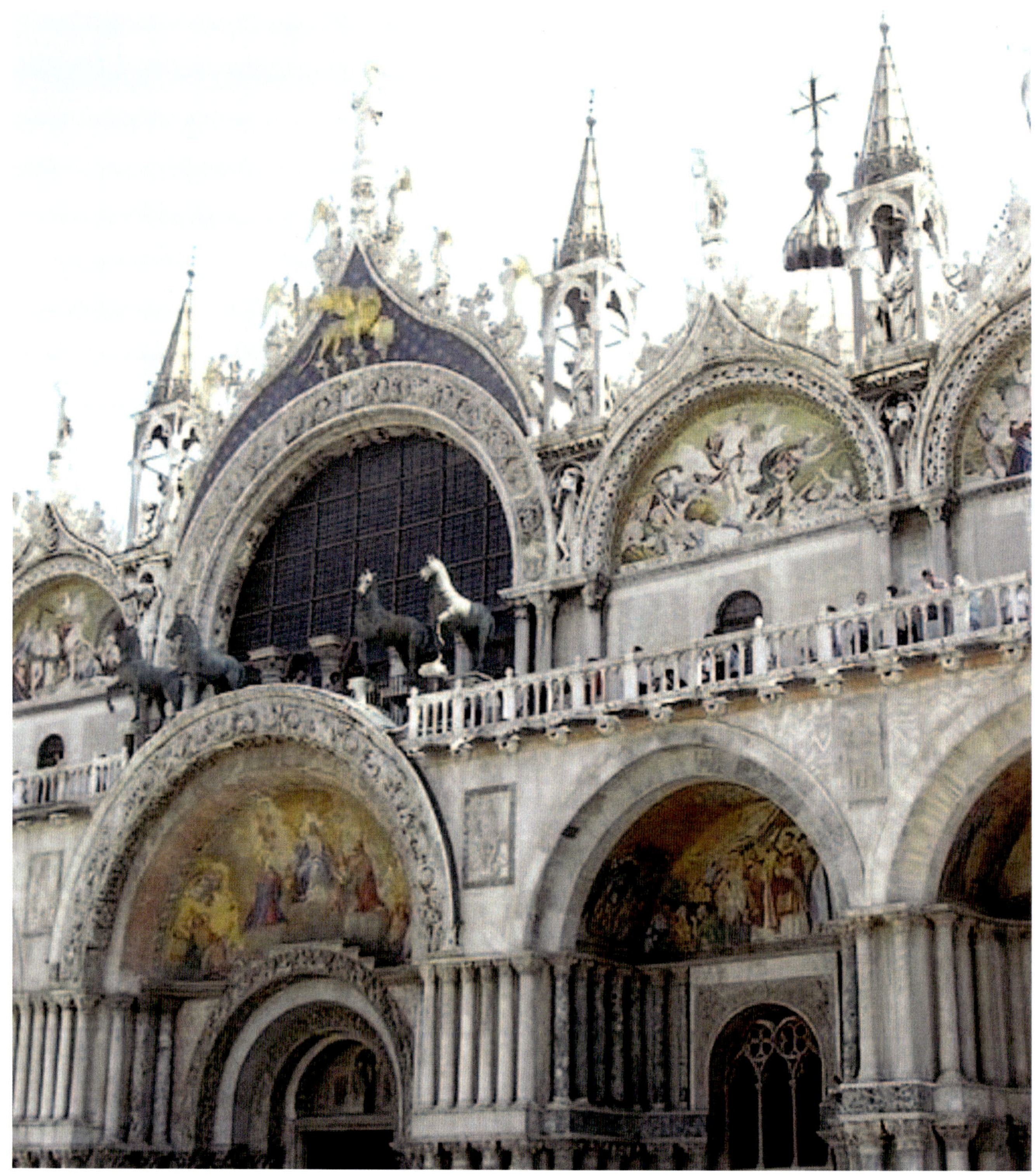

Windmills in Holland

A windmill is a machine designed to convert the energy of the wind into more useful forms using rotating blades. When we think of windmills, we usually think of the country of windmills and tulips, Holland. In much of Europe, windmills served to grind grain, later applications include pumping water. The picture below has many wonderful elements of art. The road in the foreground gets smaller as it goes back. You can see a variety of textures. For a wonderful free lesson on drawing a windmill go to: hhttp://www.teachartathome.com/images99/Windmillprojectlarge.pdfttp://www.teachartathome.com/images99/Windmillprojectlarge.pdf

The picture below was done by the master artist Gustave Dore. Do you see the windmill in the **background**?

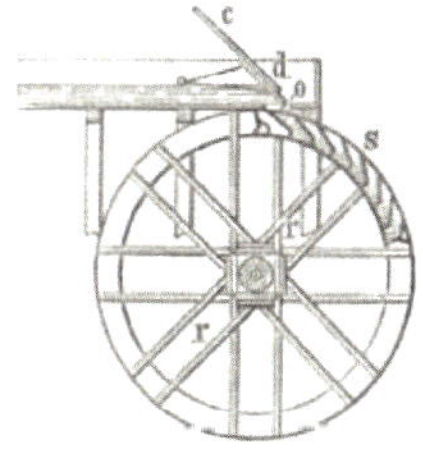

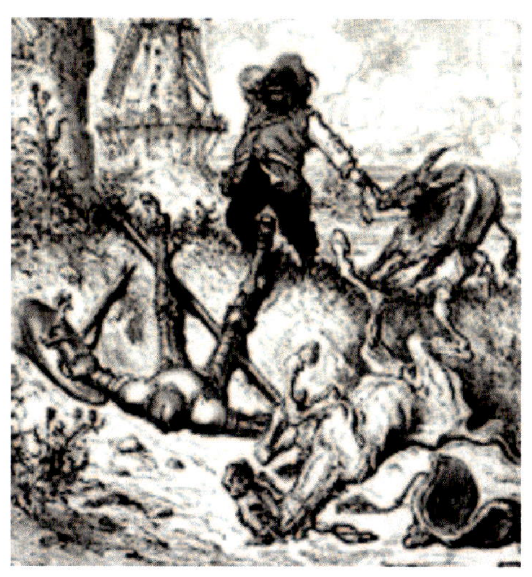

Draw a windmill using the guideline above. Add action to the picture similar to the one on the below by putting people or animals in the picture. If you put them directly beside your windmill, you will be showing scale in the picture. What do you notice about the color of the sky and the photograph? Practice copying the above picture just using pencil. Younger children love to use a brad and make a windmill so the arms of the windmill can go around.

Cities of the world

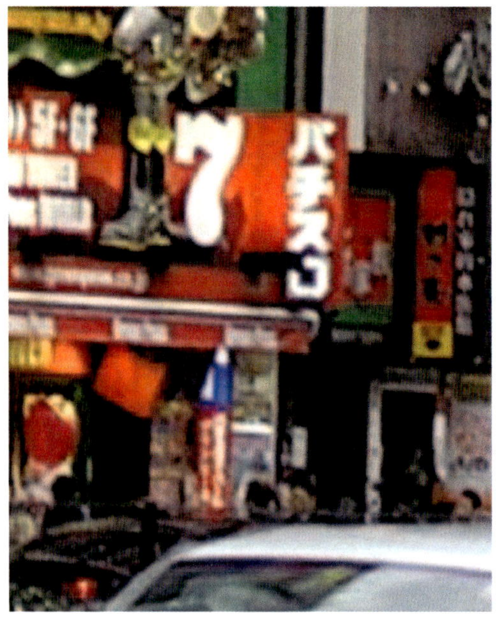

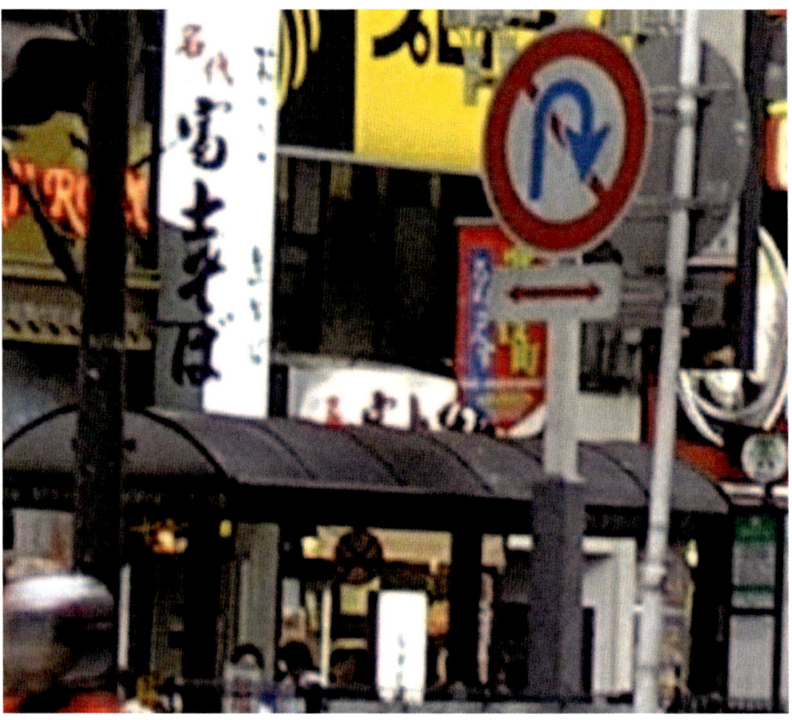

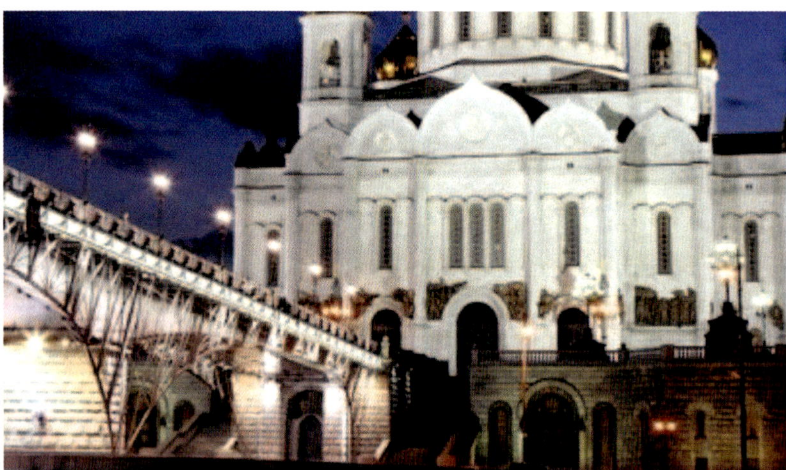

Listed below are the ten largest cities in the world and their populations.

1 Tokyo
35,197,000
2 Mexico City
19,411,000
3 New York City-Newark
18,718,000
4 São Paulo
18,333,000
5 Mumbai
18,196,000
6 Delhi
15,048,000
7 Shanghai
14,503,000
8 Kolkata
14,277,000
9 Jakarta (Jabodetabek)
13,215,000
10 Buenos Aires
12,550,000

The picture above is New York City. This is an example of a photograph that tells a story. In the foreground is a city worker. In the background is one of the largest cities in the world. What are some things you could put in a city picture to make it personal and give information? Go to this wonderful website to see examples of them in cities all over the world. Draw a building in the city with a gargoyle or griffin attached to it. http://en.wikipedia.org/wiki/Gargoyle

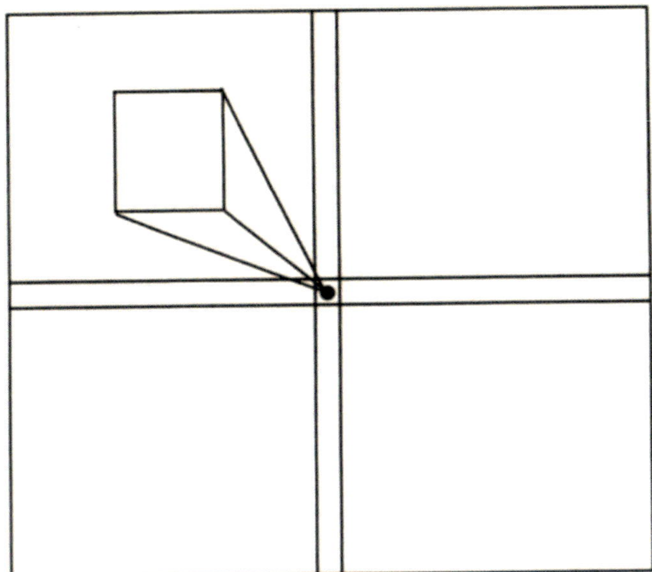

meet.

One thing that you need to make sure of is that the tops of the buildings need to be parallel to the streets. An easy way to do the buildings is to draw the top of the building and then draw lines from the corner of the roof top to the vanishing point. This is even easier than the first lesson, where you drew three cubes. It is easier because you don't even need a horizon line.

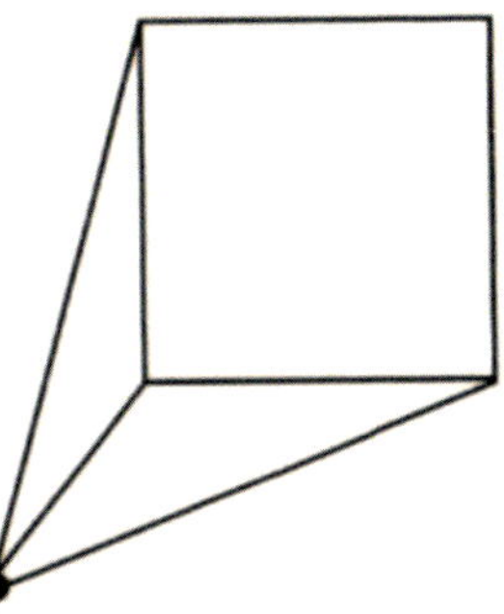

See the next page for the complete city.

The vanishing point represents the eye level in any picture. It is the place you are looking in the picture. What if you were looking straight down? Looking straight down from a very tall building sometimes makes people sick, so be careful. Place a street intersection in the shape of an "X" or "T" on your paper. It is often more interesting to place it off center of the page. You can see in fig.1 the streets are in the very center. This makes for a poor composition. In fig.2, I tilted the streets and placed them off center. This makes for a more interesting picture but will be a little harder to accomplish. When you do this kind of picture, you can start with the streets. The size or width of these streets determines how high your buildings are. A wide street makes you nearer the ground and the narrower the street the higher the building looks. One problem, if you get too high it is difficult to see the sidewalks, or cars. Also very tall buildings make it hard to see any separations between the bases of the buildings.

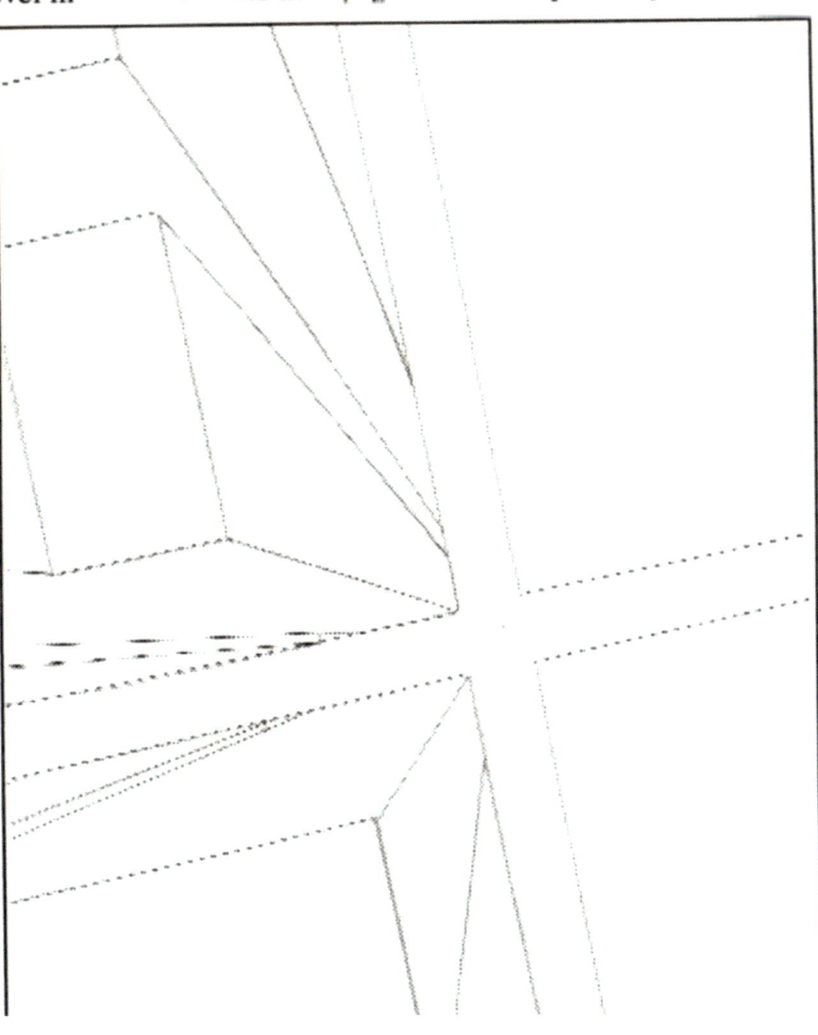

Go to this website for a lesson on how to draw a cityscape with skyscrapers. http://www.artgraphica.net/images/wetcanvas/basic-perspective/One-Point-Perspective.gif. Put a person on the building when you have drawn it. The size of the person will show **scale** in the picture. The smaller you make the person, the larger the building will appear.

Chicago

A city can be a melting pot of different cultures. The seal of a city usually expresses what it is about. Draw a cityscape by using rectangles. Each building should express some fact about Chicago. It is said that Chicago produced the first steel skyscraper, the first McDonalds Fast Food Restaurant, the first Dunkin Donuts, the first Butterfinger and Baby Ruth candy bars. It is called the "City of Big Shoulders," "The Windy City," and the "City That Works." You can draw a picture by expressing this by using rectangles in a row of different sizes. Do not even worry about perspective. Allow each rectangle representing a building represent a symbol of Chicago.

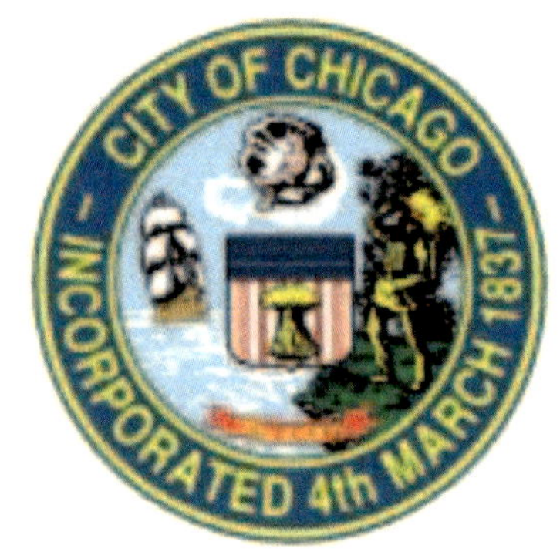

Hog Butcher for the World,
Tool Maker, Stacker of Wheat,
Player with Railroads and the Nation's
Freight Handler;
Stormy, husky, brawling,
City of the Big Shoulders.

Carl Sandburg wrote the poem about Chicago above in 1916.

A **cityscape** is a thing of great beauty. I have always heard that people are the true lights in a city. A very famous and beloved city in America is Chicago. The seal on the left belongs to the city of Chicago. Design a seal for the city or town you live in. The city below is Chicago. Go to this website for an excellent lesson on drawing a city:http://www.geocities.com/~jlhagan/K9-14/draw_one.htm

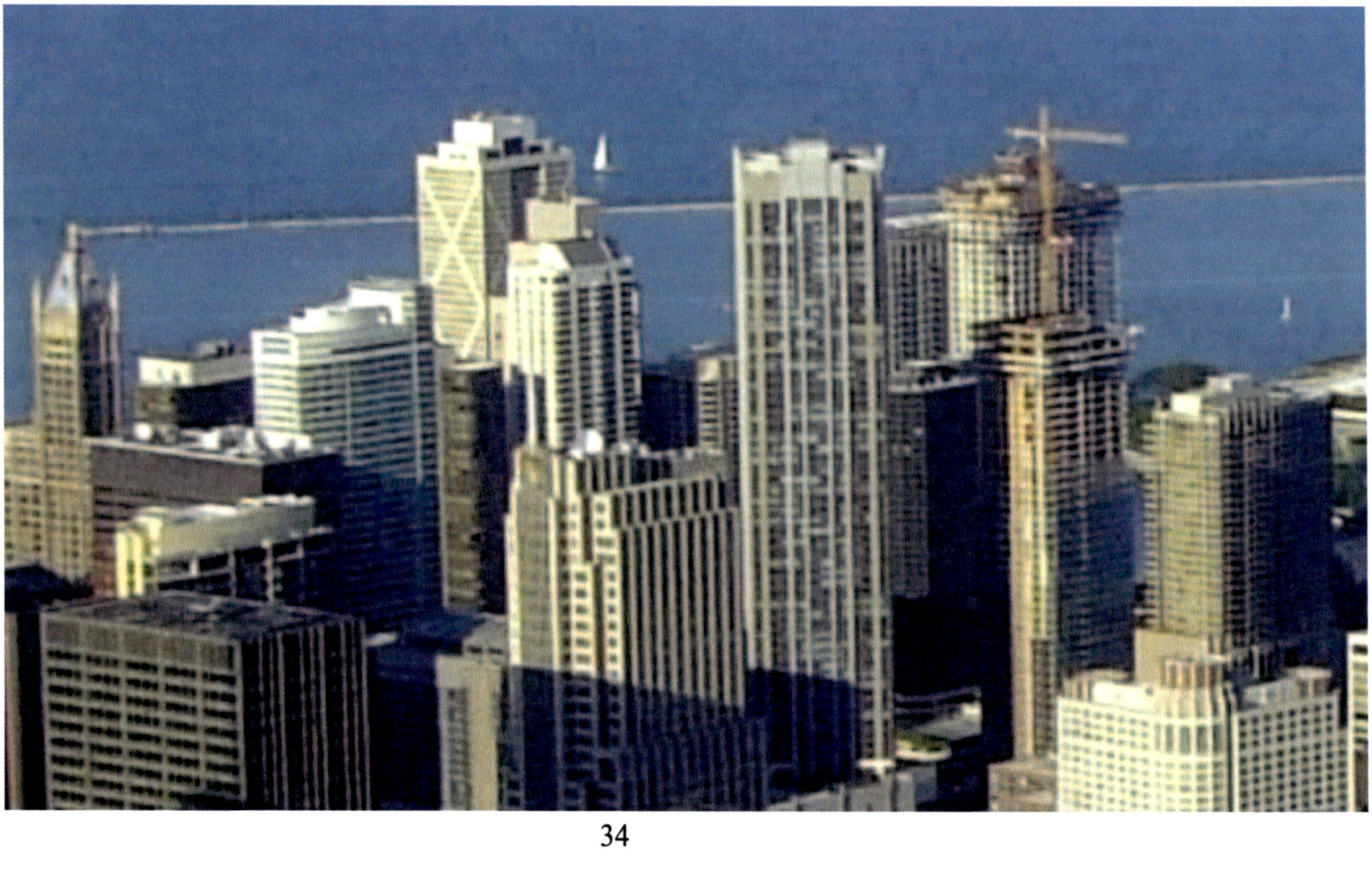

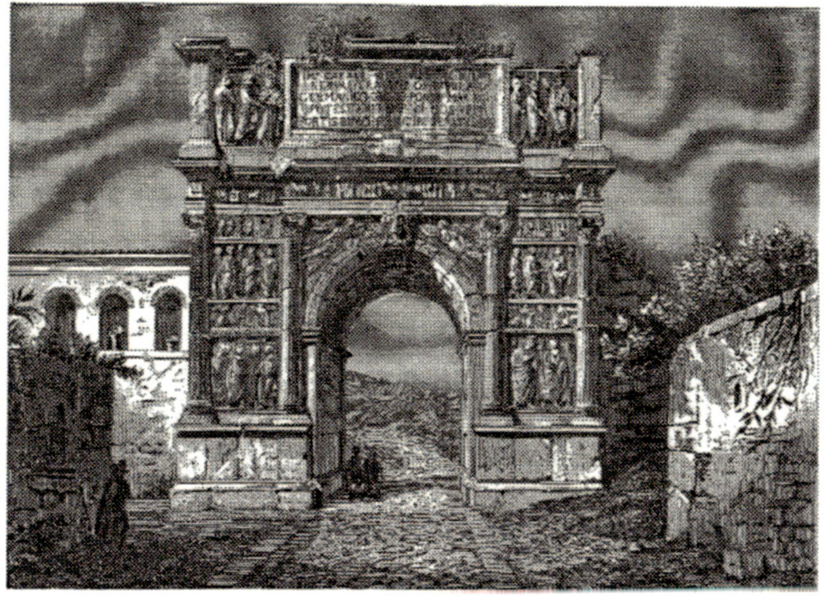

Trajan's triumphal arch in Beneventum

Architecture is art you can go inside of!

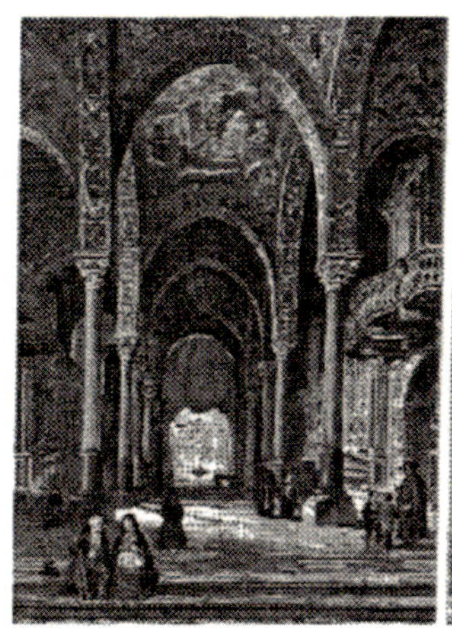

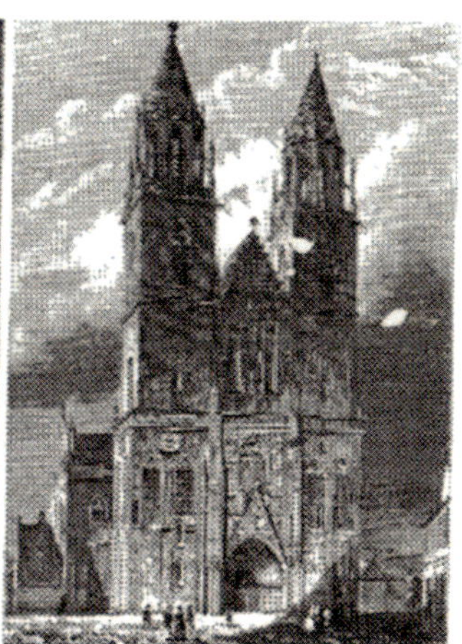

On the left is the interior of the church St. Simon at Palermo. On the right is the Cathedral of Magdeburg.

The house on the right is from the Victorian era. These three types of architecture are from different eras in history. Which do you suppose is the most difficult to reproduce today and why?

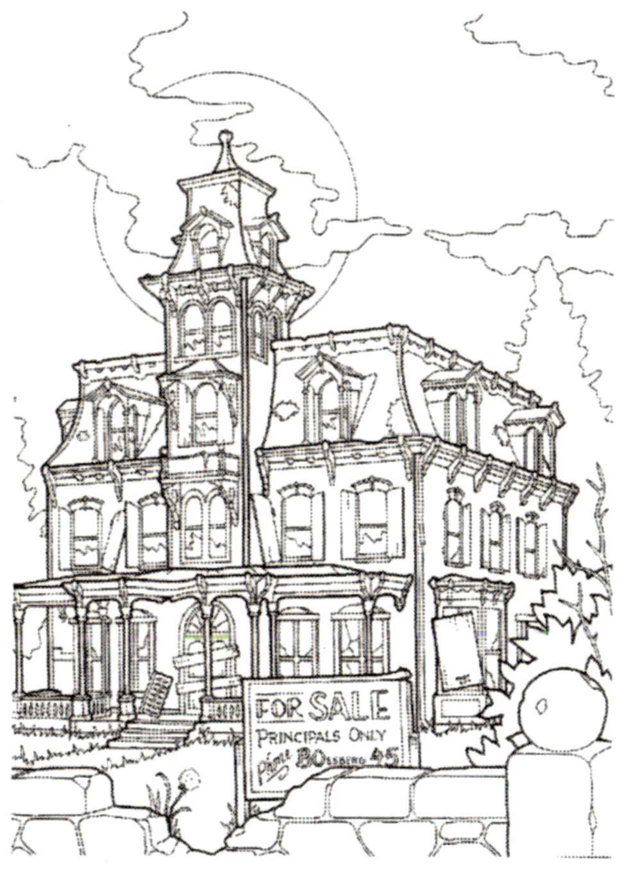

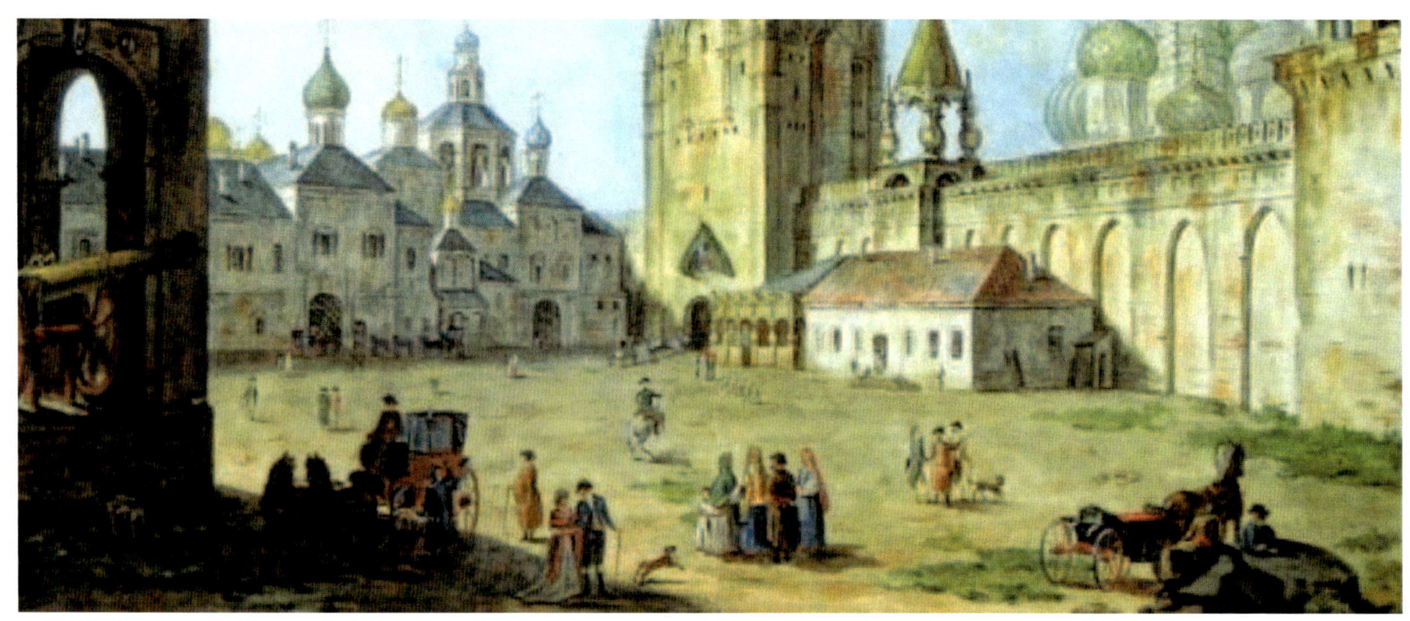

Russia
The painting above is Alekseev's Red Square painted in 1801.

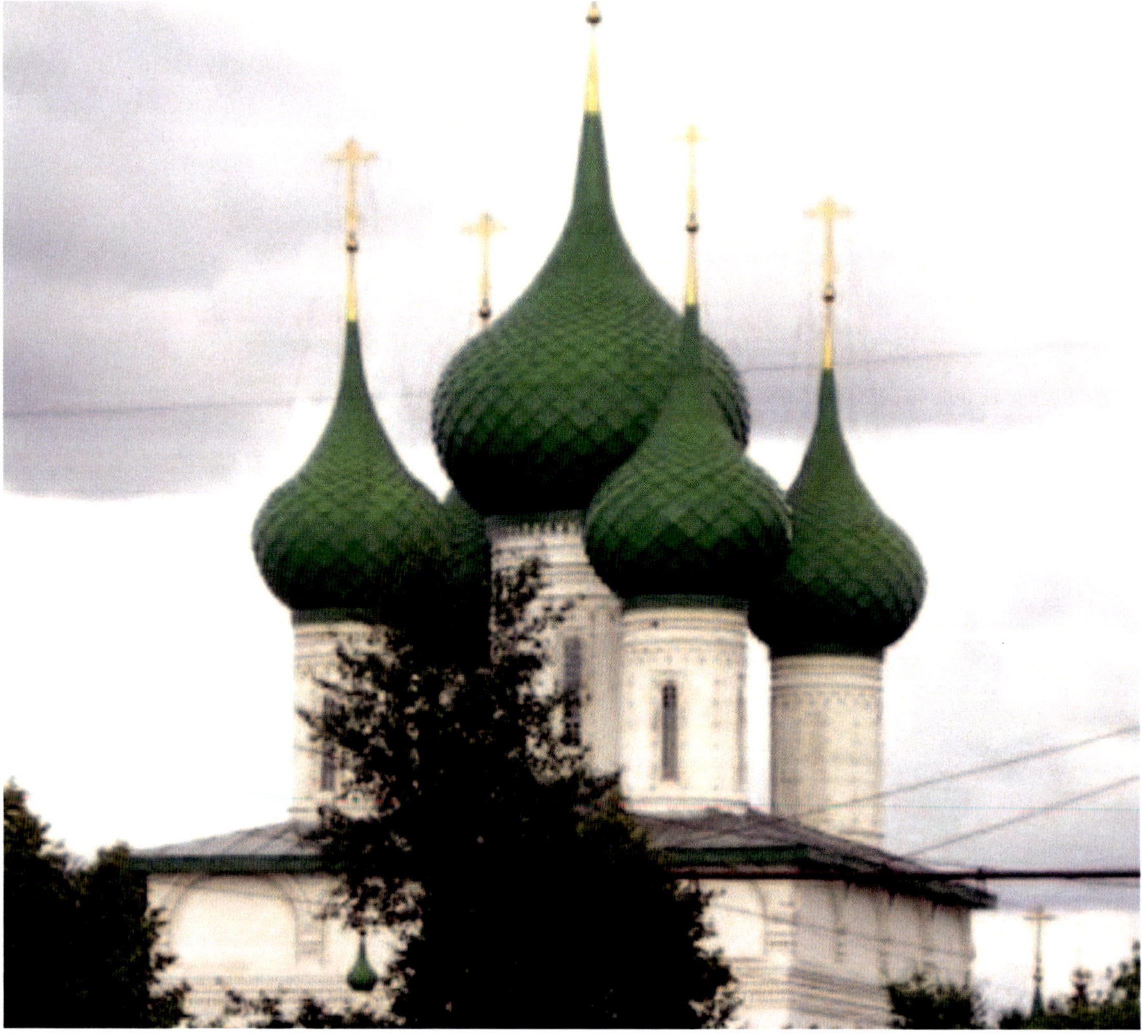

You can see an onion dome above.

Gothic Architecture

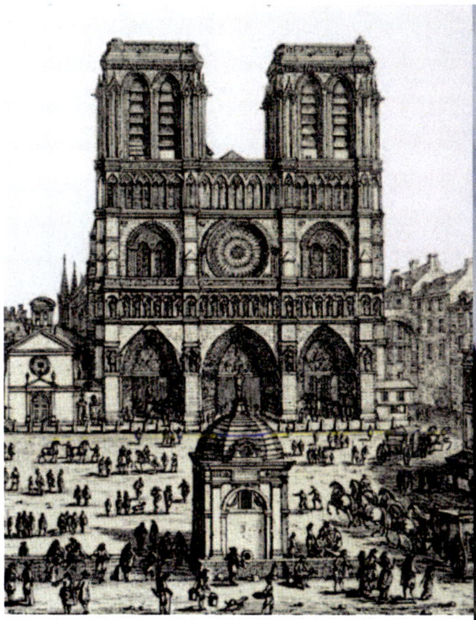

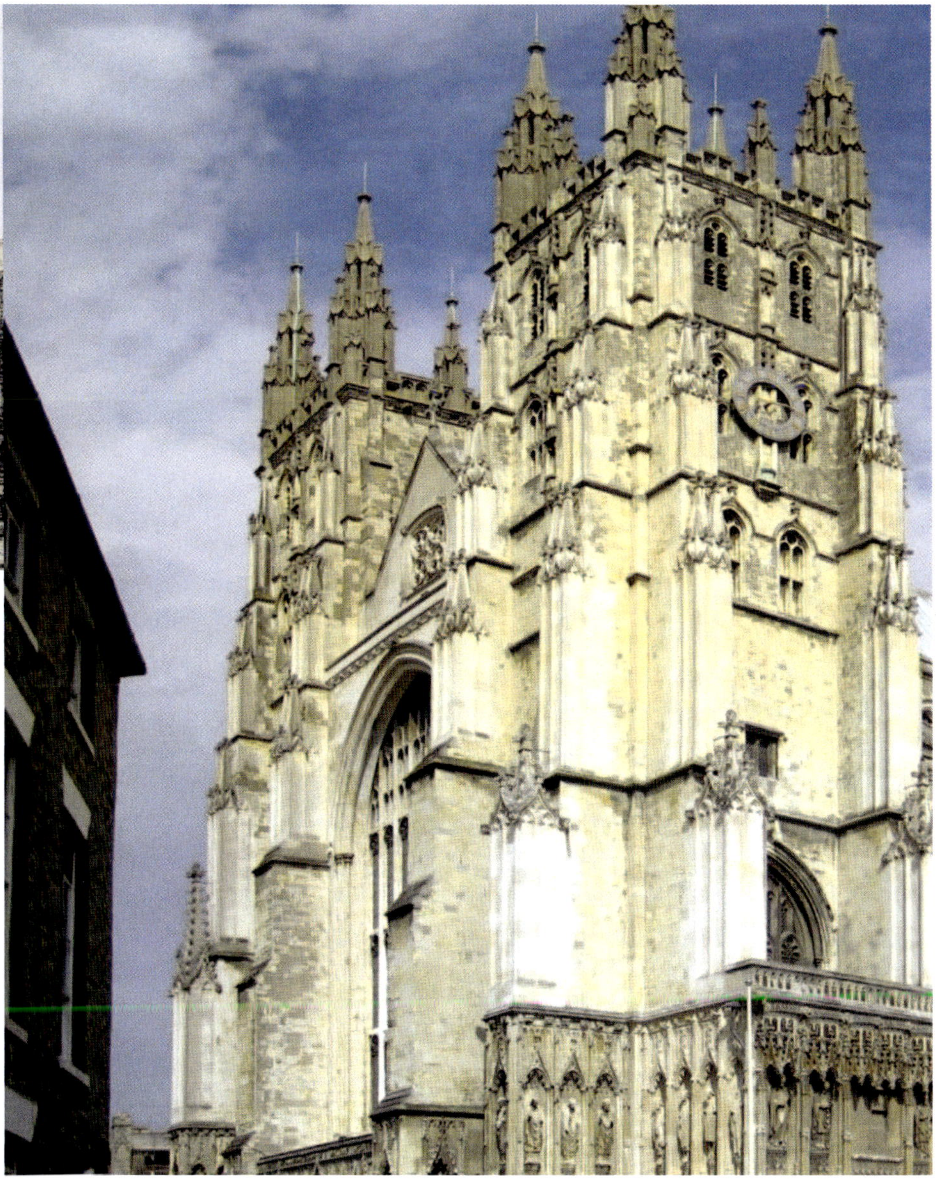

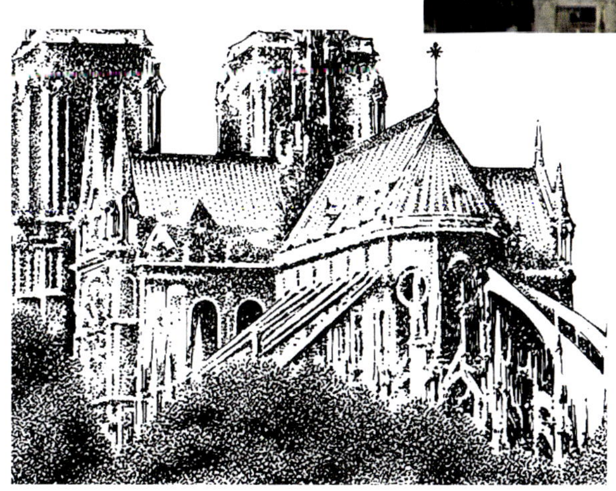

An important element of architecture are **flying butresses**. In the picture of the church on the left, you can see how they look like they are propping up the building. Go to this website to tour a Gothic cathedral: http://www3.iath.virginia.edu/salisbury/docs/cathedral.html and then try to draw the famous Notre-Dame Cathedral on the left, notice triangles and retangles as you draw.

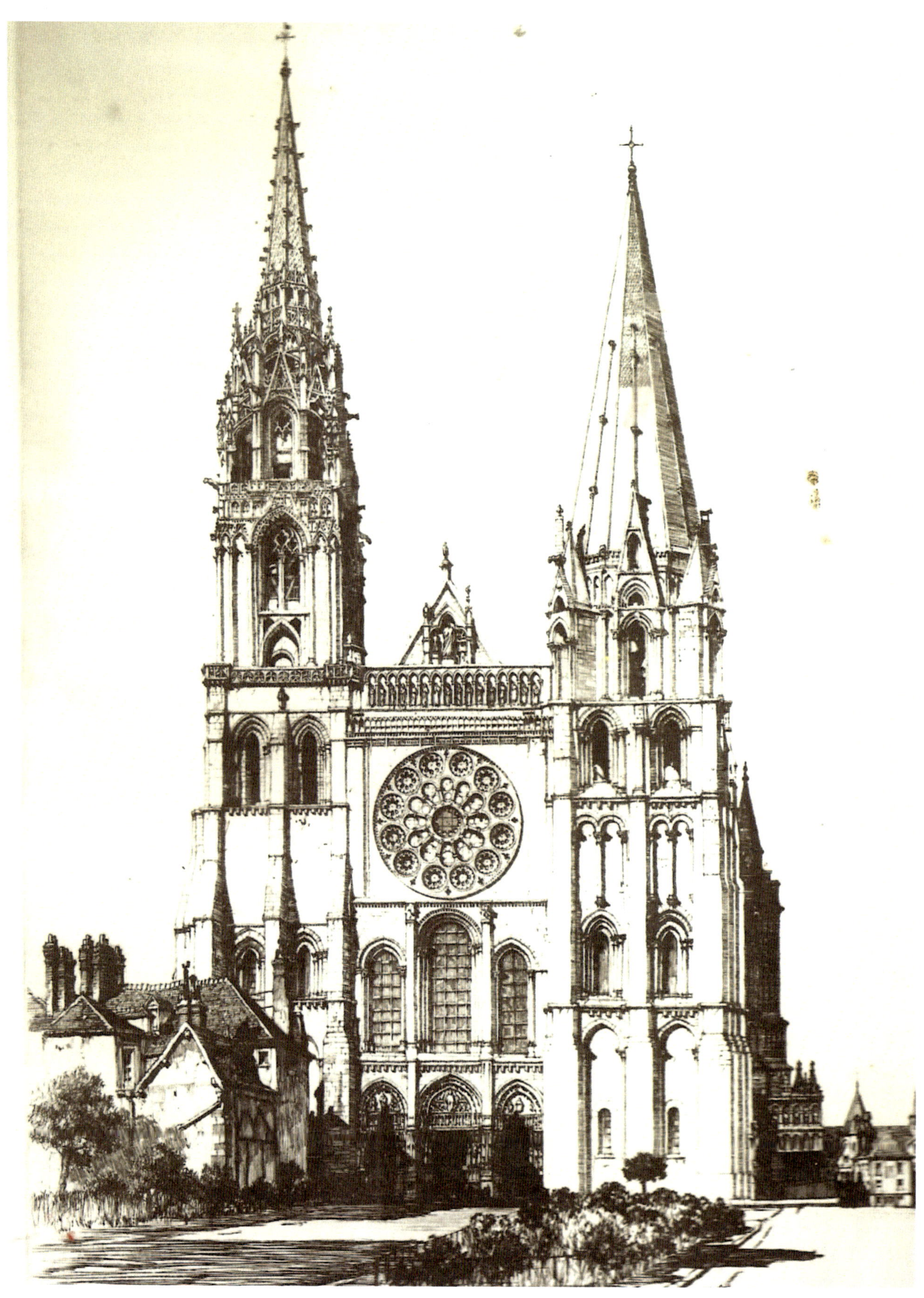

Go to the next page and finish the drawing of this building.

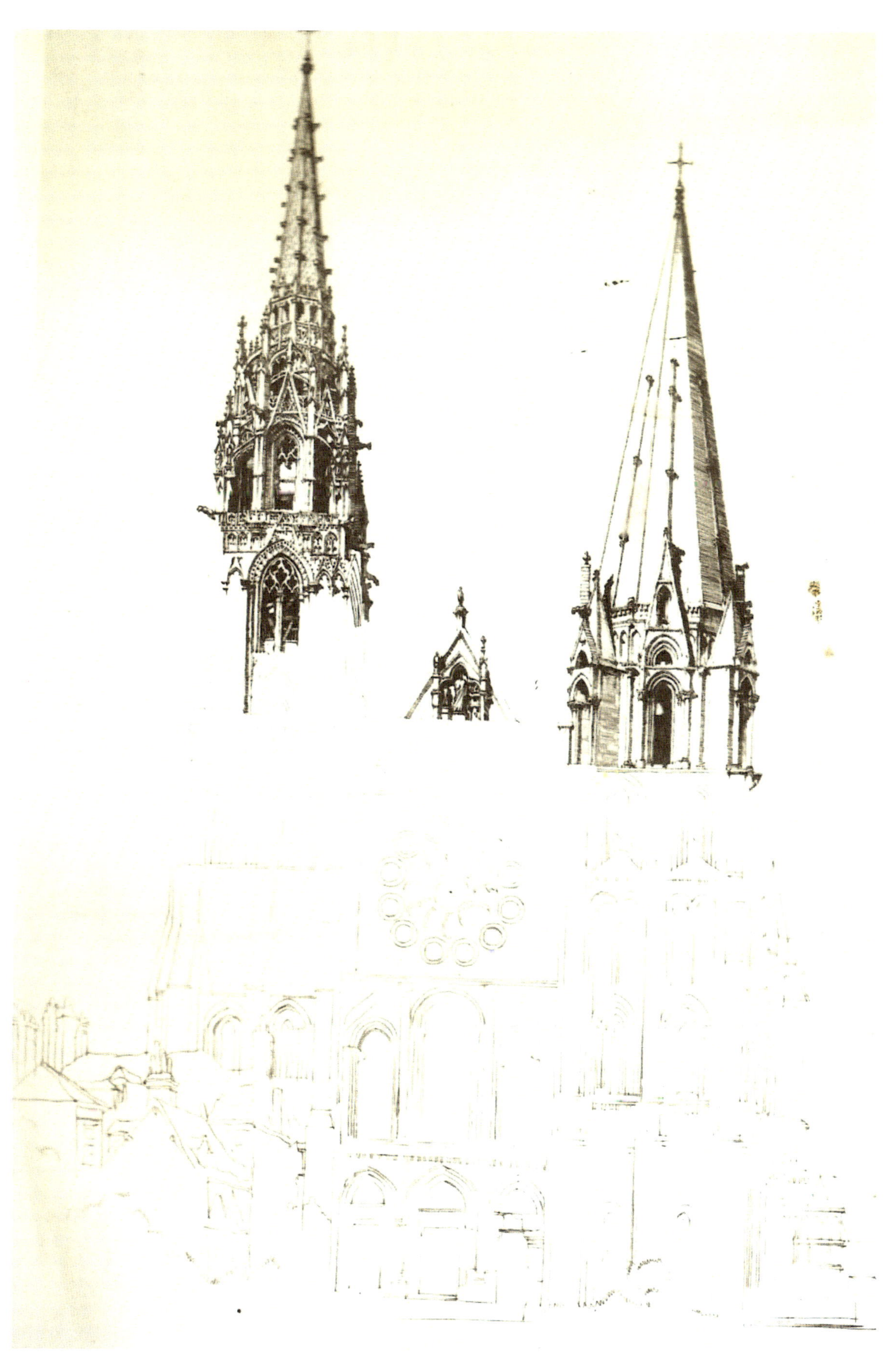

Sometimes it is helpful to remember elements of architecture by sketching them. Finish this building.

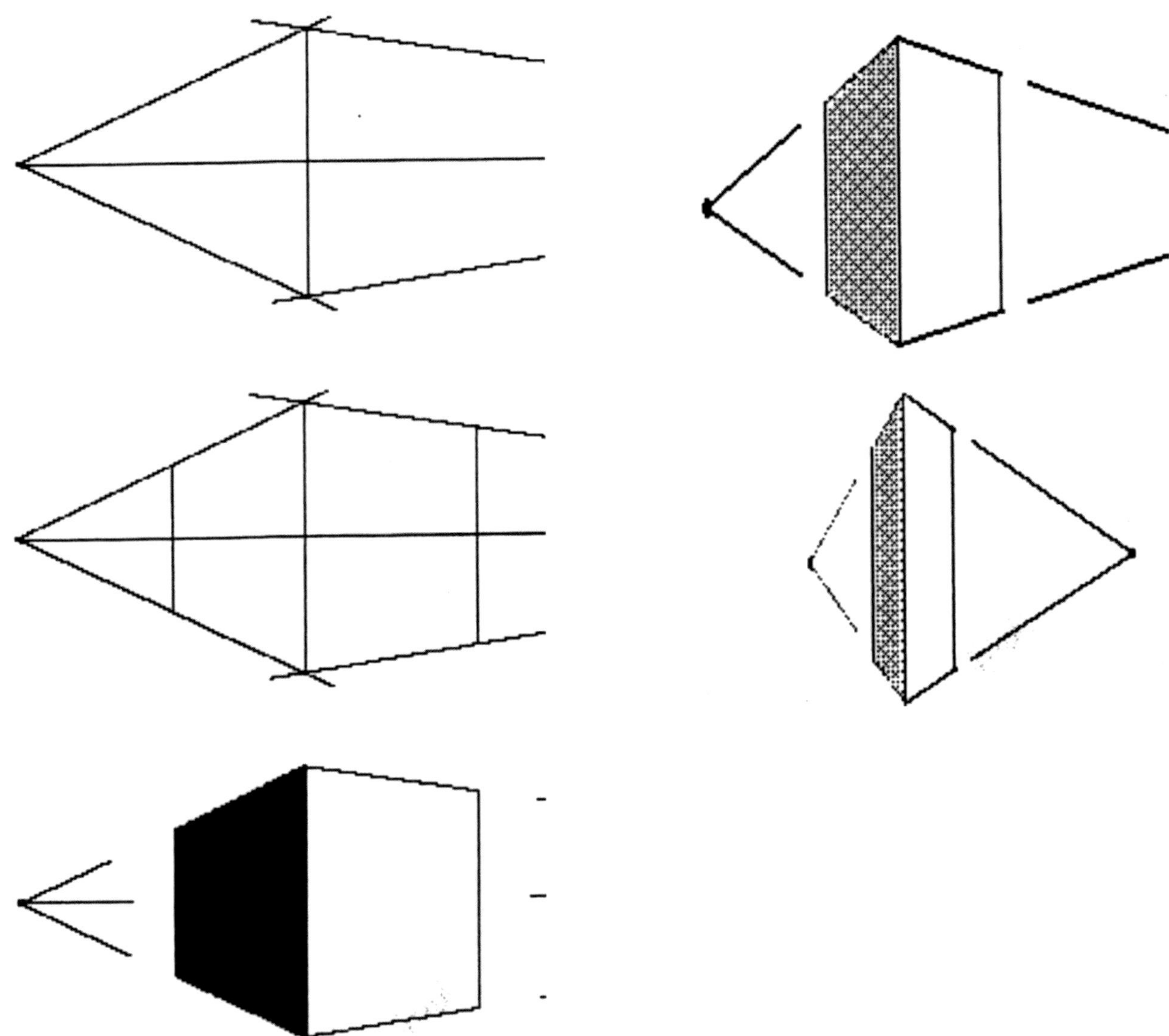

In a two point perspective picture, all verticals are vertical and all other lines meet at one of the two vanishing points. You are standing at the corner of the building and looking down both sides. Start with the two structures on this page and create details to do a skyscraper and a Gothic cathedral.

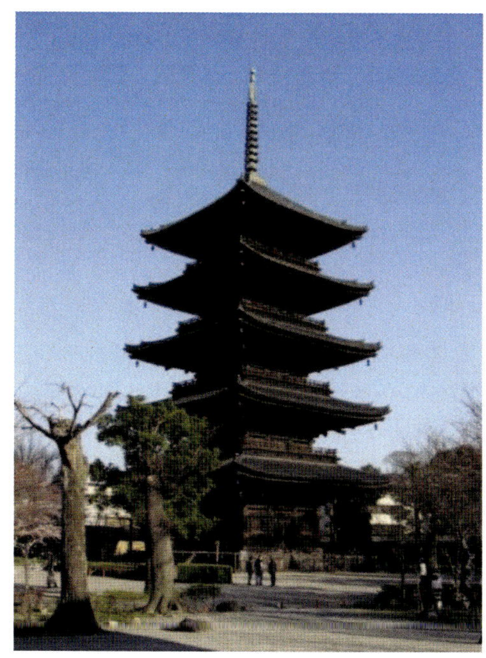

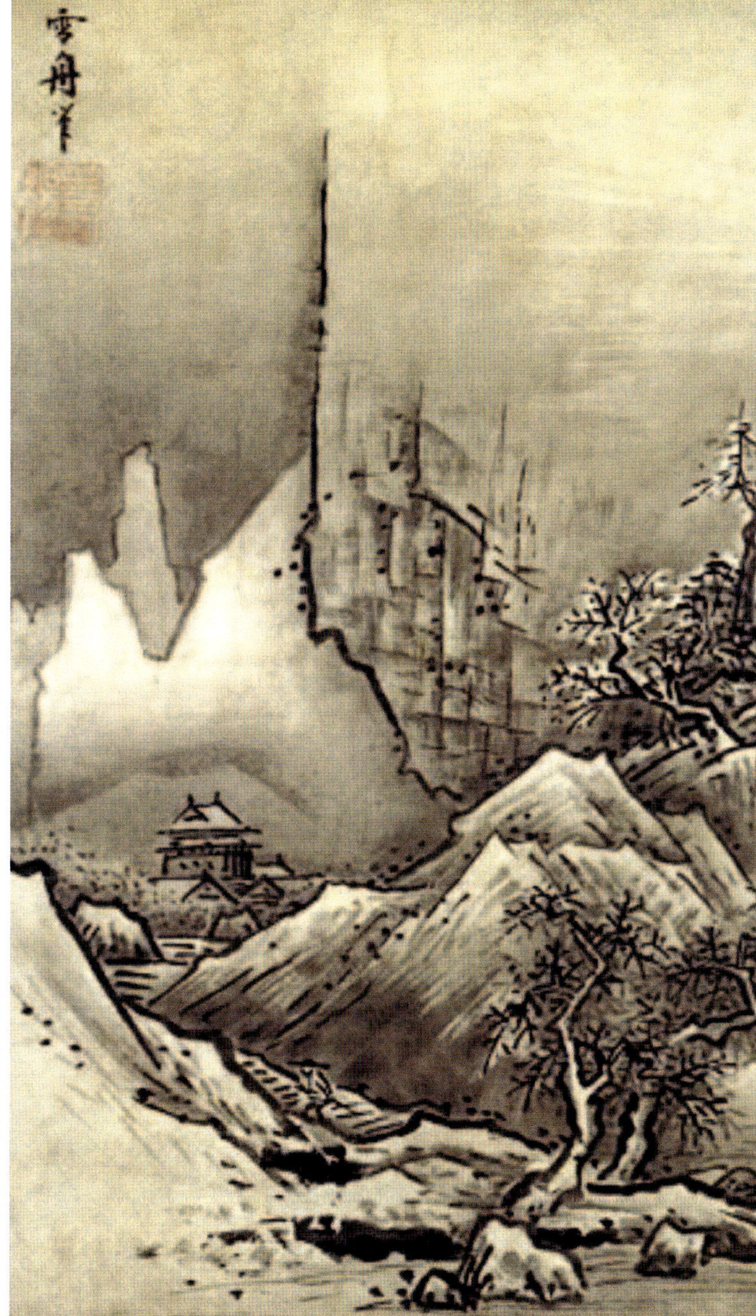

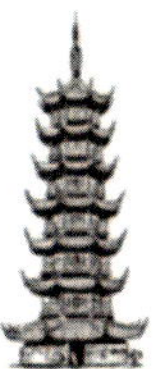

Pagodas are Oriental style buildings. According to the encyclopedia, in the same way that nutcrackers were used as guards to the home, the roofs of the pagodas would allow evil things to just slide off of them and out of the house. Pagodas are seen in all of the countries of the orient. Do a one page report on pagodas. Go to http://www.ehow.com/how_make-pagoda.html to learn how to make one.

Airports

The largest airport in the world is the King Khalid International Airport in Riyadh, Saudi Arabia. It takes up some 81 square miles This airport has four terminals, yet only three have ever been used.

The second biggest airport in the world is Denver International, which takes up 53 square miles. By comparison, London Heathrow takes up around 3,000 acres, or just 4.7 square miles. Be creative and design an airport. The picture below is a design for an airport. When you design your airport, remember that the pilots see it from the sky. Design it from above.

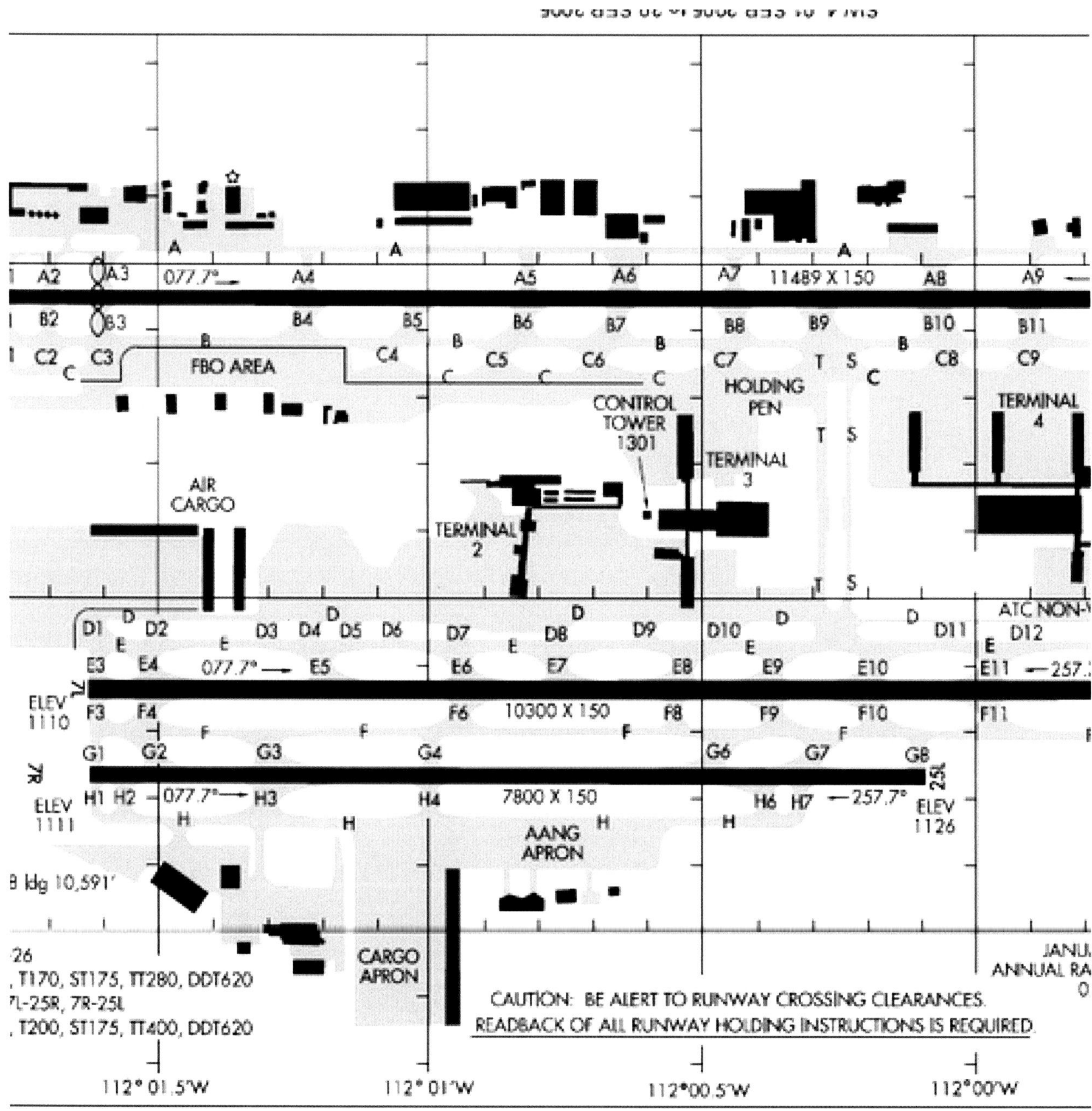

Mountains of the World

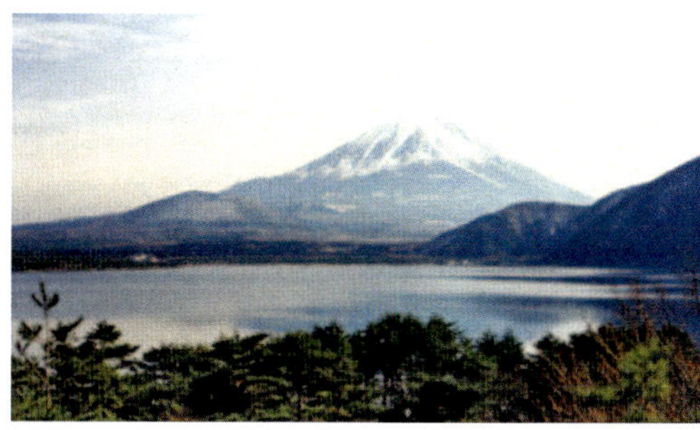

On the left is the very famous Mt. Fuji in Japan. Notice the clouds you see in the sky. The pictures below are also of Mt. Fuji. Do you see any similarities? The picture below is a print. You can do a print of Mt. Fuji by taking a foam meat tray cleaned and dried and draw a picture of this mountain. Choose three colors to do your picture in. Can you color blue, red and white in the picture below? Paint one area of your print at a time, print and wash until you have all your colors on the print. Go to this website for detailed instructions:
http://www.kinderart.com/printmaking/print101.shtml

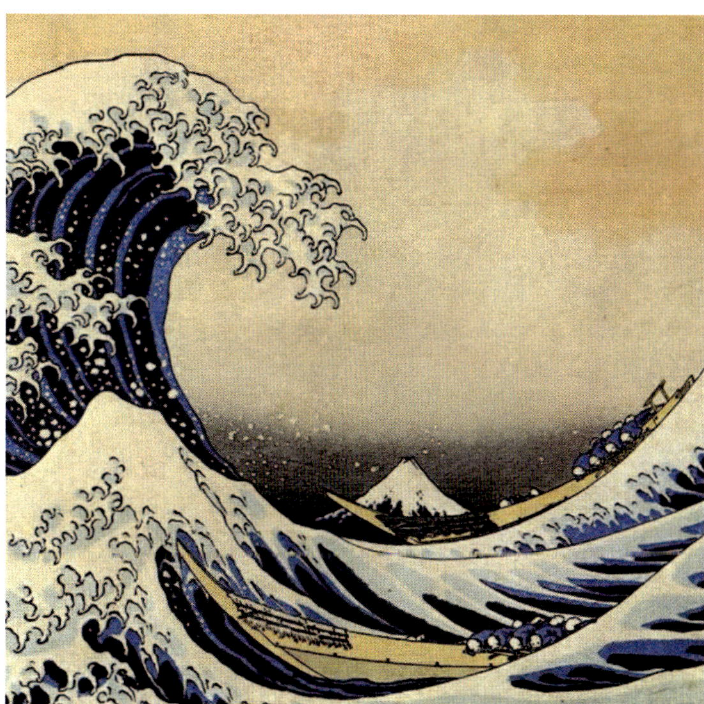

Primary colors are red, yellow and blue. **Secondary colors** are green, orange and purple. Do one print of the mountain above in primary colors. Do one print in secondary colors.

The picture below is of the Andes Mountain Range in Peru. Notice the snow covered peaks. Go to this website for a wonderful lesson on painting mountains: http://www.skjoldbroder.dk/nucleus/index.php?itemid=16&catid=3 and paint a mountain range from the following pages of examples.

Mountain- A mountain is high, rocky land that is higher than a hill.
Mountain Range- A mountain range is a row of connected mountains.

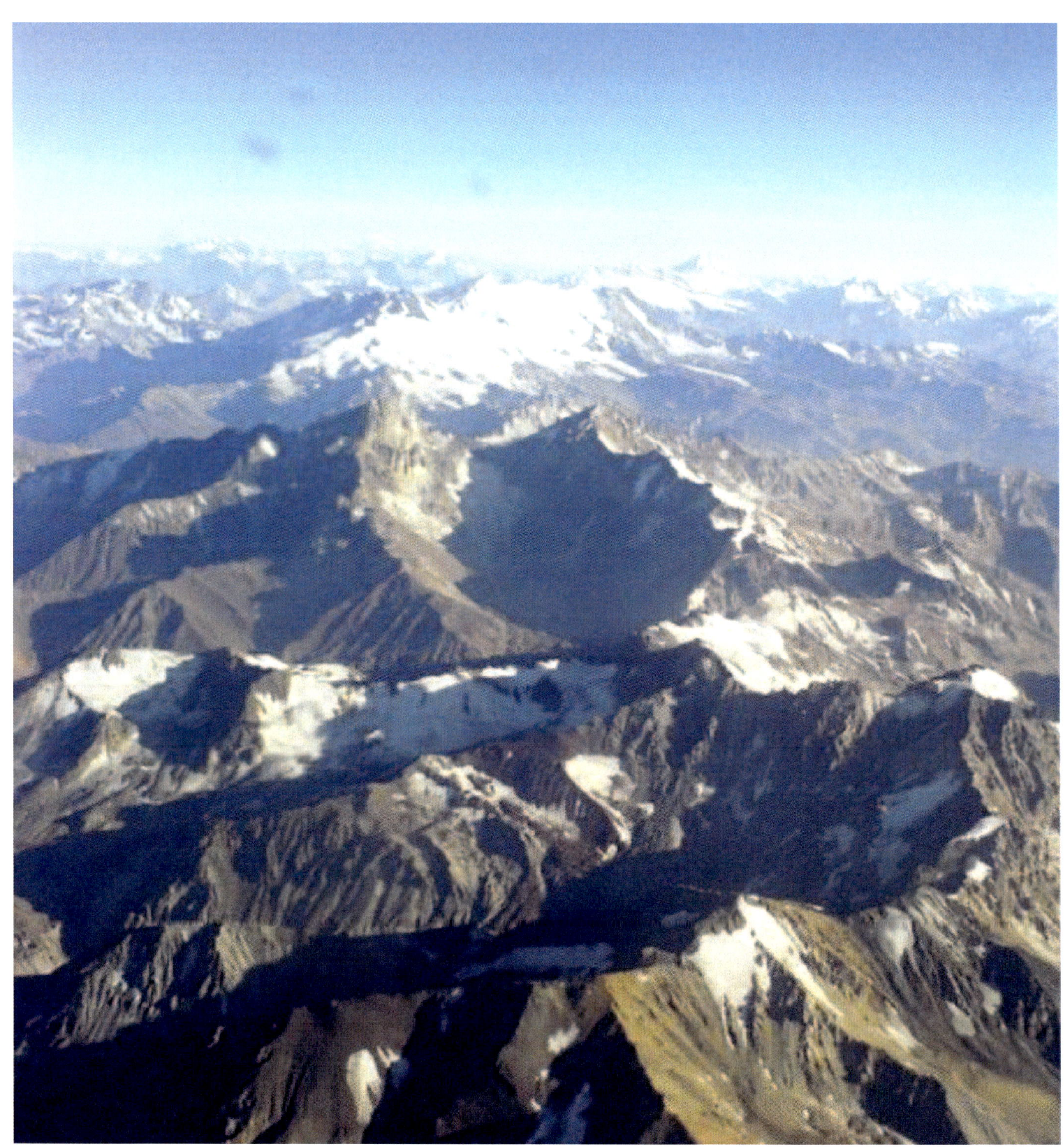

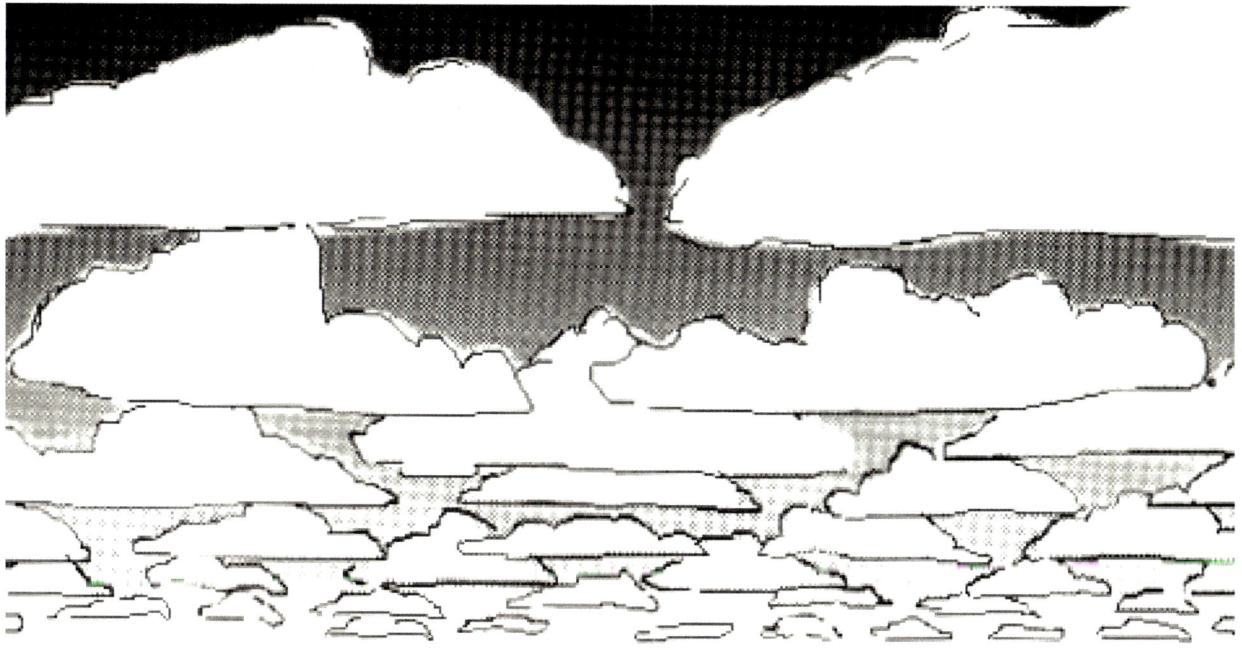

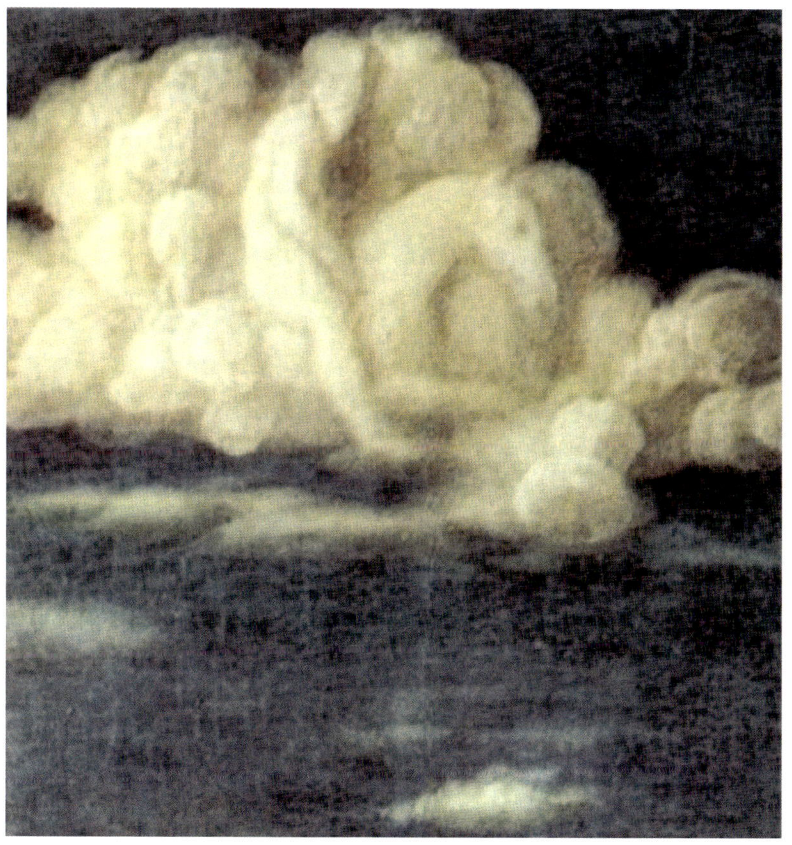

If you look at the sky on a bright clear day, you will see that it is a darker blue at the top and gets lighter as it goes to the horizon line. The clouds closest to us are larger and get smaller as they get further away. Notice on the left how an artist just shades one side of a mountain. Draw and shade one of the pictures on this page. Be sure and notice the difference in dark and light values.

hill- A hill is a raised part of the earth's surface that is smaller than a mountain.

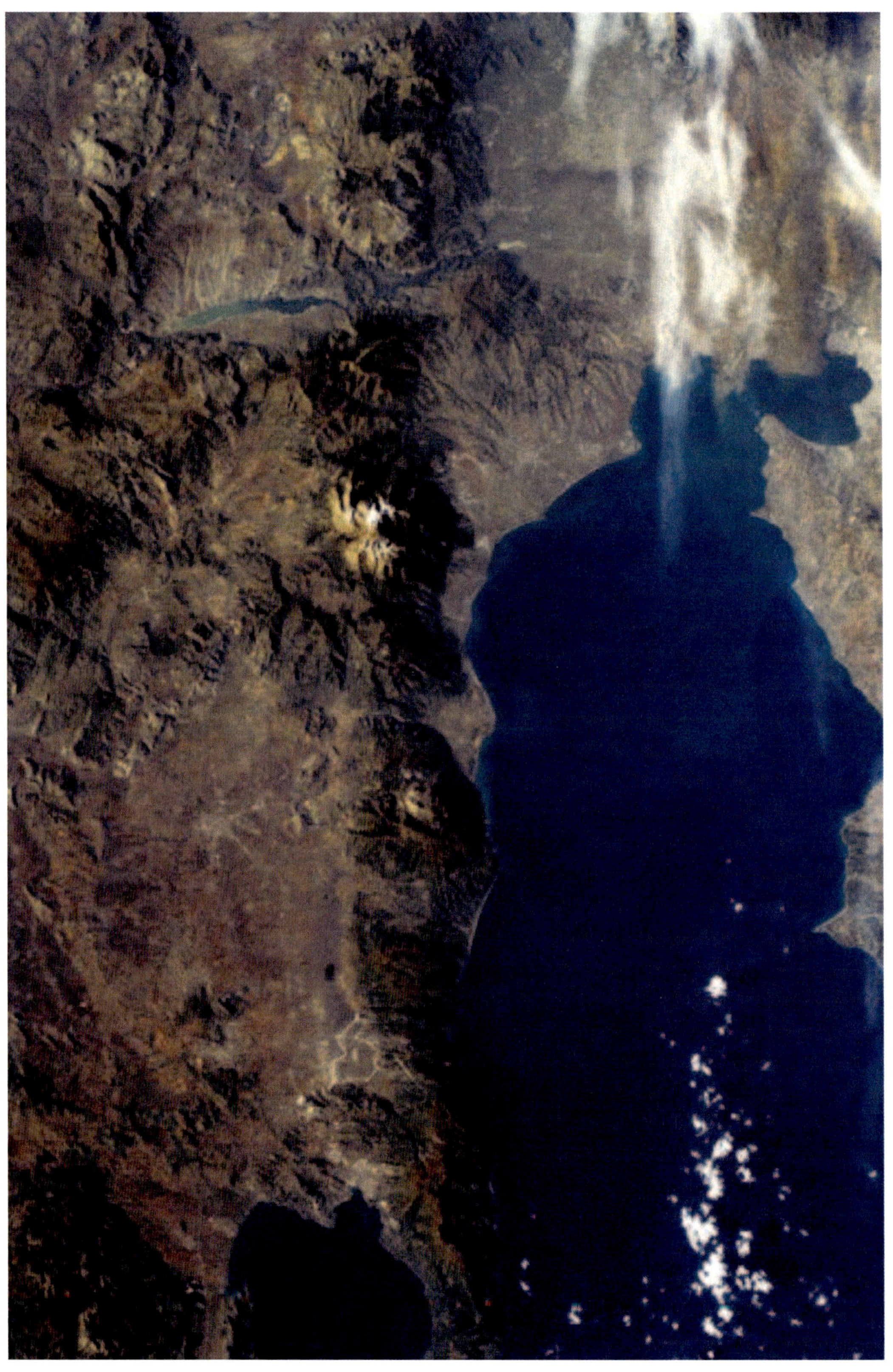

Mt. Olympus in Greece was thought to be the home of the Gods. How do you compare this mountain to the one on the previous page? **"Mountains are the beginning and the end of all natural scenery."**
John Ruskin Modern Painters (1856) Vol. 4, part 5, ch. 2. Do you agree with that?

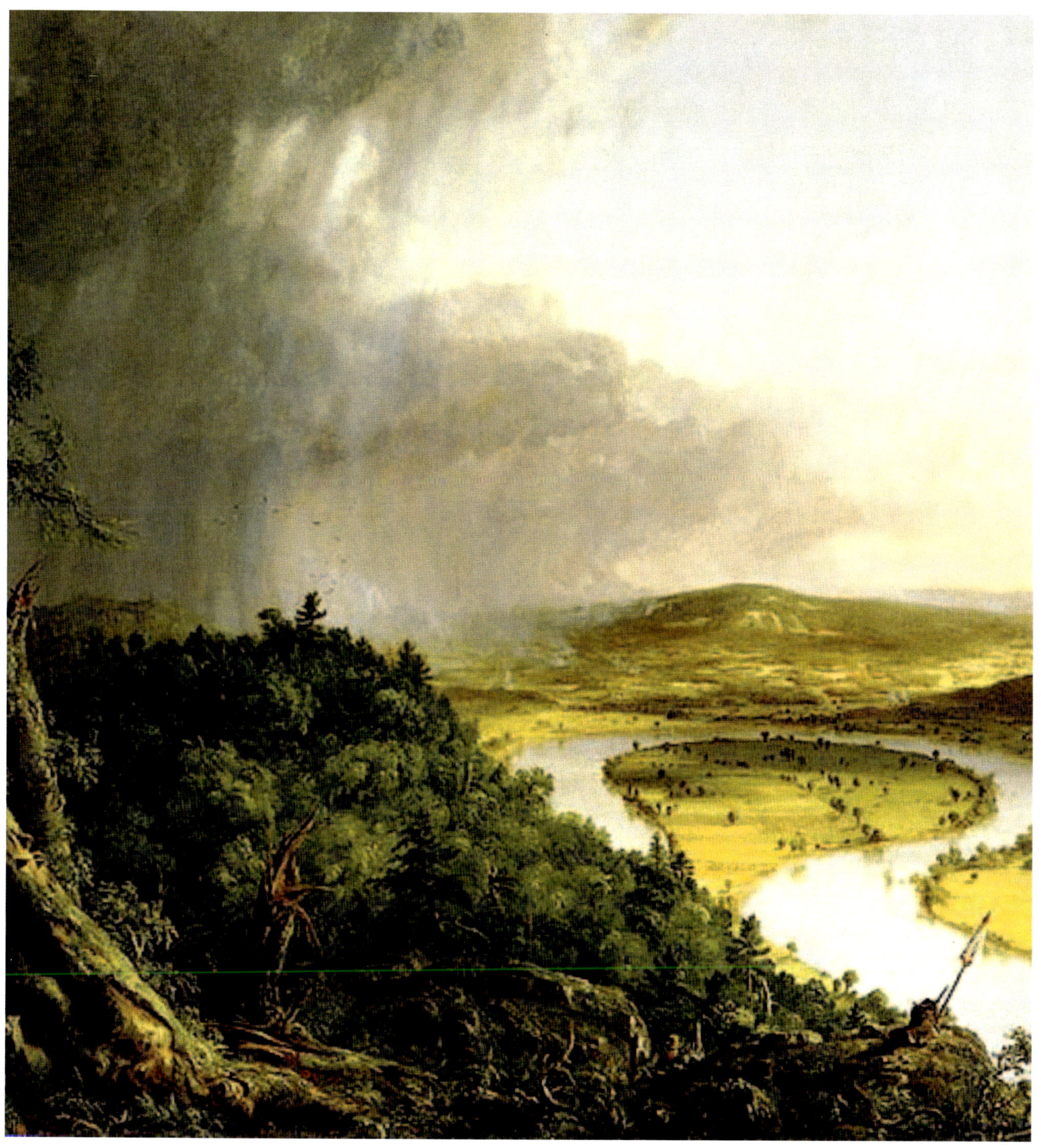

Thomas Cole did the above picture. He did many landscapes. You can see his skill as an artist by looking at the reflection in the water. The mountain in the background is lighter in color than the objects in the foreground. You can even see a small bit of smoke on the mountains above. Do you think they are the Smokey Mountain range? Cole was a founder of the Hudson River School of painting, wanting to paint realistic pictures of nature, and did many pictures of the Catskill Mountains in New York. http://en.wikipedia.org/wiki/Catskill_Mountains

lake- A lake is a body of water that is surrounded by land on all sides.

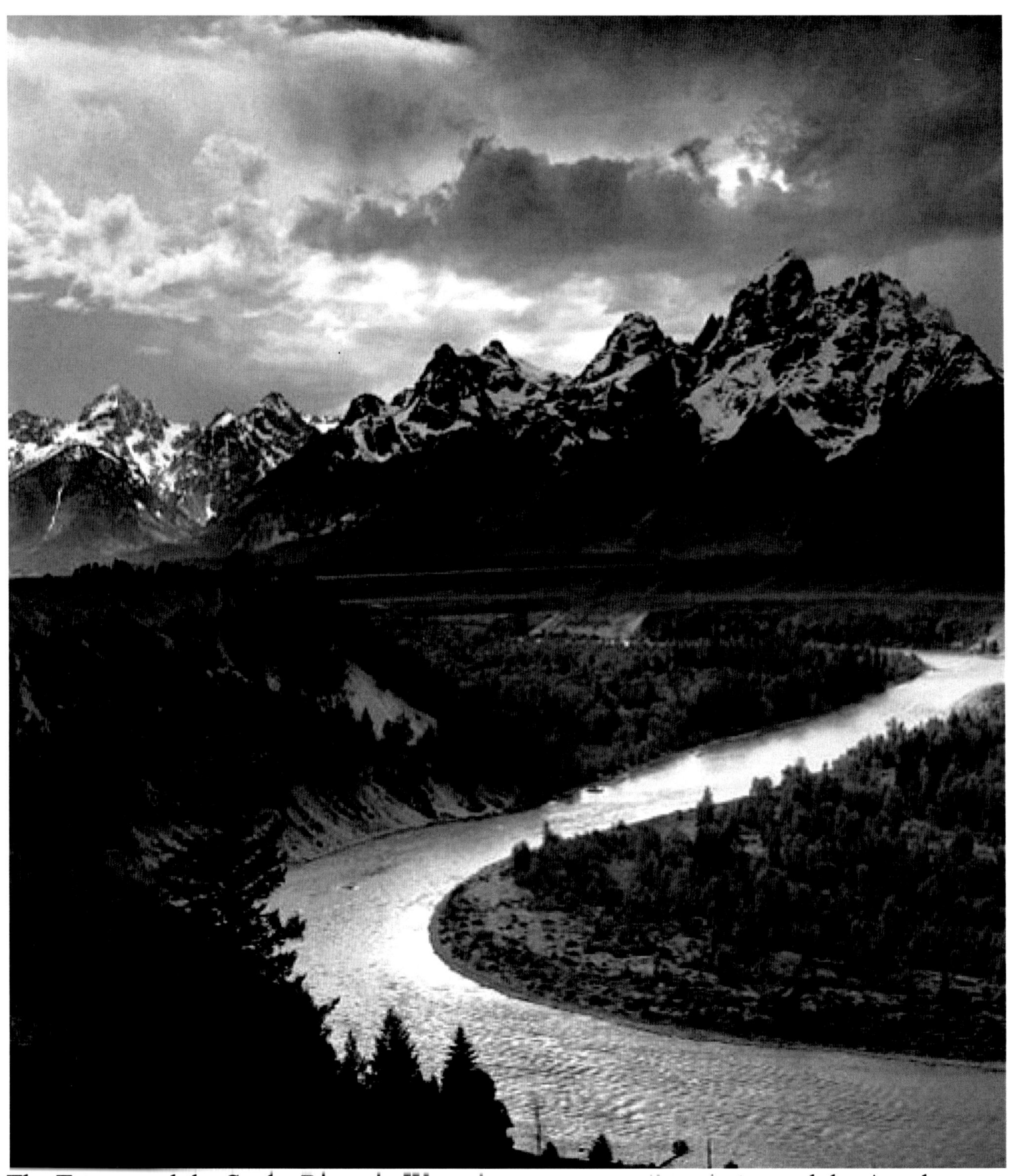

The Tetons and the Snake River in Wyoming are seen in this photograph by Ansel Adams, one of the master photographers of the world. His photos of nature are unsurpassed. Notice how the mountains closer to us are darker and the ones further away get lighter. This is called **atmospheric perspective**. Go to this great website for lessons on photography and the history of camera. http://www.kodak.com/US/en/corp/features/brownieCam/

river- A river is a large stream of water that flows through the land.

The artist who did the picture on the right was George Caleb Bingham. He was famous for doing pictures of the Mississippi and Missouri Rivers in the mid 1800's. Draw a famous river in America that is close to you. Label the parts seen below.

Delta- A delta is land where the mouth of a river flows into an ocean, sea, estuary, lake or another river.

Tributary-This is a stream that flows into a larger river.

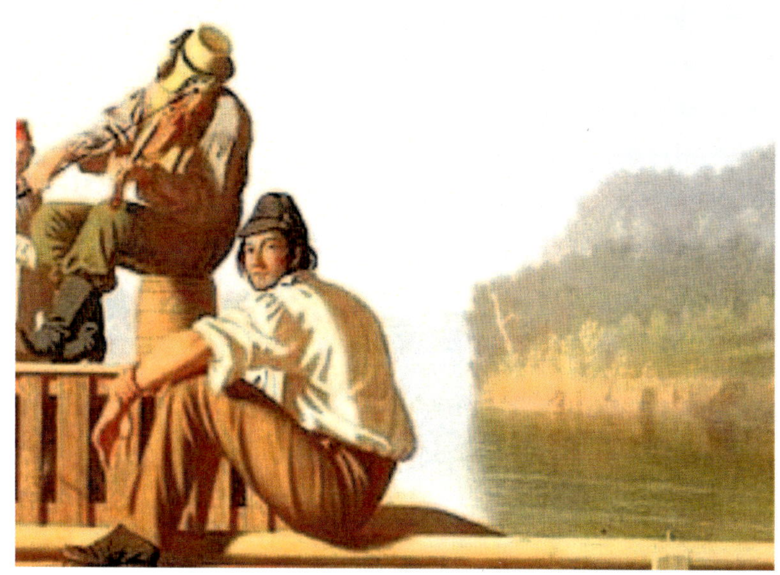

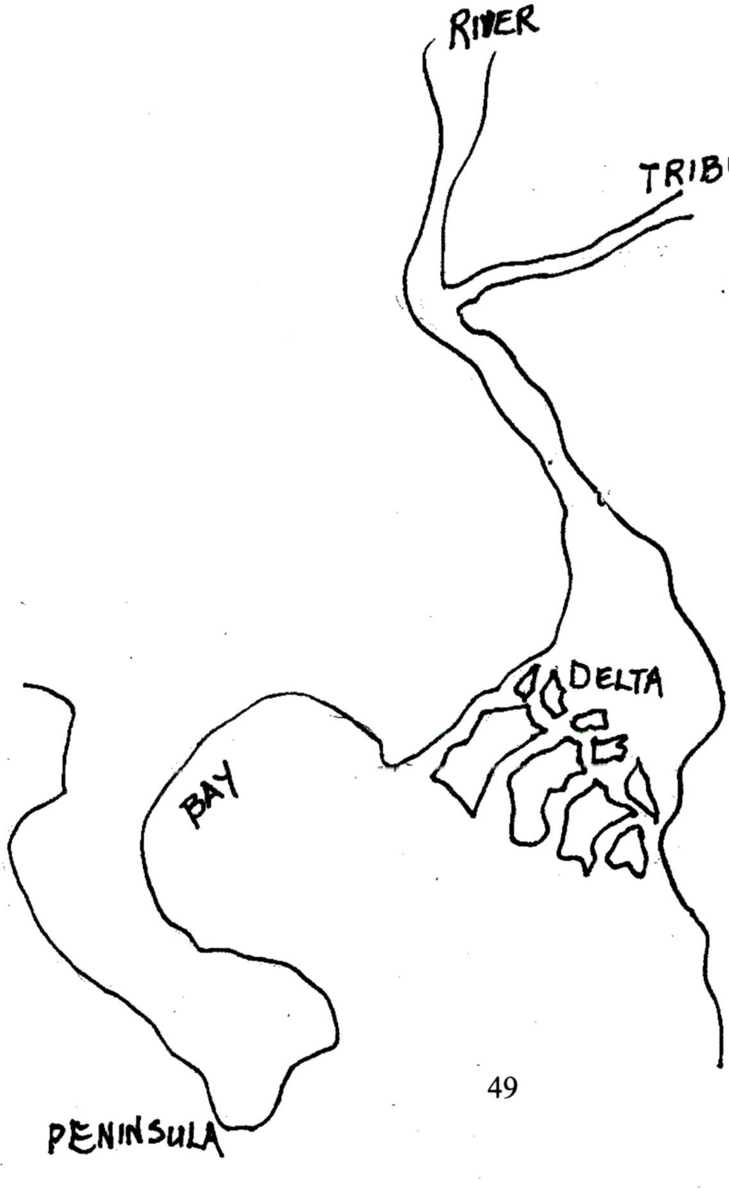

RIVER

TRIBUTARY

DELTA

BAY

PENINSULA

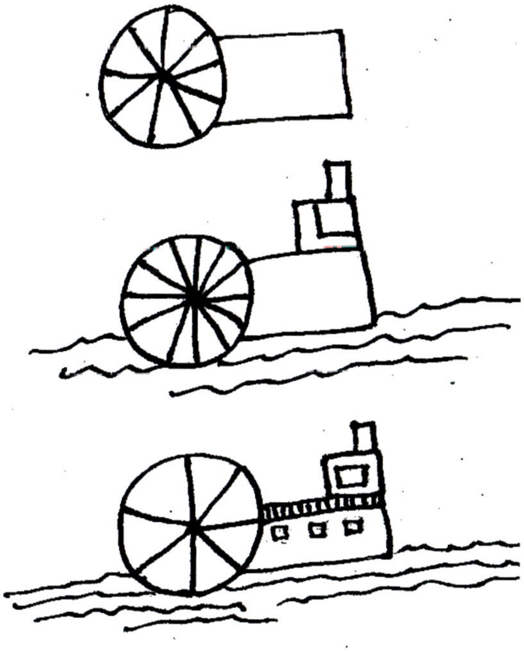

Covered Bridges

Some people travel around America and do pictures of covered bridges.

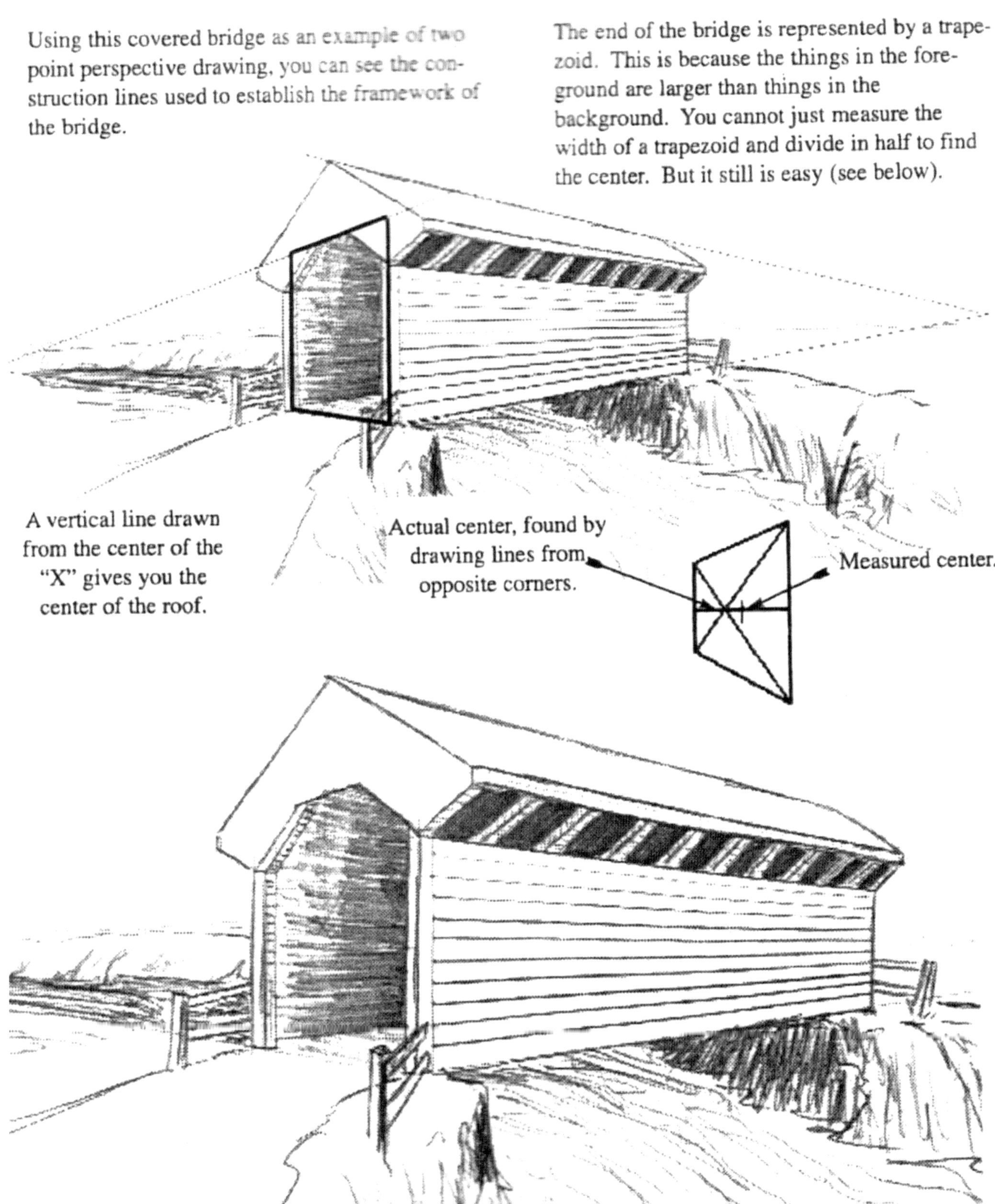

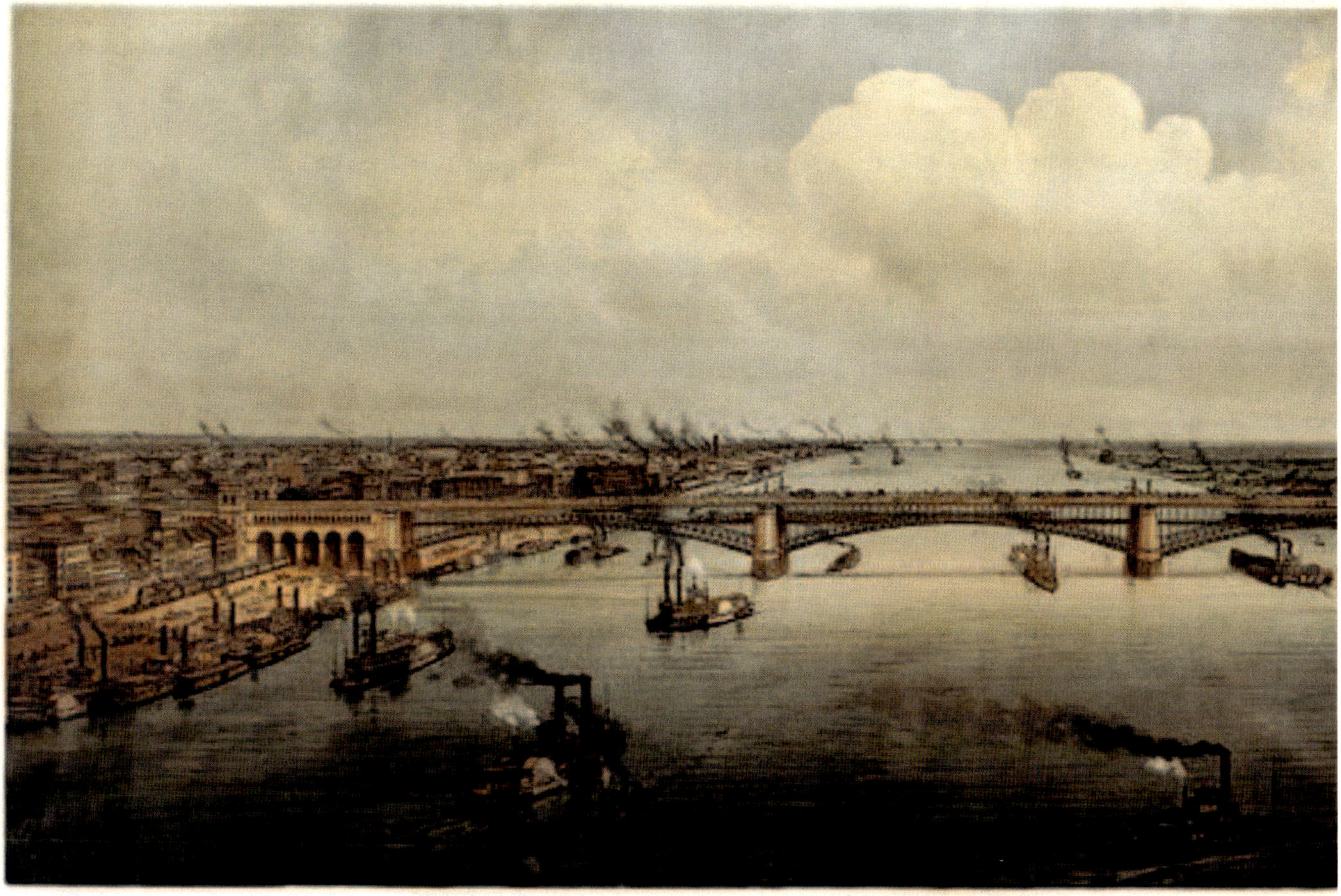

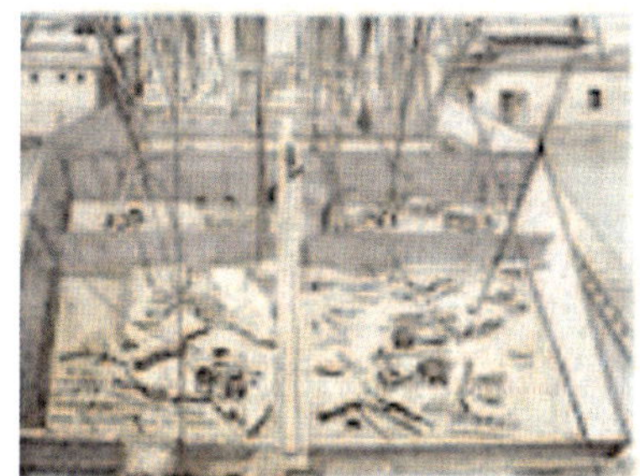

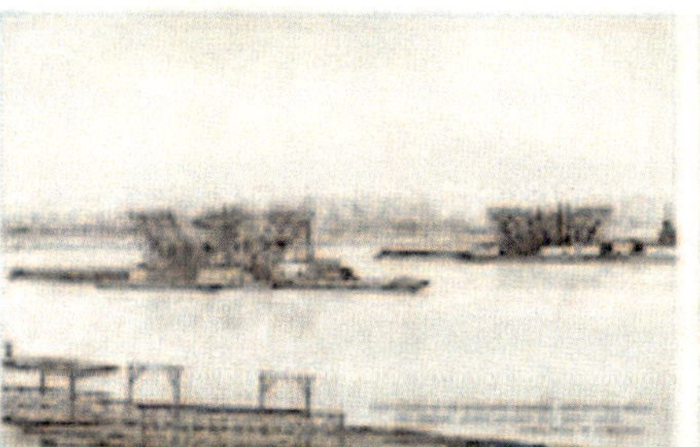

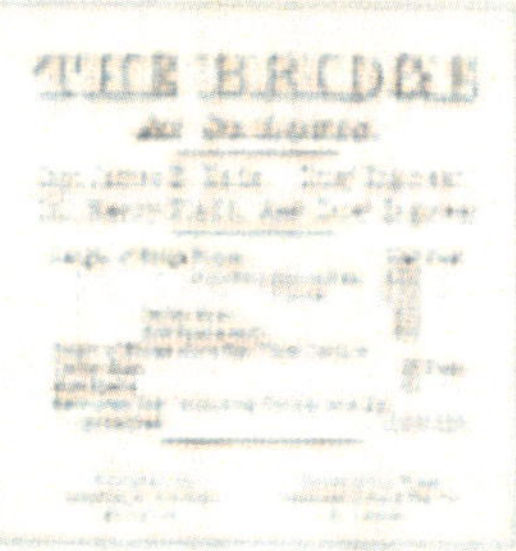

THE BRIDGE

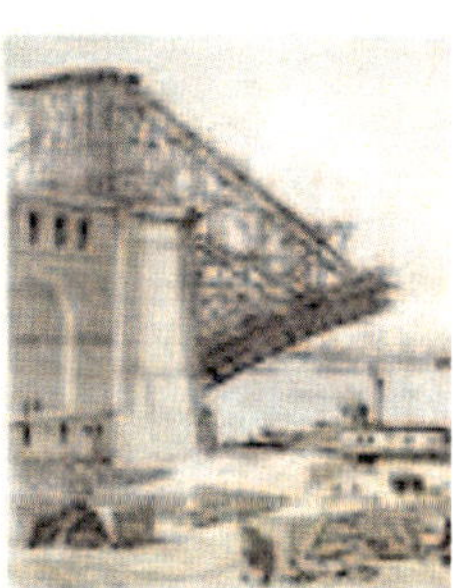

Above is an example of one point perspective. The bridge is larger if it is closer to us. It gets smaller in the distance. The picture above and one the left are also examples of perspective. The picture above is of the Eads Bridge in St.Louis, MO. You can go to this website to read all about it: http://www.sensato.com/1921/25eadsbr.htm
Engineers design and build bridges. Leonardo da Vinci was an artist/engineer who designed a bridge that was recently used in Norway. An architect took Leonardo's "Golden Horn" bridge and built it in 2001 in Norway. Read about this at http://www.vebjorn-sand.com/press_release/20011101.htm.

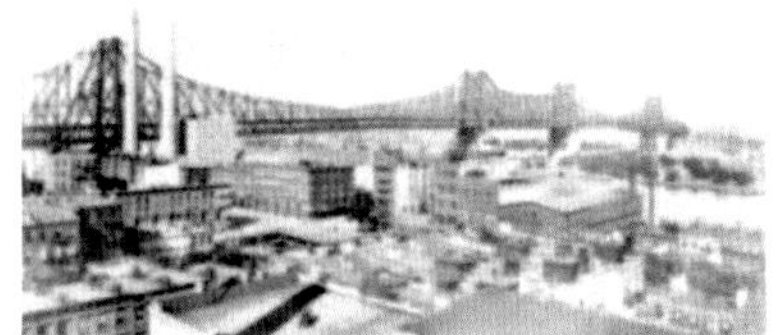

The bridge below is the Queensboro Bridge in New York City. It is one of the most ornate bridges in America. The bridge was completed in 1909 by architect Gustav Lindenthal. Architecture is art that you can walk inside of. The picture below is not only an example of perspective, but also an example of scale. If you look at the boat beside the bridge, you can get an idea of how large the bridge really is. The bridge on the left is an example of a **reflection** in the water. Take a piece of dark blue paper and use light colors to draw the bridge on the left. If you want to know the details of the bridge, draw it like the one below.

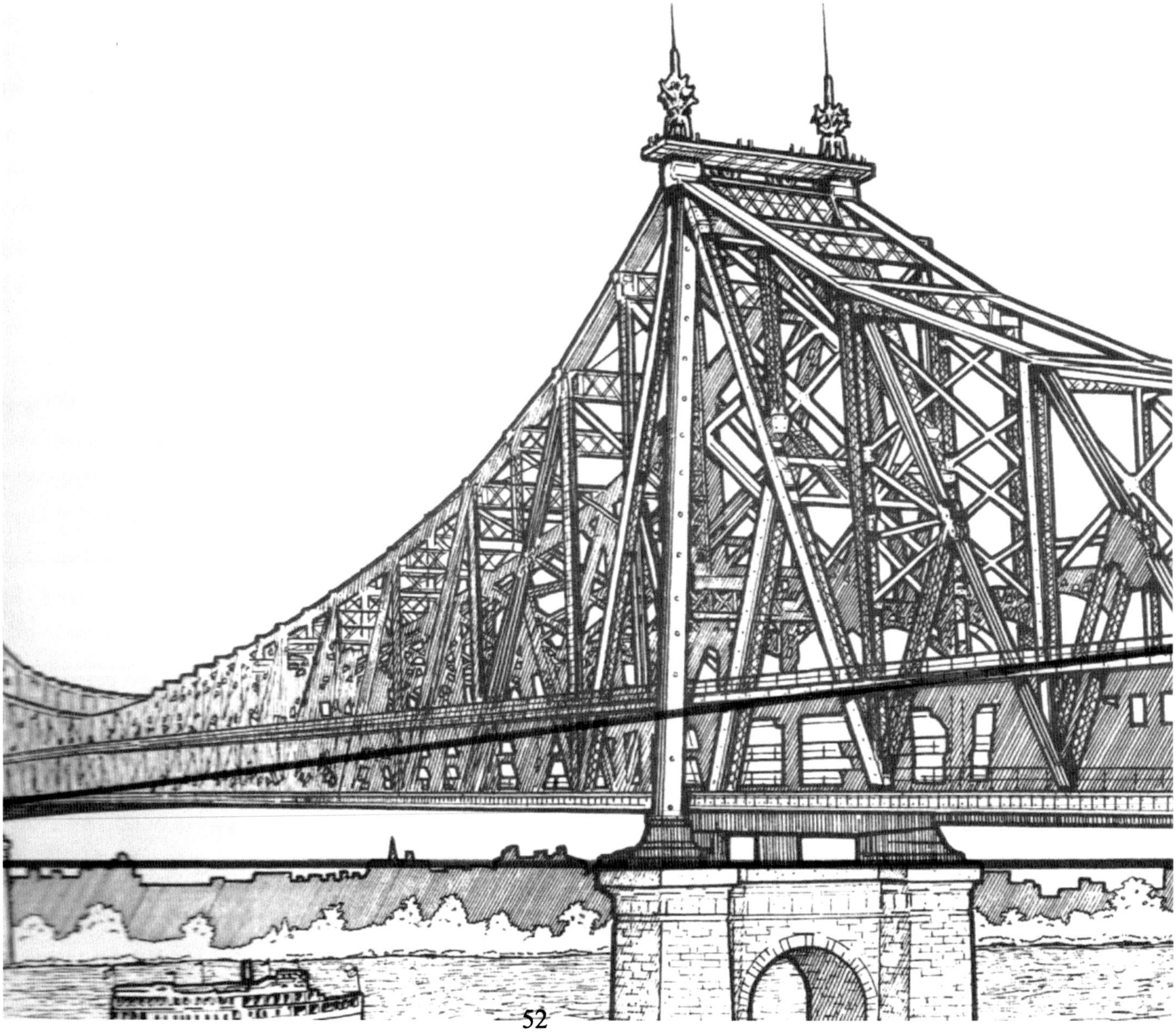

Deserts of the World

For a wonderful lesson on how to draw a cactus go to this website:http://entertainment.howstuffworks.com/how-to-draw-landscapes2.htm Notice in the desert below how the hills are slightly different in color. One side is darker and one side is lighter. Put a boat of some kind in this desert picture. A desert sometimes looks alot like an ocean. Andrew Wyeth did a painting similar to this.

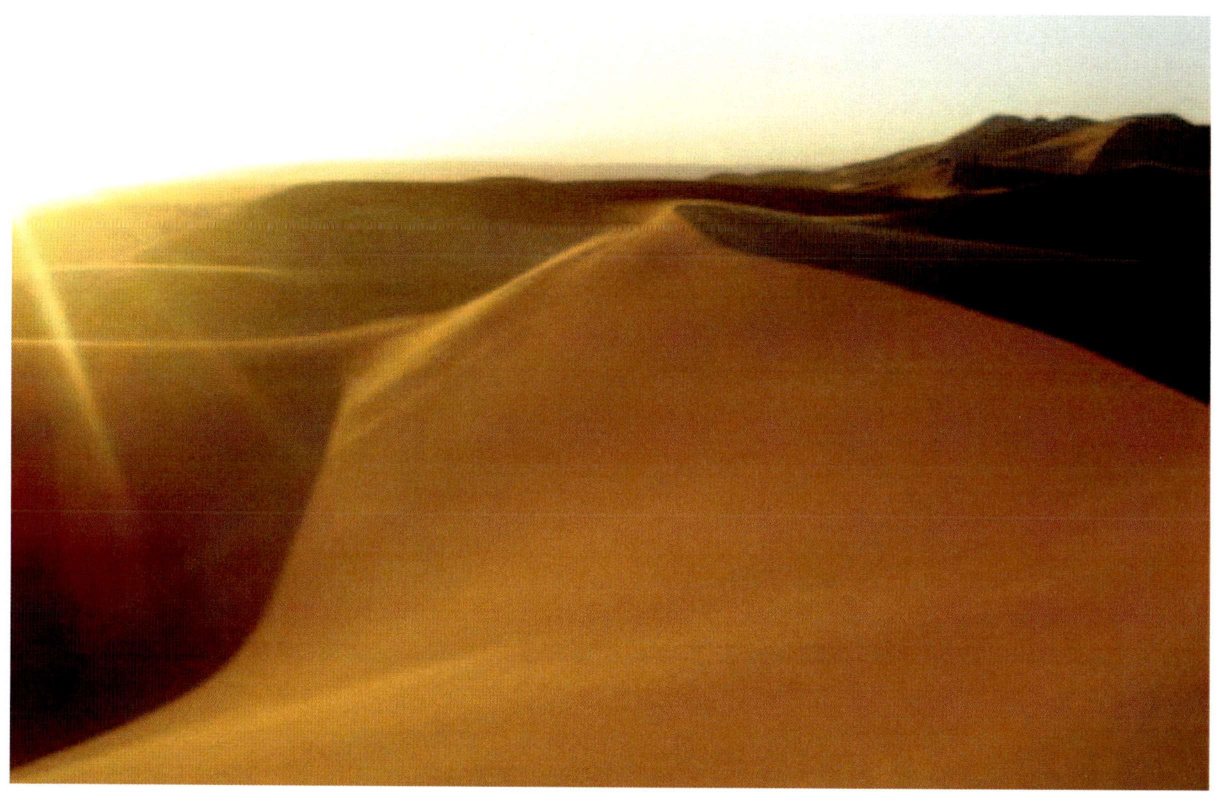

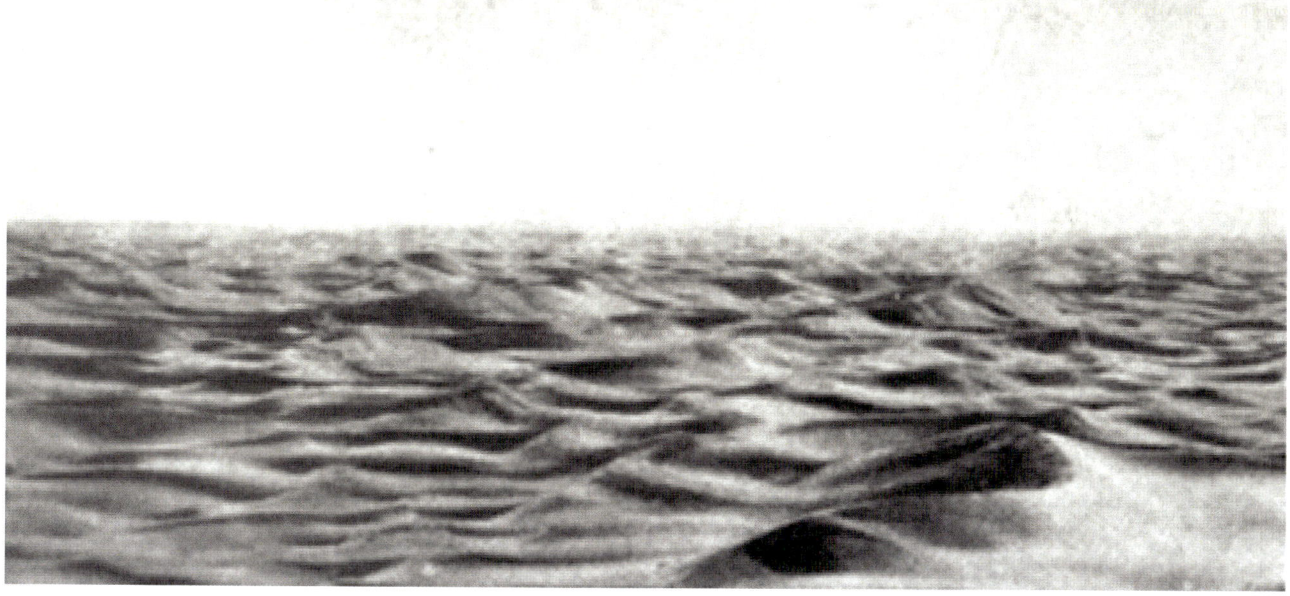

You can go to the website to see Mt. Rushmore where four presidents were carved out of the solid rock of a mountain.
http://www.nps.gov/moru/
Carving rock is called **subtractive sculpture**. You can't add to it. Who could imagine you could carve a mountain using dynamite and come up with something like this? Draw this grouping with a different group of famous people.

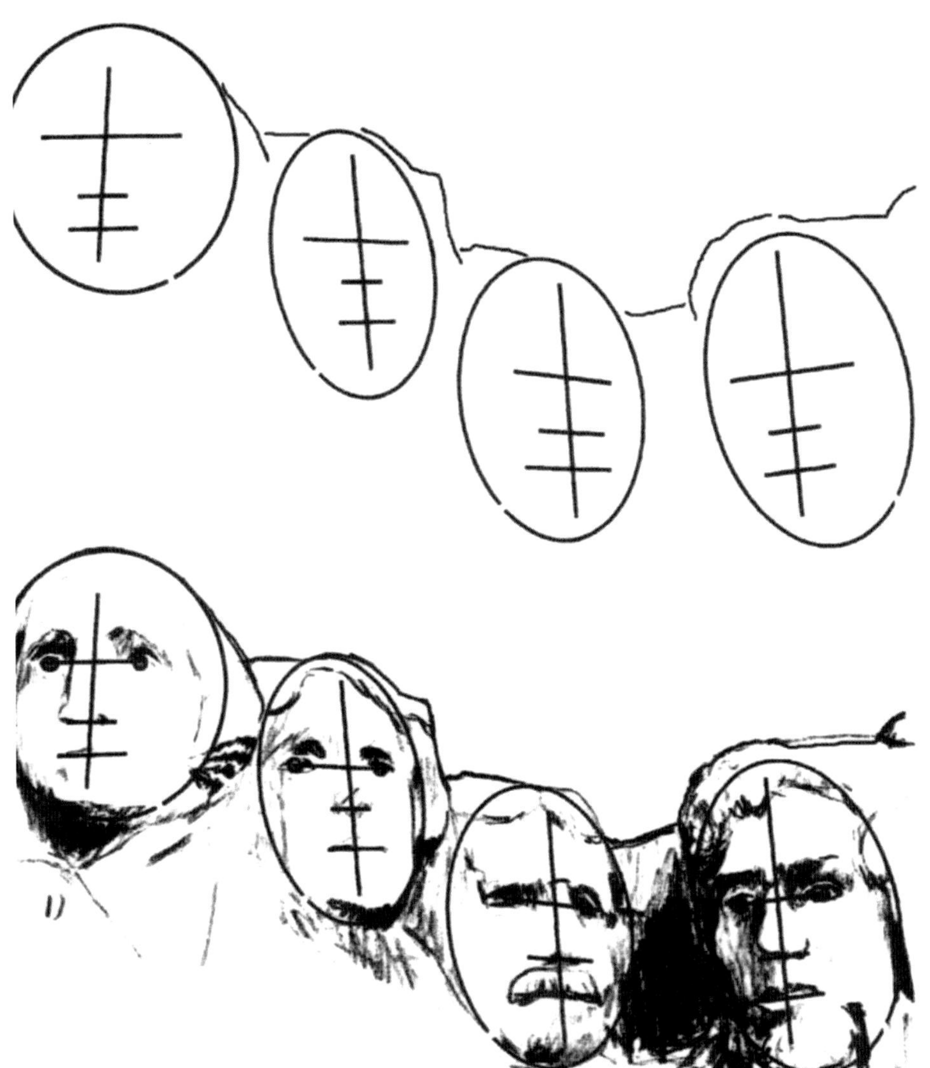

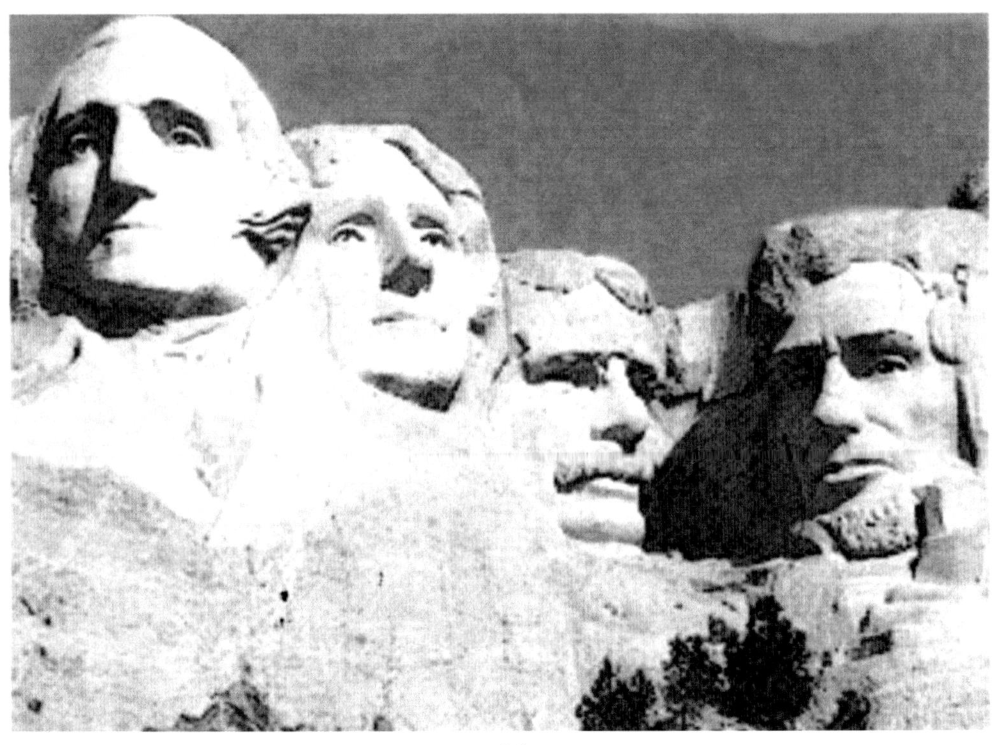

Frederic Remington was a master artist who pictured the American desert. The picture on the right is done by Remington. The Navajo and Hopi Indians live in the American southwest desert areas. Remington pictured the American cowboy and the west. The horned lizard is a creature you would see in the American desert.

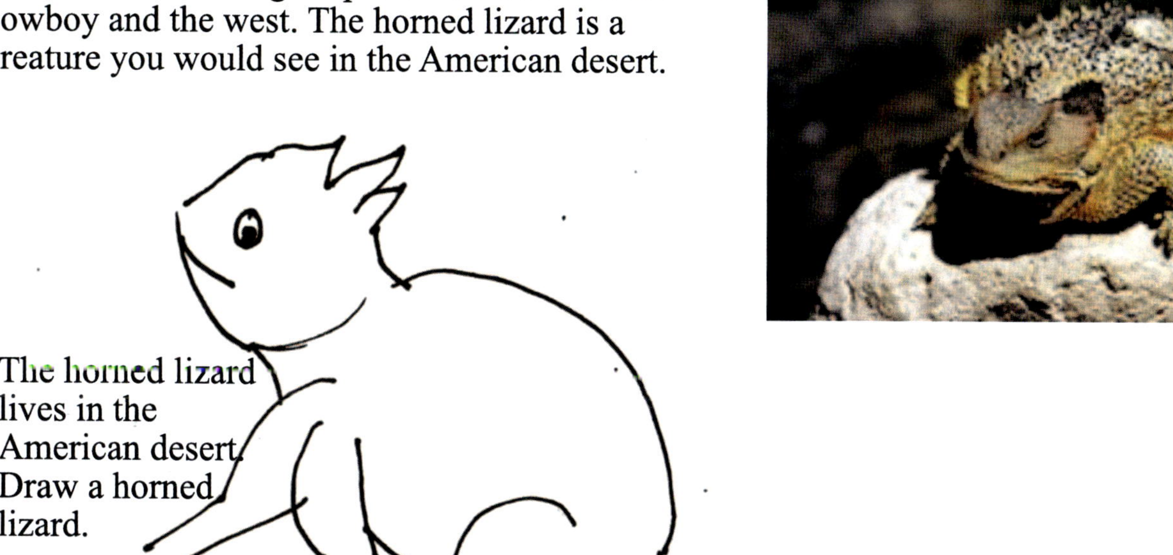

The horned lizard lives in the American desert. Draw a horned lizard.

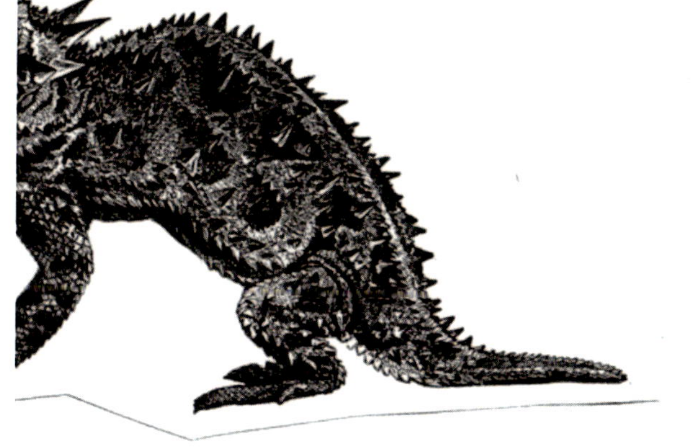

Always define your space with simple lines, and then add the implied texture. **Shading, shadow and texture** make things look real.

Look at the skin of the lizards. They have an **implied texture**. Do you see how the horns are shaded?

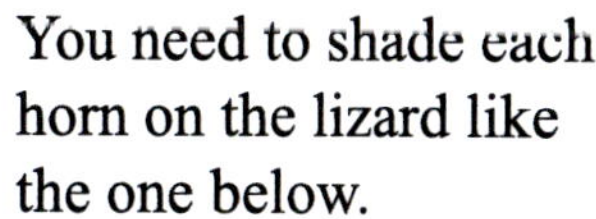

You need to shade each horn on the lizard like the one below.

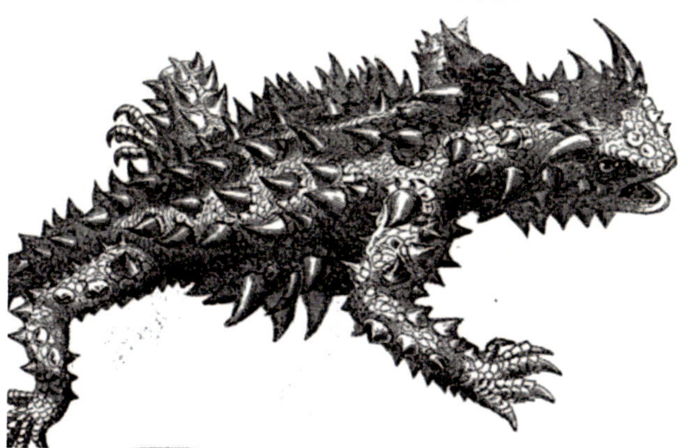

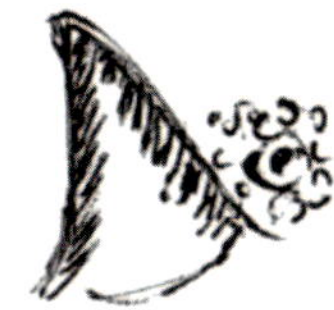

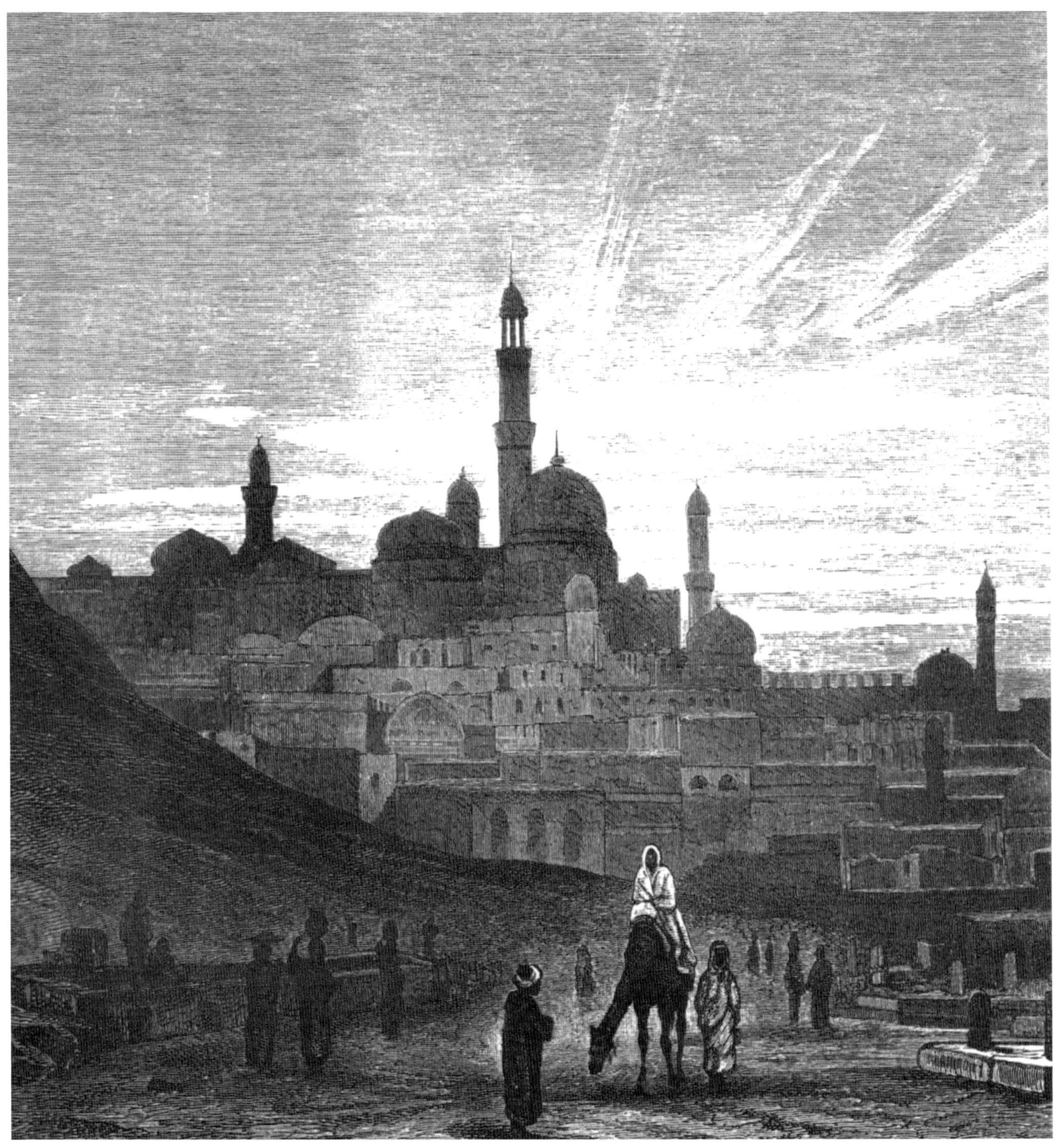

The wonderful picture above is of Jerusalem. The domes you see are called onion domes. Do you think they look like an onion dome from Russia? Draw the picture above, but start with the light background. You can get a yellow oil pastel, or chalk pastel, and draw the color out to the edges of the paper. You can add orange and red color. The edges of the sky do in blue. Be sure and blend the colors well. You can do the horizon line with a charcoal pencil and do the rest of the picture in willow charcoal and regular charcoal. You color will be in the sky. The effect will be dazzling.

Jaffa

The city of Jaffa is famous in history. During the crusades, Jaffa was captured. Go to this website and read about Jaffa: http://en.wikipedia.org/wiki/Jaffa

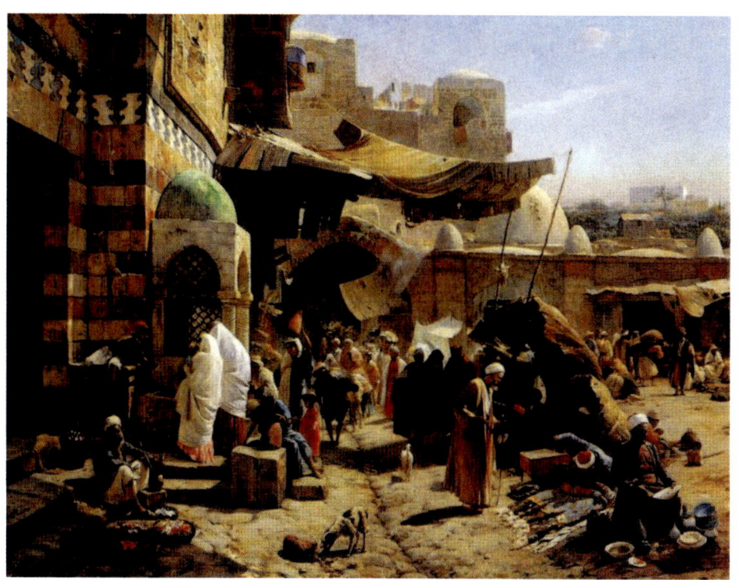

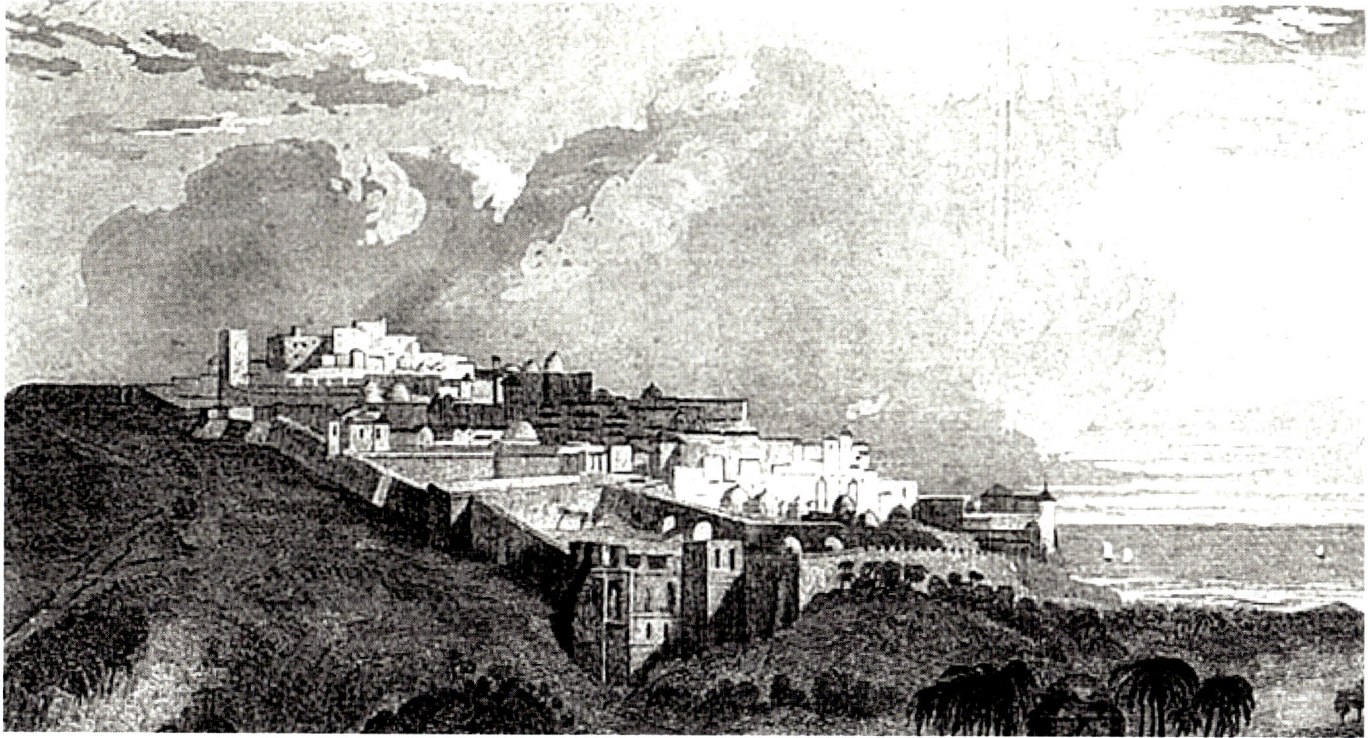

On this page are pictures of Jaffa in Israel. Each is from a different perspective. On the top right, history is pictured. Above the artist captures the beauty of the city. On the right, modern Jaffa is shown in a photography. Can you live in a desert and have a coast on the sea? Read about Jaffa. The first-century historian Flavius Josephus was so impressed by the area that he wrote, "One may call this place the ambition of Nature." Josephus also reported a thriving fishing industry at this time, with 230 boats regularly working in the lake, according to the Wikipedia. Allow students to choose one of these pictures and ways to communicate about the city, and do a picture of Jaffa.

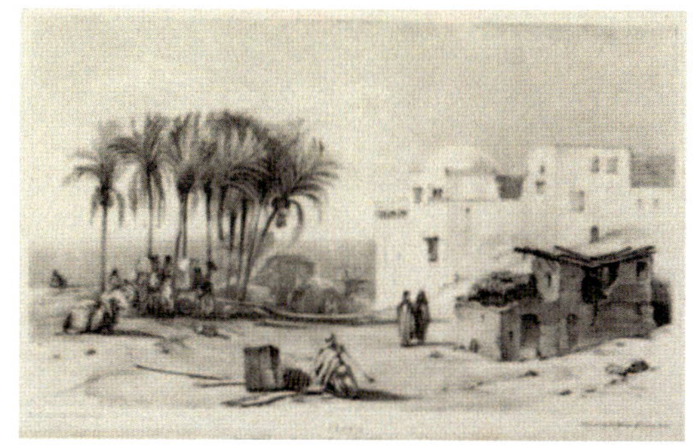

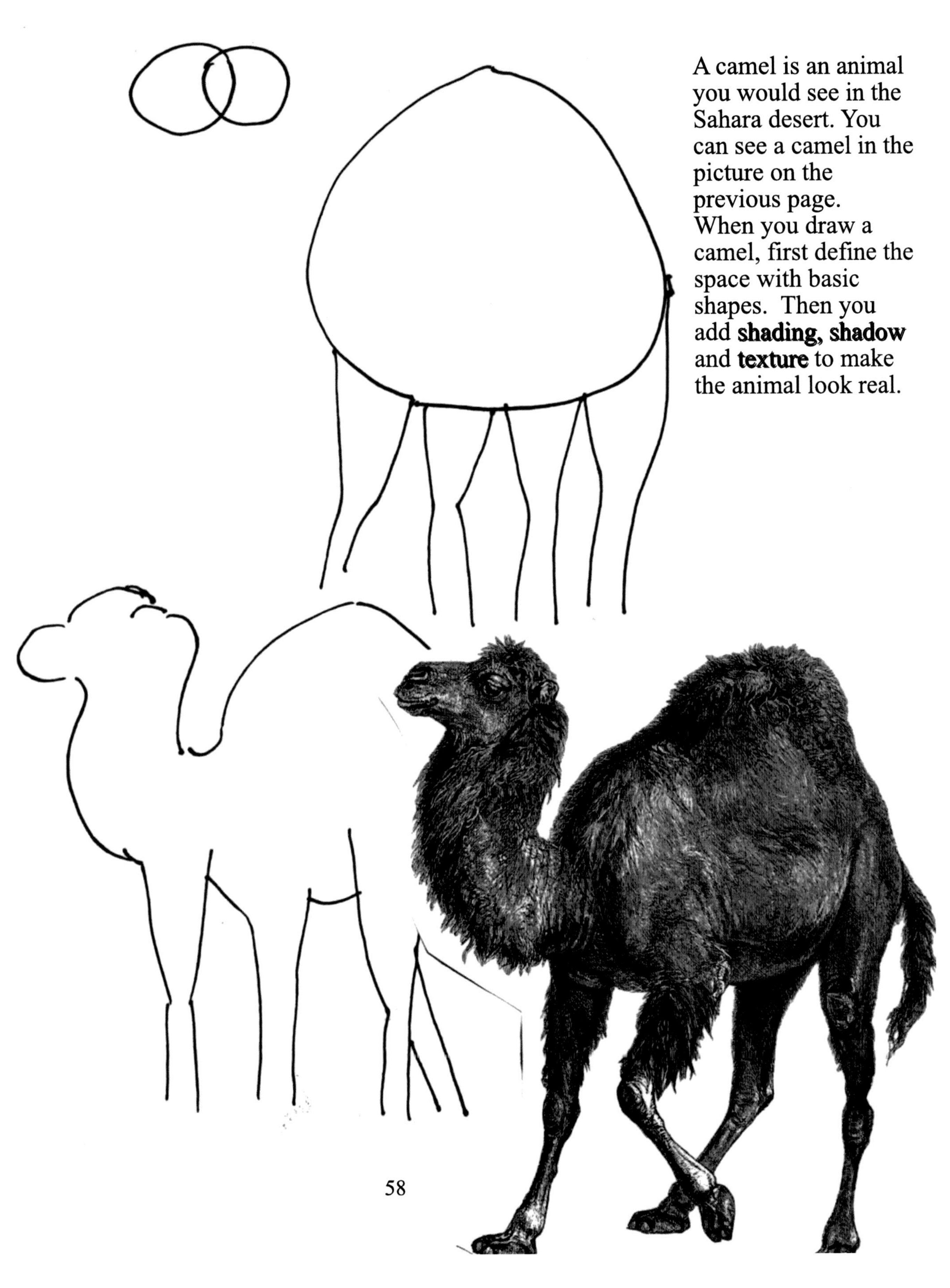

A camel is an animal you would see in the Sahara desert. You can see a camel in the picture on the previous page. When you draw a camel, first define the space with basic shapes. Then you add **shading, shadow** and **texture** to make the animal look real.

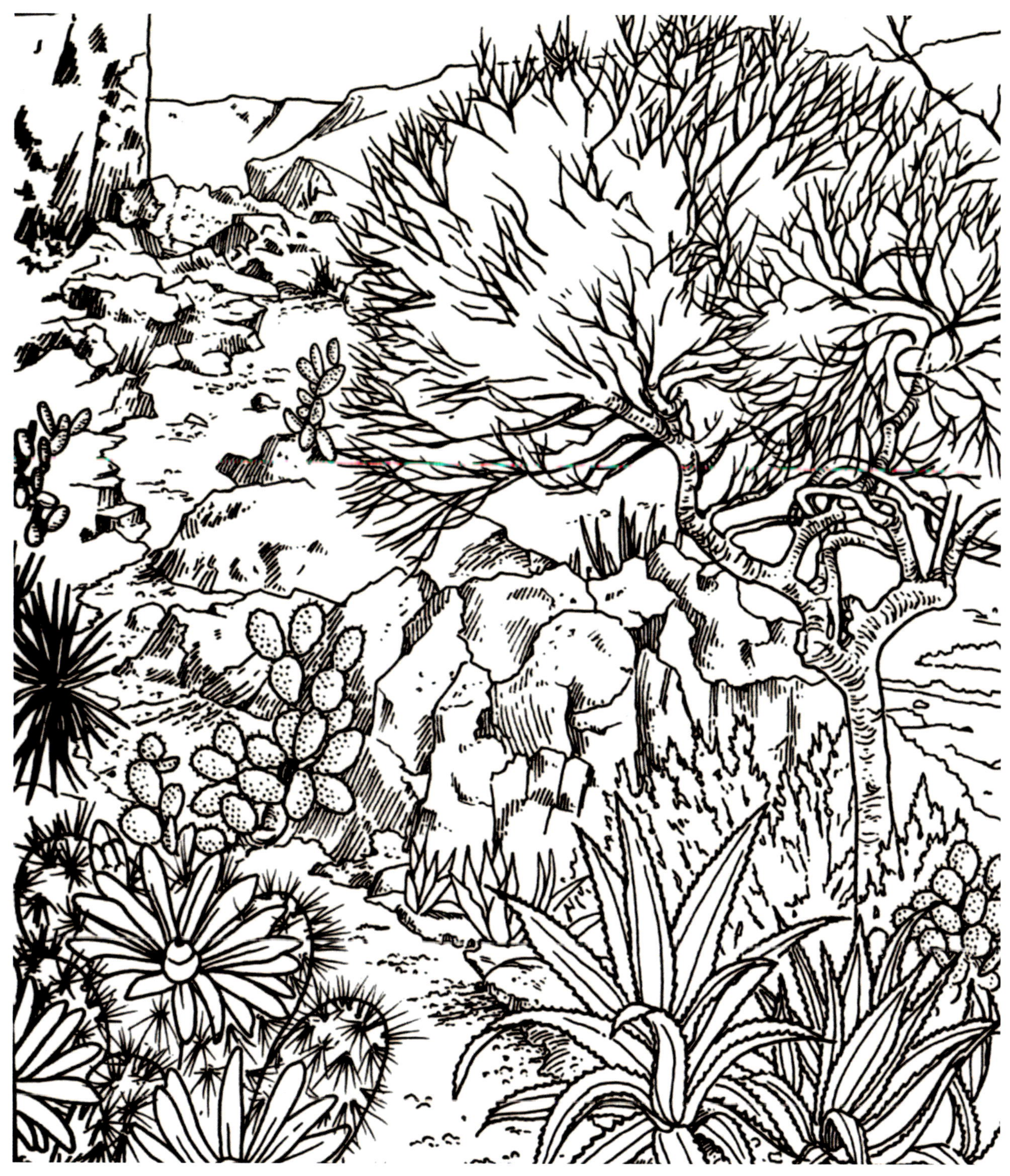

The picture above is desert **flora** and **fauna** you could see in the American desert of the southwest. Plants you see in the desert can be a variety of beautiful cactus with lovely flowers. There is such a contrast between the beauty of a desert flower and the prickly points of a cactus.

Go to this website to see one of the great artists of the American west including the desert. Charles Russell did many pictures of the American Indians living in the desert: http://commons.wikimedia.org/wiki/Category:Charles_Marion_Russell

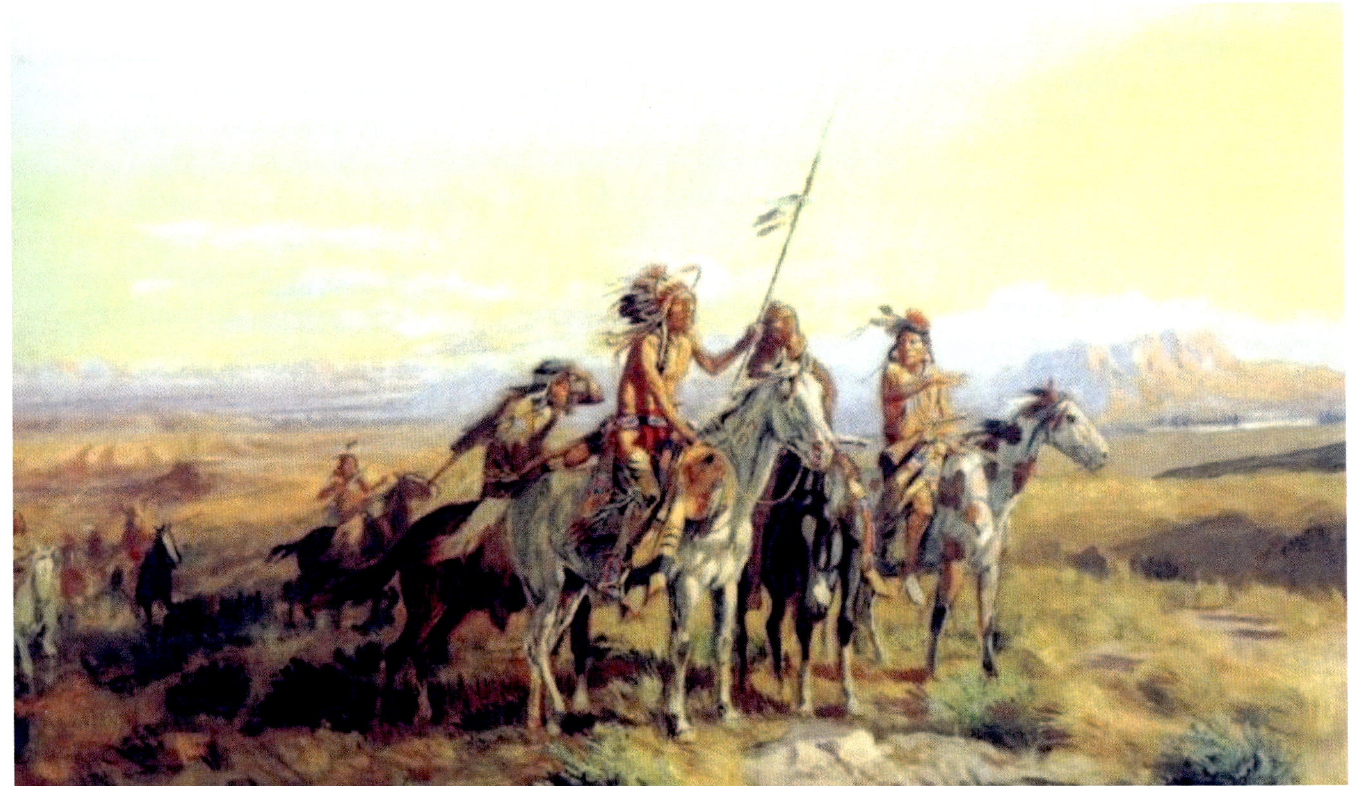

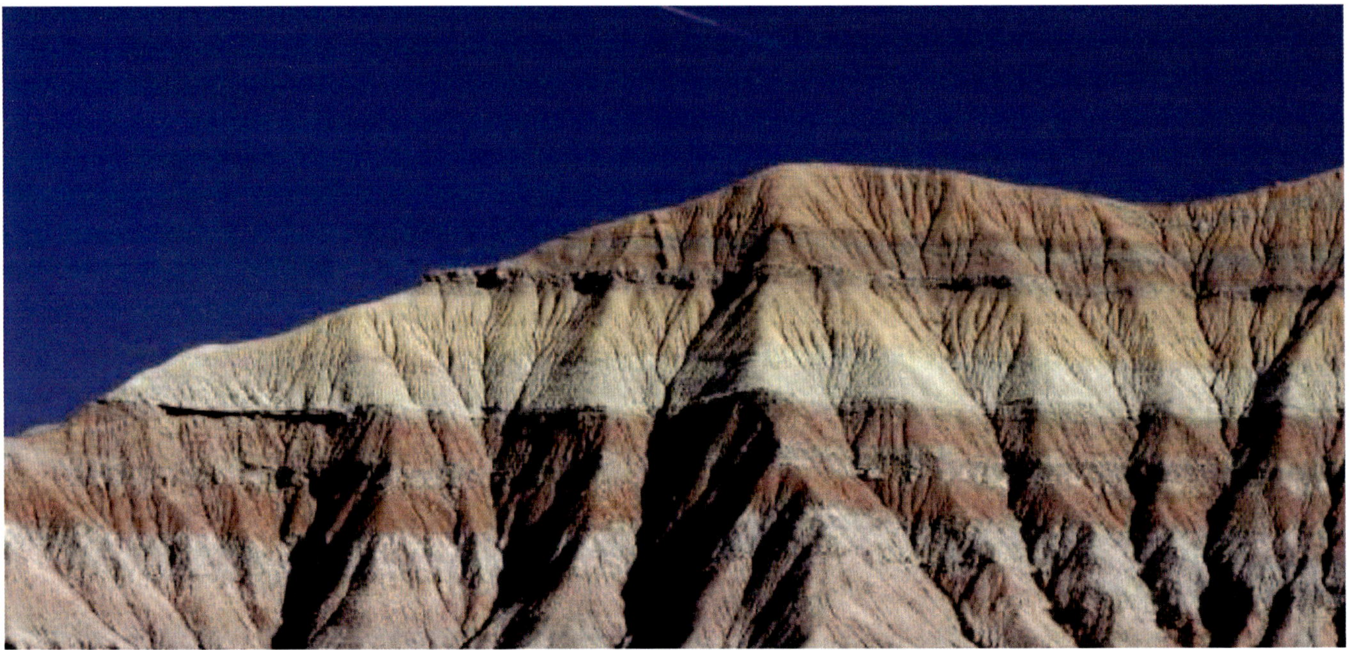

The painting on the top of the page was done by the master artist Charles Russell. He did pictures of the early American west and gave us historical pictures of the flora and fauna and the cowboys and Indians of that period. The mountains in the photo above, are in the background of the picture at the top of the page. In America, we have what is known as the "Painted Desert."

canyon- A canyon is a narrow valley with steep high sides.

plain- A plain is a flat stretch of land.

plateau- A plateau is a flat or gently rolling piece of land that is above sea level.

Draw a horse first and put on a desert background. Layer the background step by step

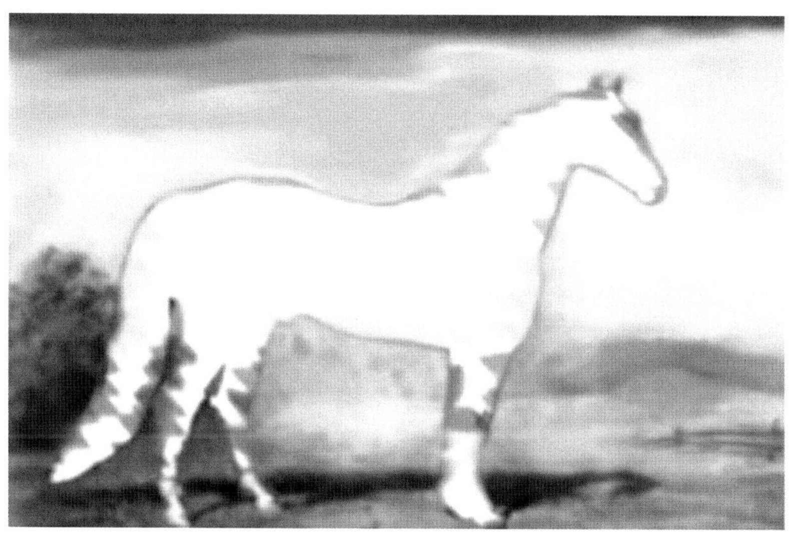

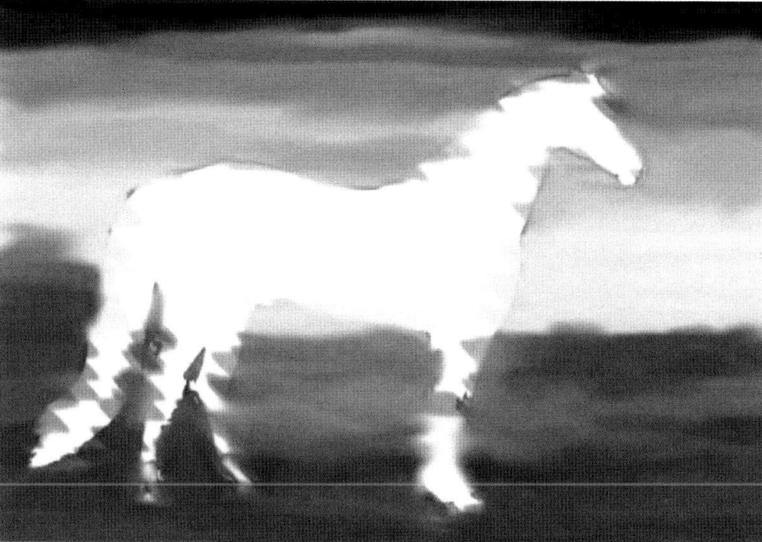

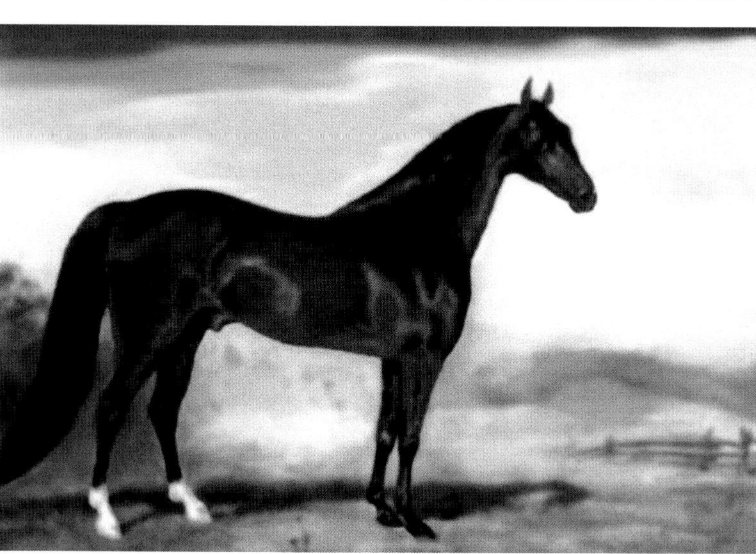

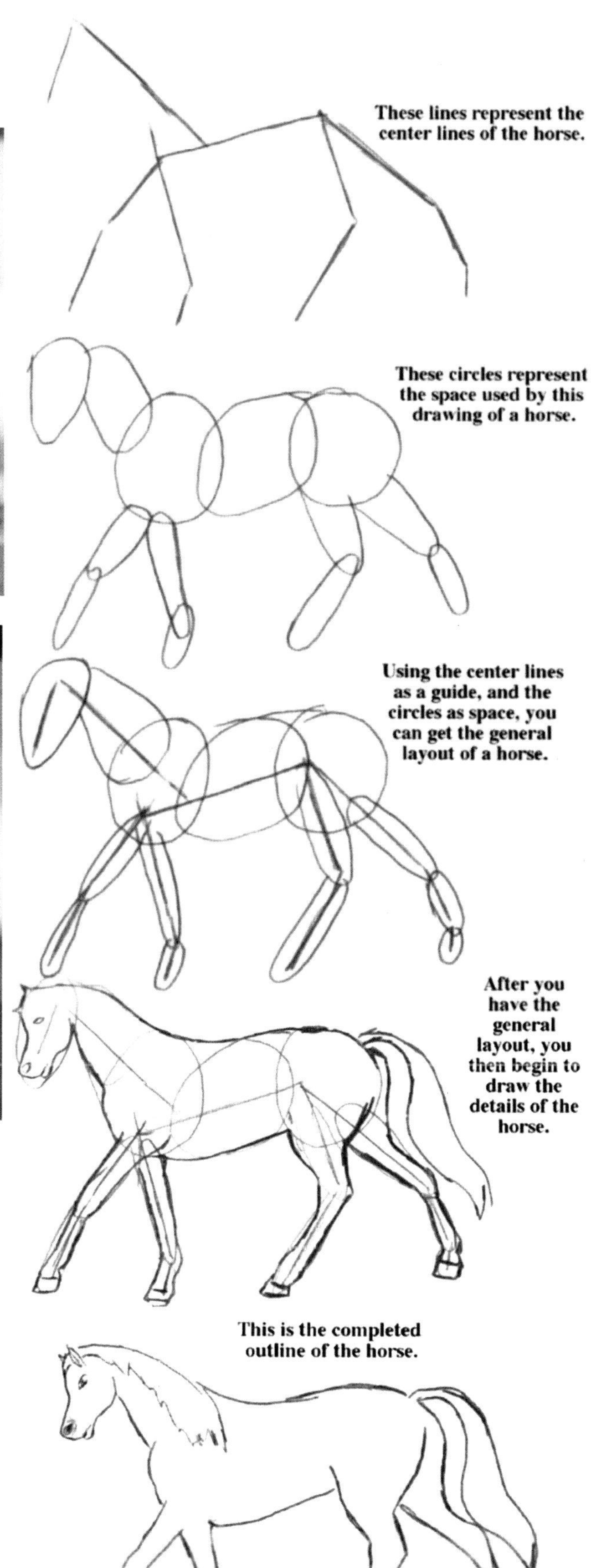

Islands of the World

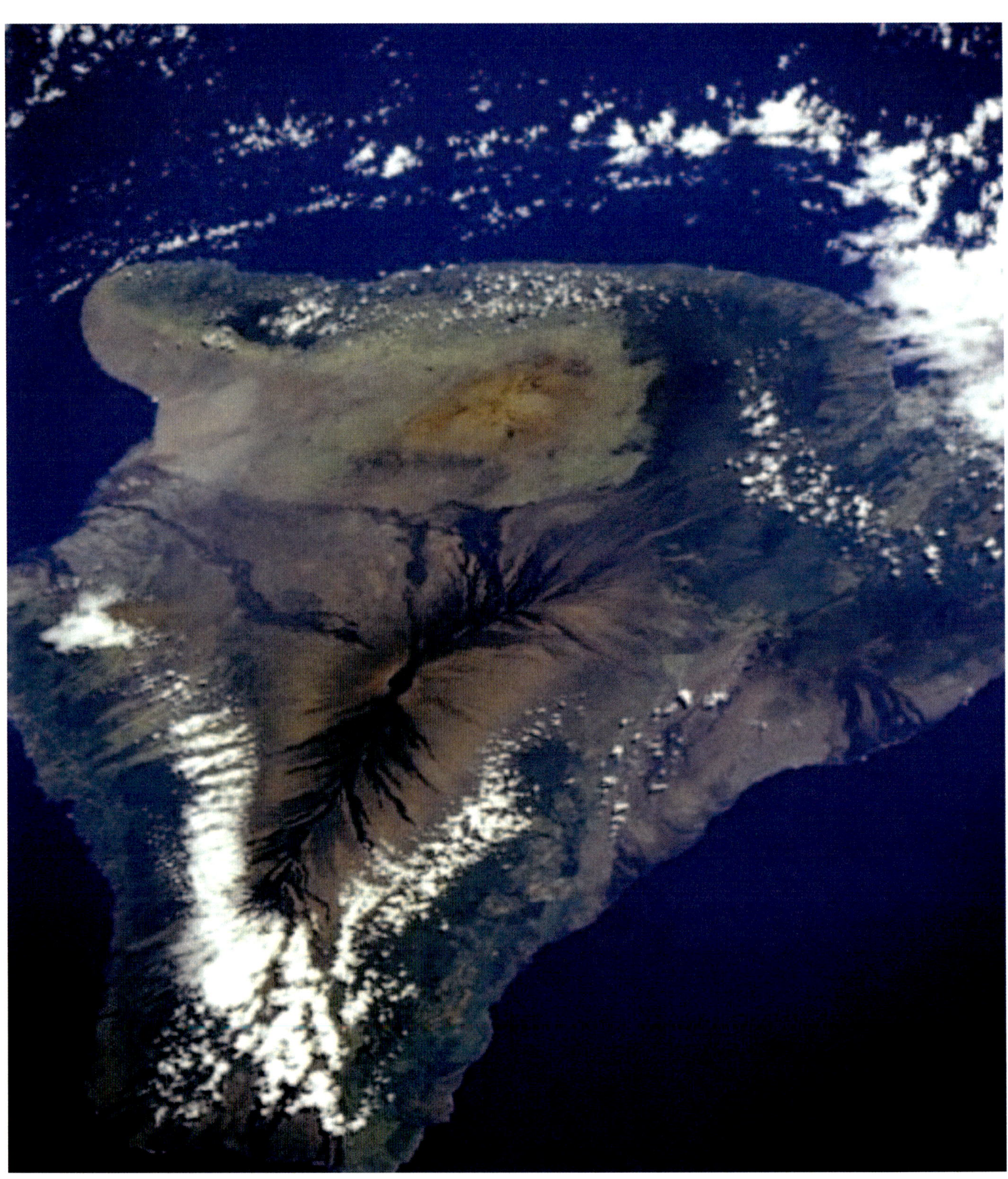

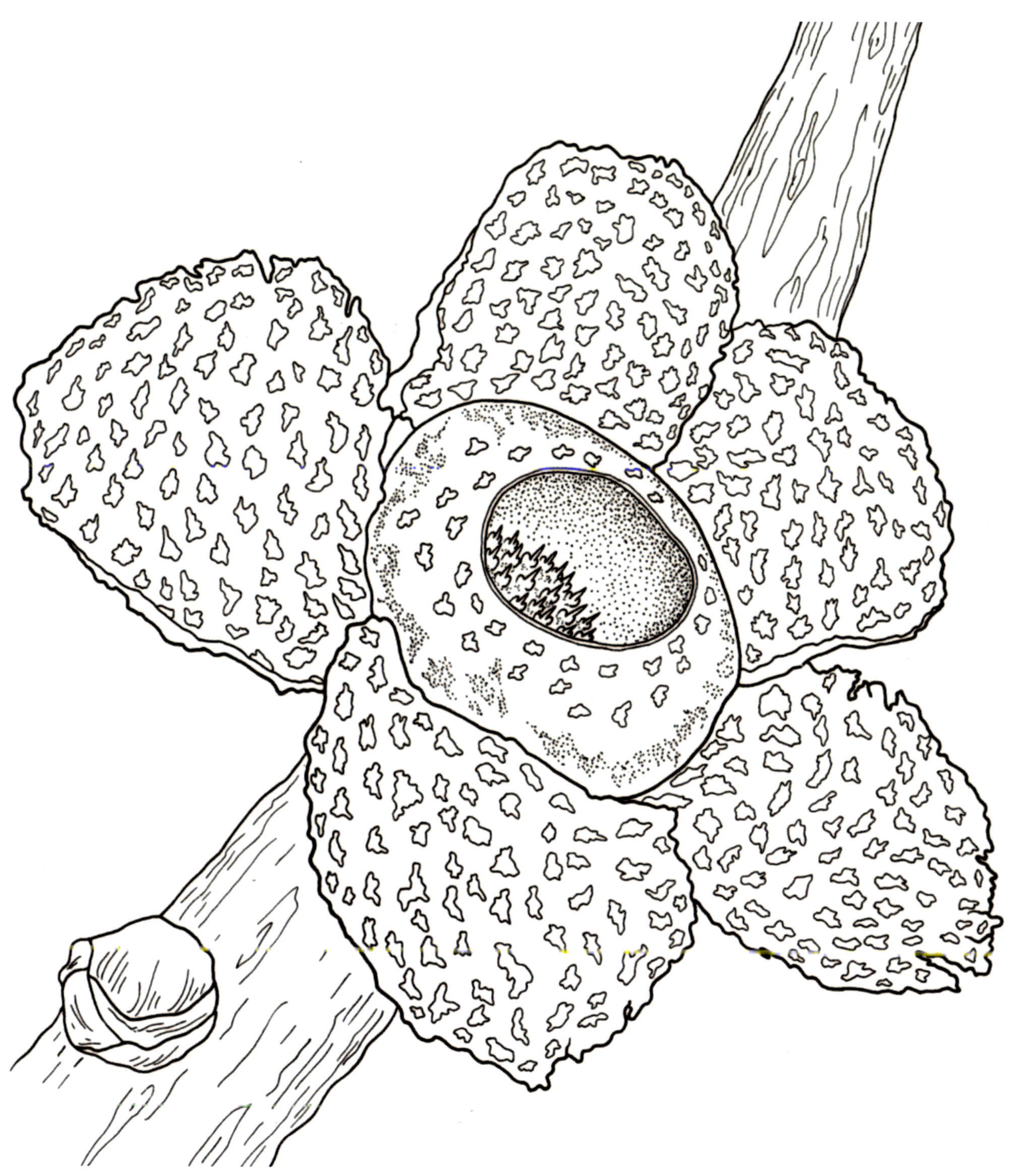

The Monster Plant is the largest plant in the world. Sometimes it is three feet across or more. It is from the islands of Sumatra or Borneo. It is brick red with a red-yellow center. The dots are raised from the surface. In art, **hot colors** are red, orange and yellow. Color this flower in hot colors. What can you draw on this flower or put beside the flower that would tell you the size of the flower. How large would a bee be? How large would a caterpillar be? Put something on the flower that shows **scale**.

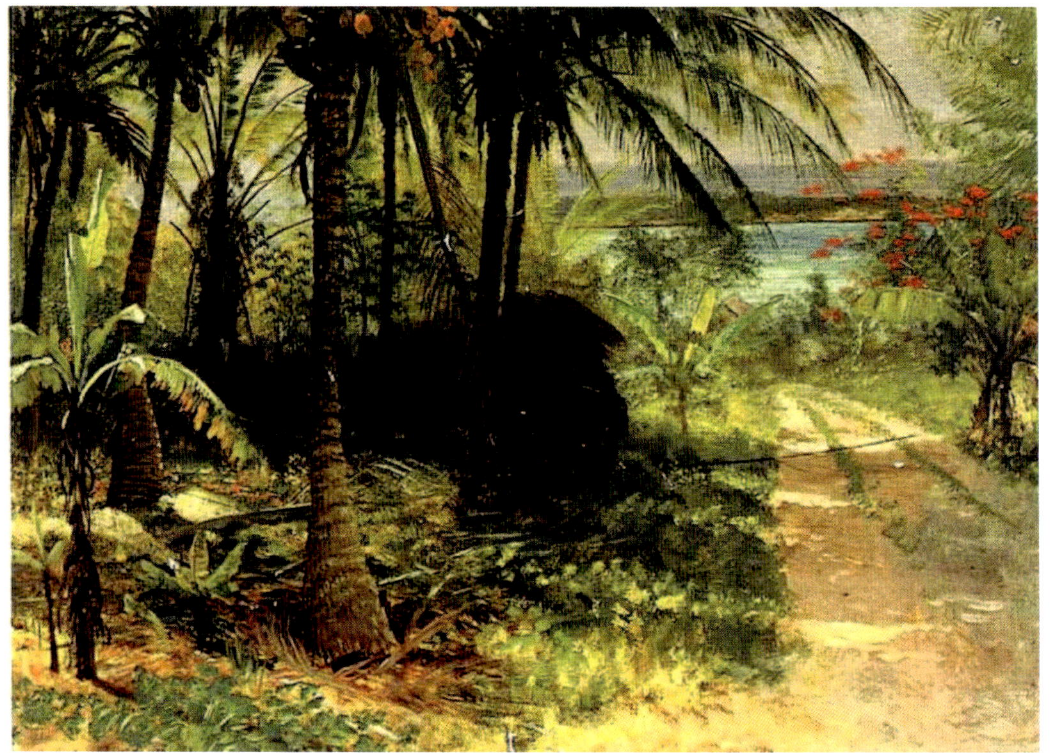

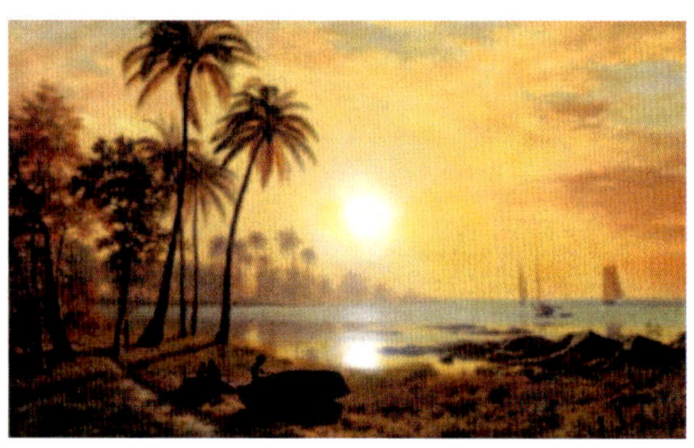

Albert Bierdstadt did the two tropical landscapes on this page. The one to my left is warm colors. The one above is cool colors. Notice his use of atmospheric perspective by making things lighter in the distance. This gives his work depth.

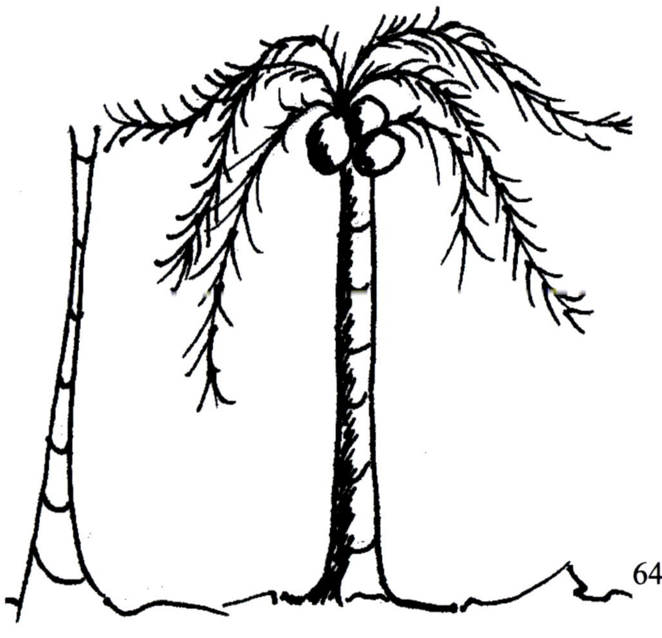

Draw an island picture with several beautiful palm trees. Use the picture on the left as a guide. Put palm trees and a large beach on your picture. You can even put a beautiful island plant in the **foreground**, or the front of the picture.
island An island is a body of land surrounded by water.
archipelago- An archipelgo is a group of islands.
coast- Coast is land beside the sea.

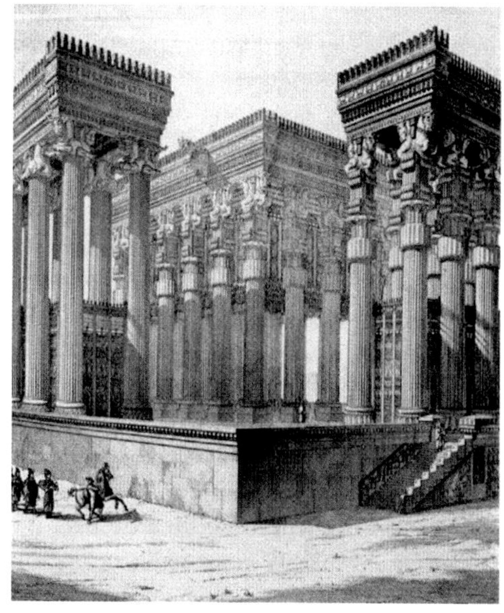

The picture on the left is of the lost city of Persepolis.Many times in the jungle explorers have found a "lost city." How exciting to explore it! Color this in bright colors and then draw yourself right in the middle.

Make observations of what you see. Be as detailed as possible. This city flourished until 330 B.C. Follow the directions to make a grid of the picture on the left. Make the squares four times as large as the original picture.

Concepts to learn:

grid
proportion
spacial relationship

A ***grid*** is a network of evenly spaced vertical and horizontal lines, often used to locate points on a map. In art, a grid can be used to break down a large complex picture into smaller, simpler parts. It can also be used to maintain the spacial integrity or proportions of a picture. Anyone can use this technique to make their art work more professional. This technique is not just a way to "copy" other peoples art work. It is a way to recognize ***spacial relationships***. Often we have seen an artist characterized as a man in a big floppy hat with his arm outstretched toward his subject eyeing his subject over his thumb. Artists do this sometimes to get a better idea of spacial relationships sometimes called ***proportion***. They are using their thumb as a measure to check the distances between objects they are trying to "copy". Sometimes people have an innate sense of proportion and place objects in relationship with each other without even a thought. This is a rare gift which only a few people are born with. Fortunately for the rest of us it is a learnable skill. Working with a grid helps us recognize proportion and teaches us to keep the objects we are copying in relationship to one another.

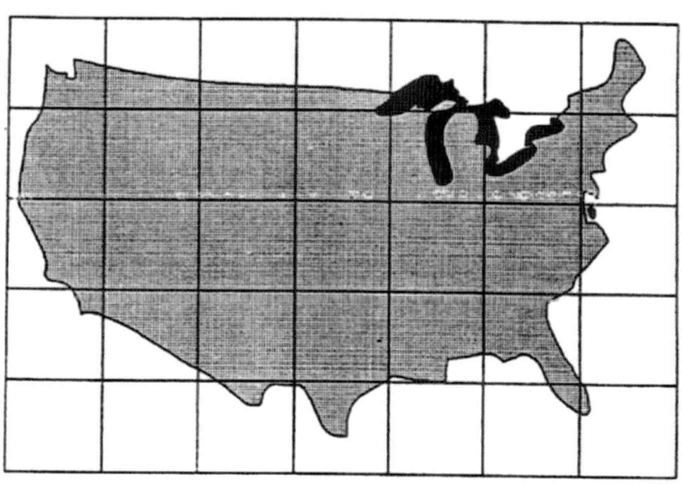

U.S.A. map with grid.

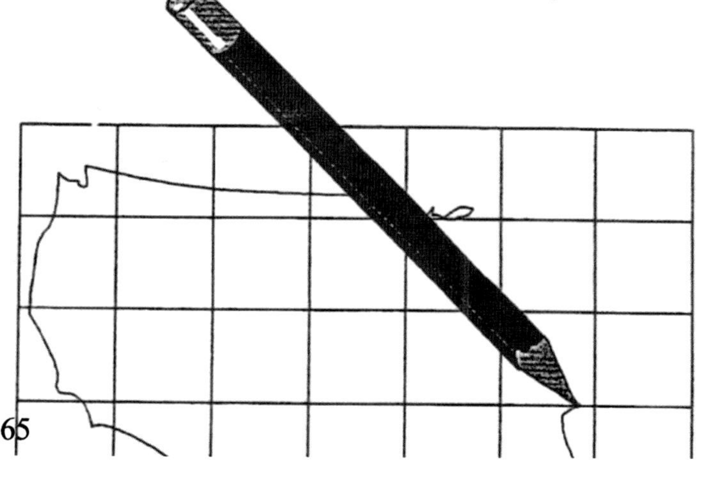

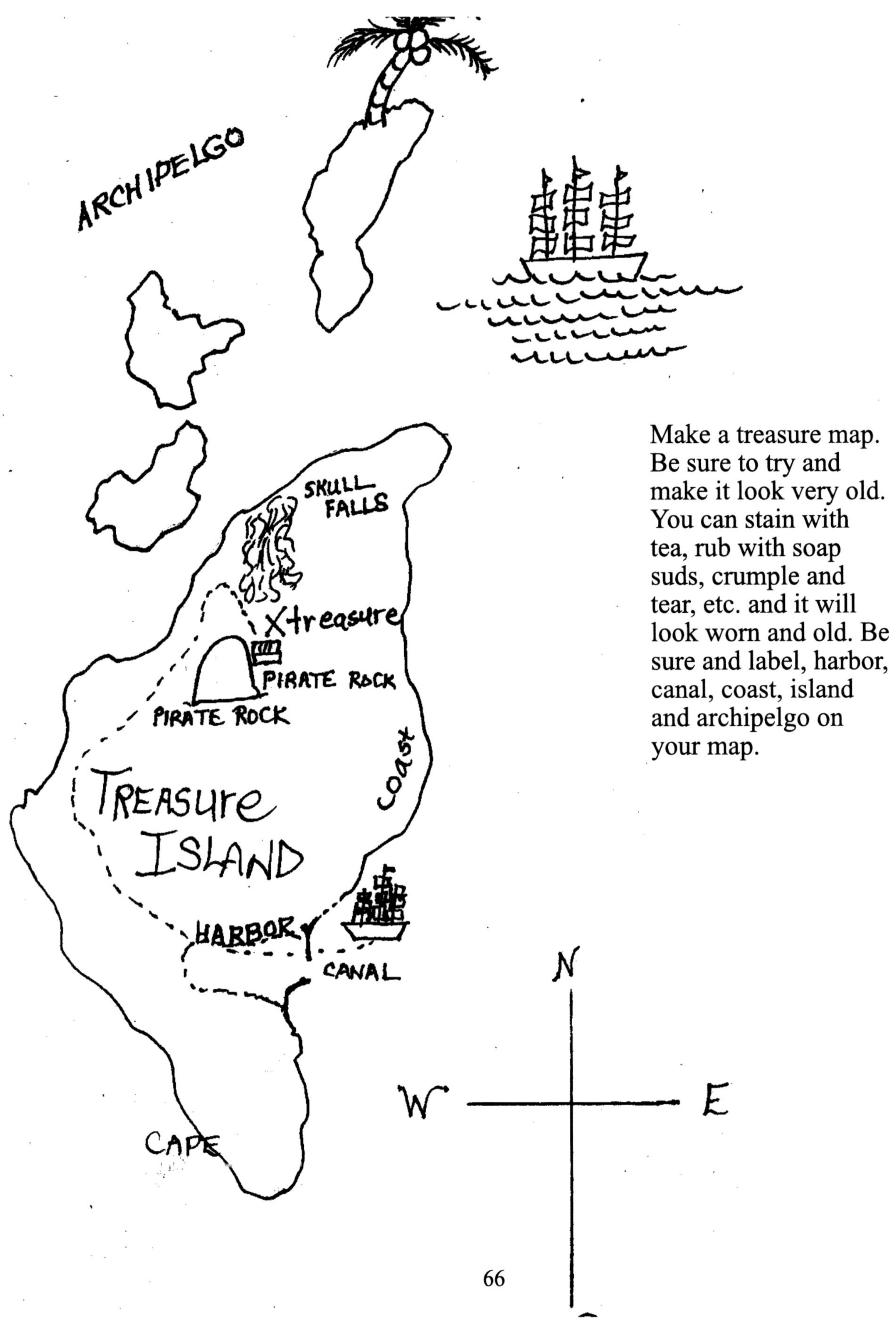

Make a treasure map. Be sure to try and make it look very old. You can stain with tea, rub with soap suds, crumple and tear, etc. and it will look worn and old. Be sure and label, harbor, canal, coast, island and archipelgo on your map.

Make and label a treasure map similar to the one above. Go to this website for wonderful information on treasure maps: http://en.wikipedia.org/wiki/Treasure_map

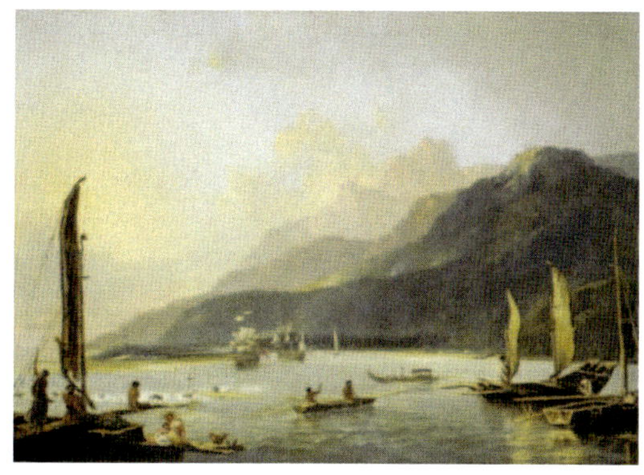

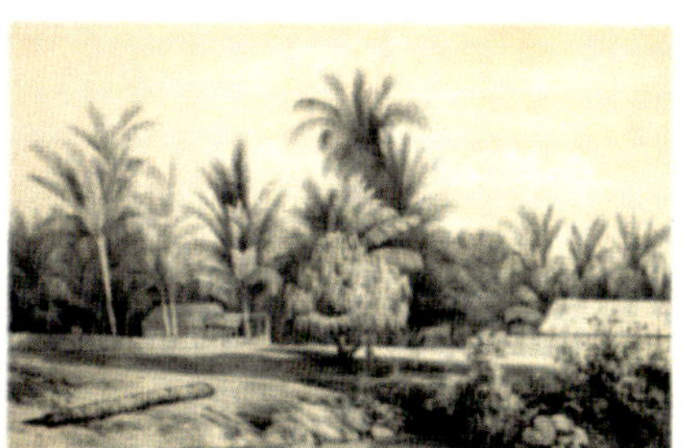

William Hodges did this pictures of Tahiti on Captain Cook's second voyage in 1776.
There are many wonderful stories in literature describing people of the South Sea Islands such as Tahiti. Mutiny on the Bounty is just one. For an exellent lesson on drawing ships go to this website:http://www.angelfire.com/ar/rogerart/seven.html
Draw and color a picture similar to the one above.
The picture on the right is by the master artist Gaugin, picturing native culture.

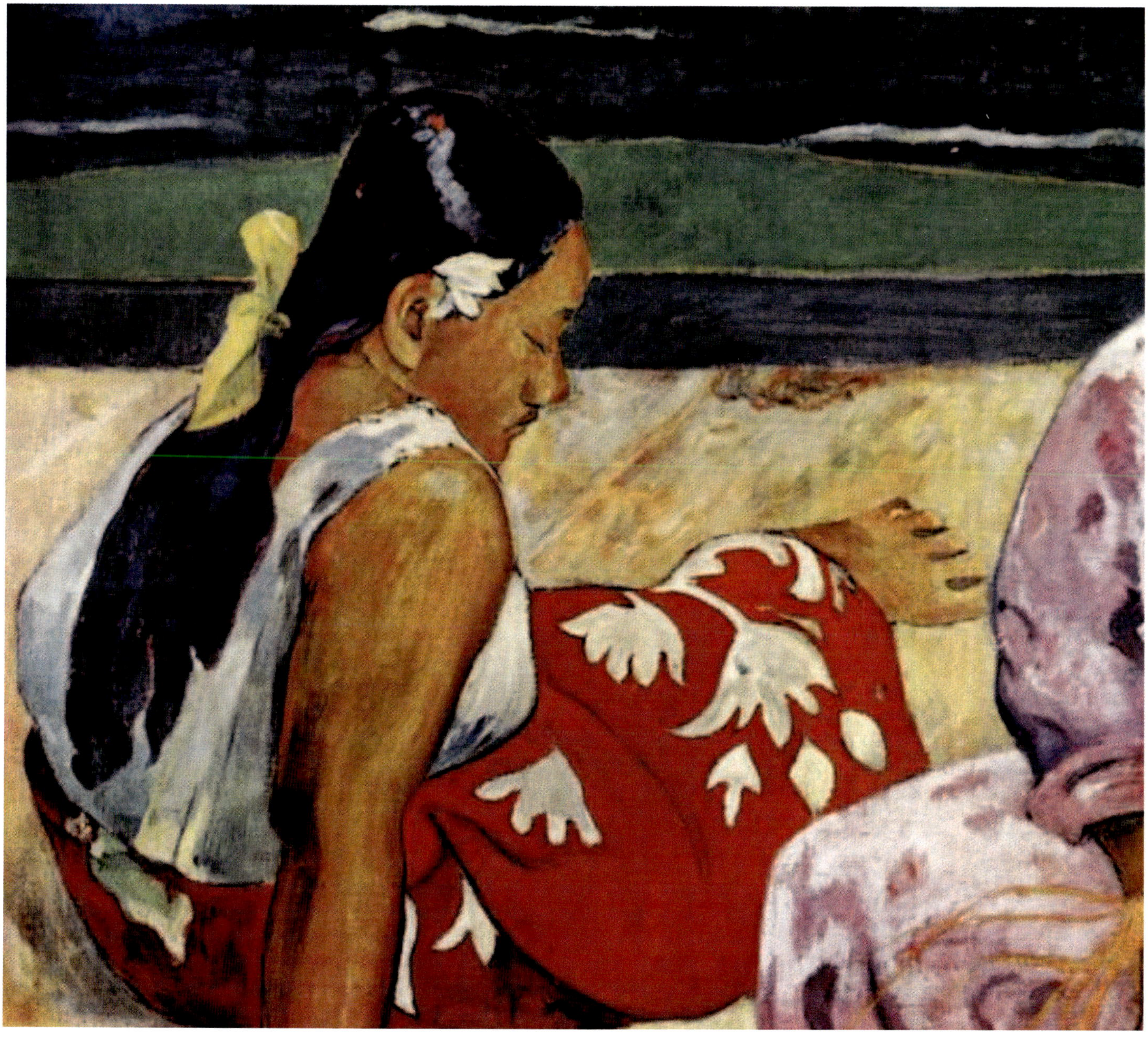

Rainforests

Rousseau was one of the artists that did magnificent jungle pictures. The flora and fauna on the islands is very important. Do a picture of leaves. Look at the way Rousseau does leaves below. Copy each kind of leave using different shades of green. Can you see where the light hits each leaf? One shade is darker and one is lighter.

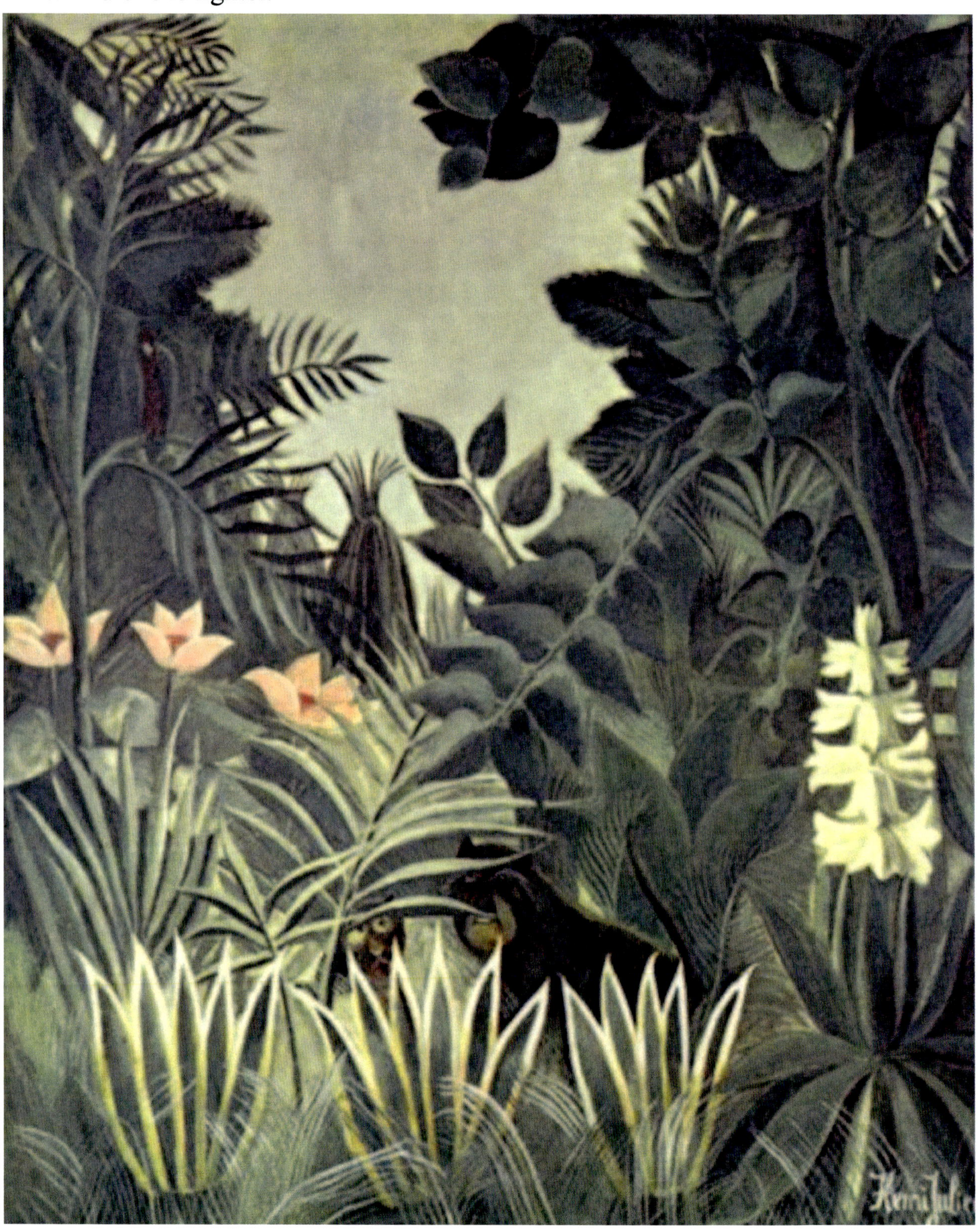

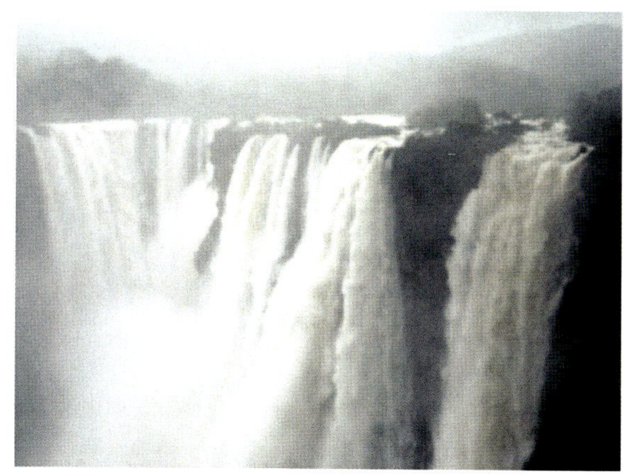

Rainforests

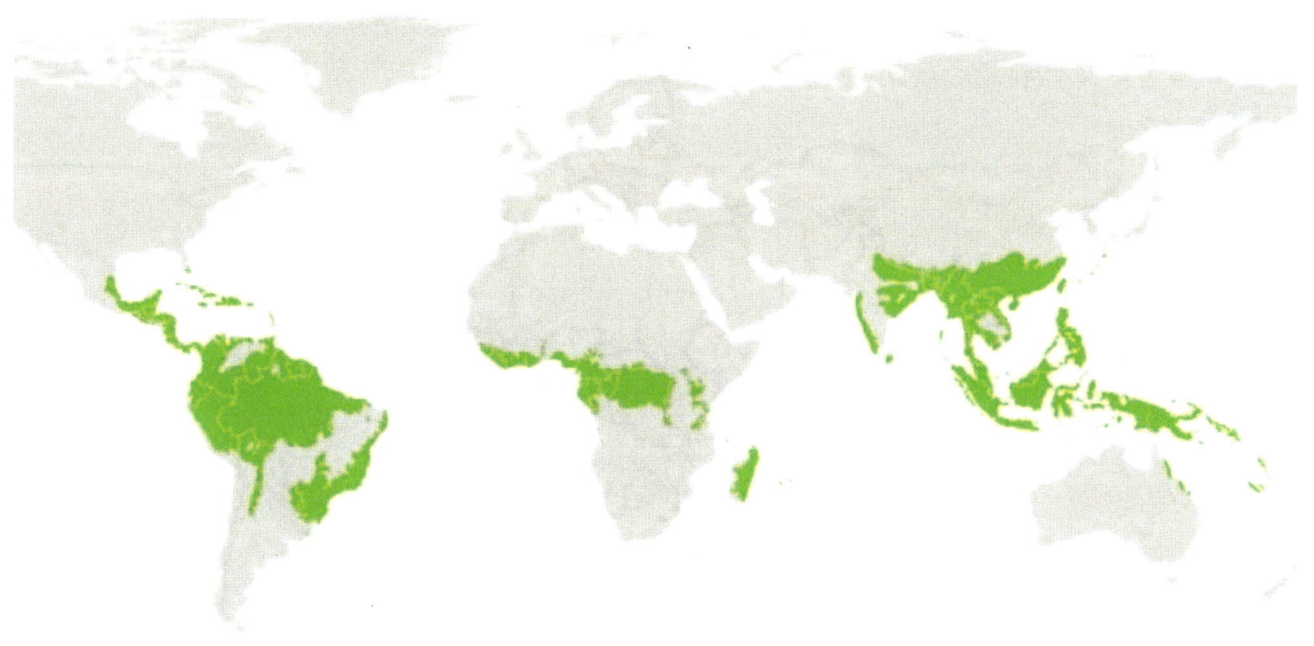

South and Central America are full of rainforests. Rainforests are characterized by high rainfall, and
are home to two thirds of all the living animal and plant species on the planet. Beautiful and colorful birds are seen in the rainforest. Toucans are seen in the rainforest. For a wonderful lesson on how to draw a toucan go to:http://peelbooks.com/draw_series/23.htm#toucan01

bog-A bog is a type of wetland that accumulates dead plant material. You could see a frog in a bog. 69

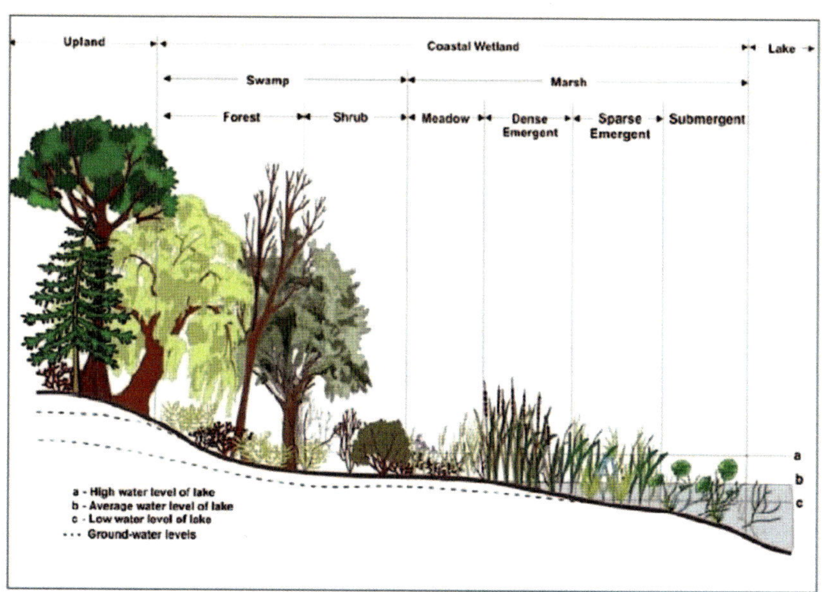

marsh- A marsh is a type of wetland which is subject to frequent or continuous flooding of water.

Anteaters

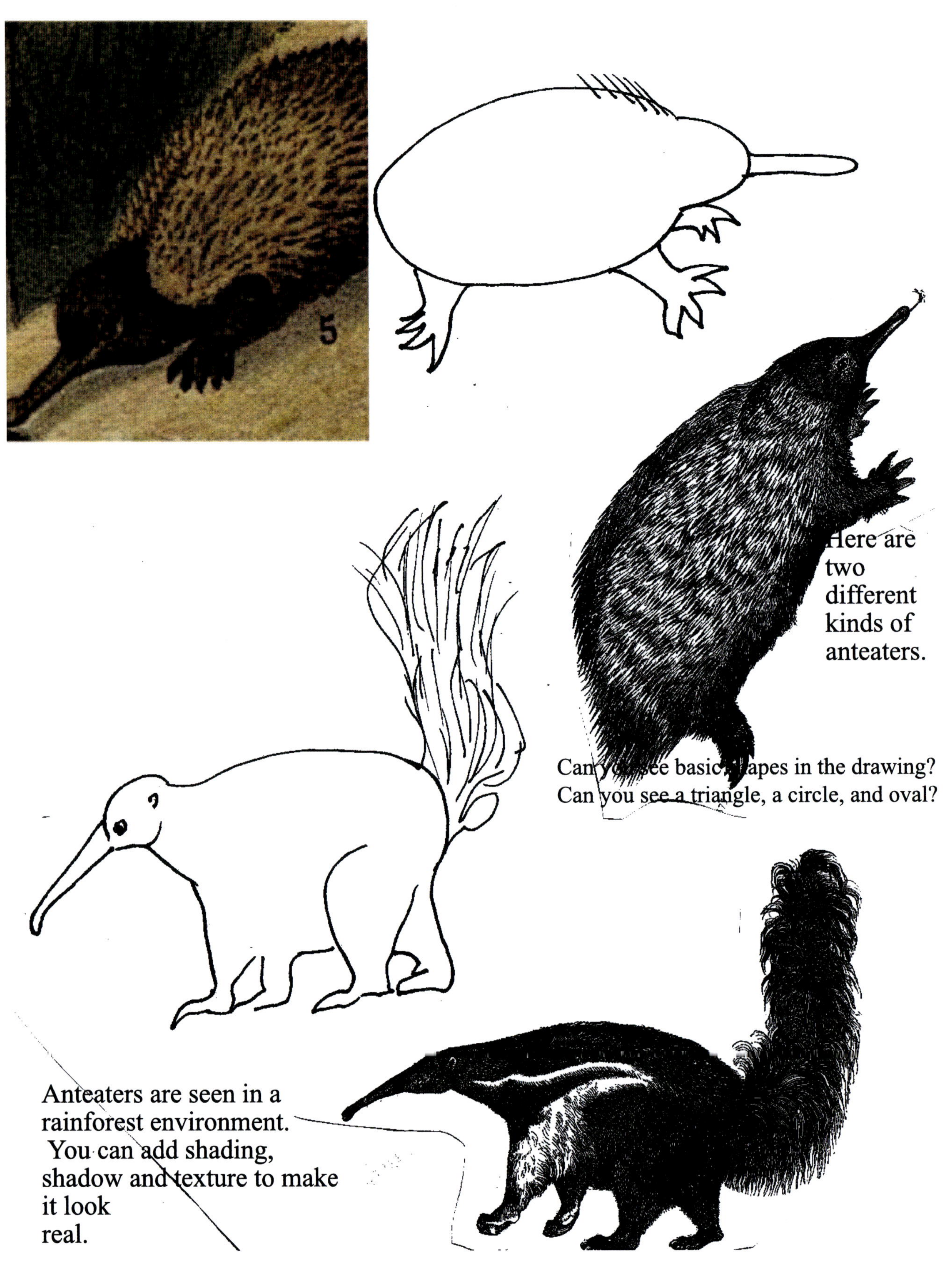

Here are two different kinds of anteaters.

Can you see basic shapes in the drawing?
Can you see a triangle, a circle, and oval?

Anteaters are seen in a rainforest environment. You can add shading, shadow and texture to make it look real.

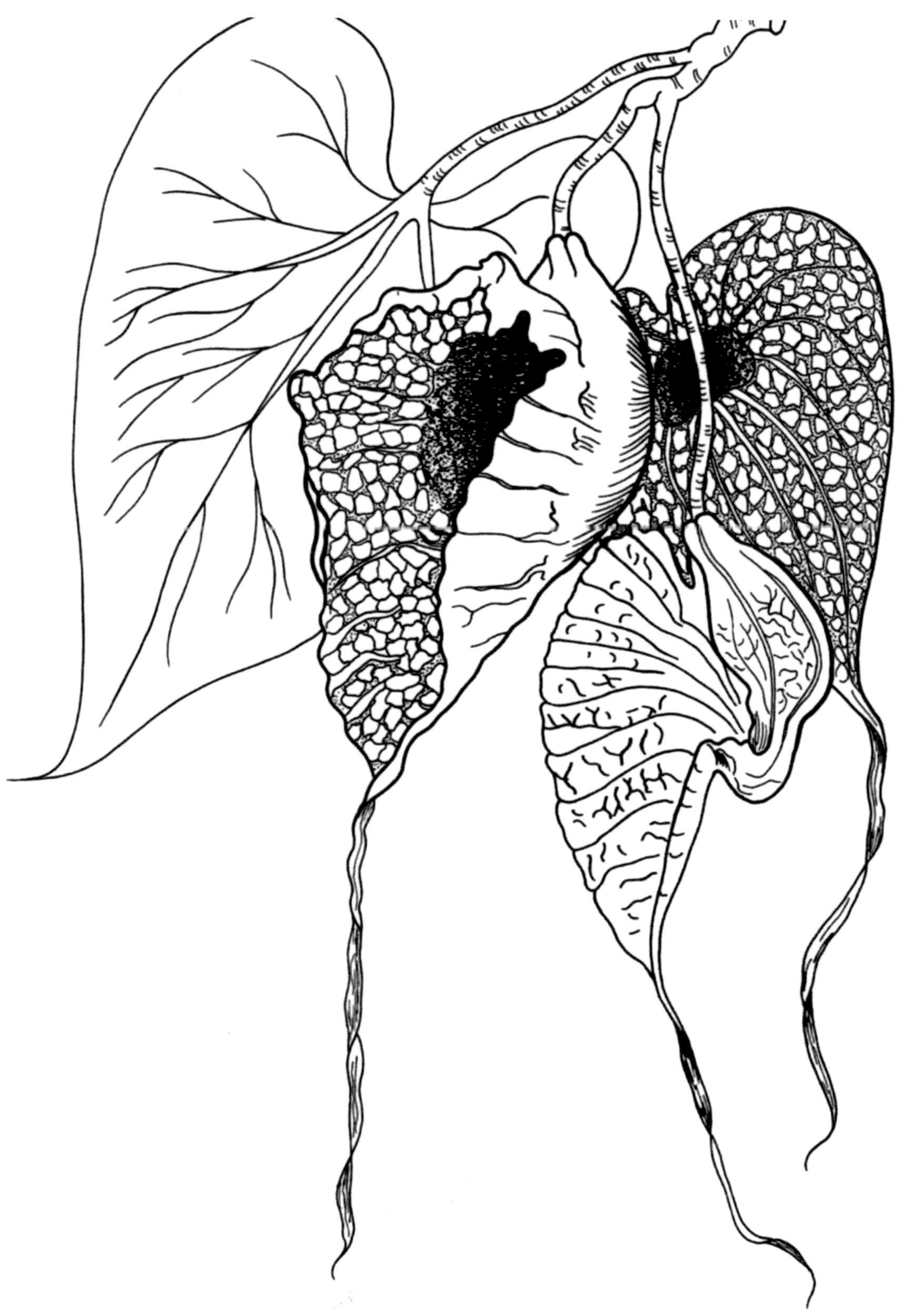

This native plant of Central and South America is called the Pelican Flower. It can be 18 inches across. Color the above picture, color the leaves green and color and the dots maroon. What color will you make the hummingbird?

These gigantic plants are three to six feet across. Their flowers are from six to eighteen inches across. The flowers are so amazing because they bloom in a white color and slowly change to pink and then red. When you mix a primary color with white, you get a pastel. Pink is a pastel color.

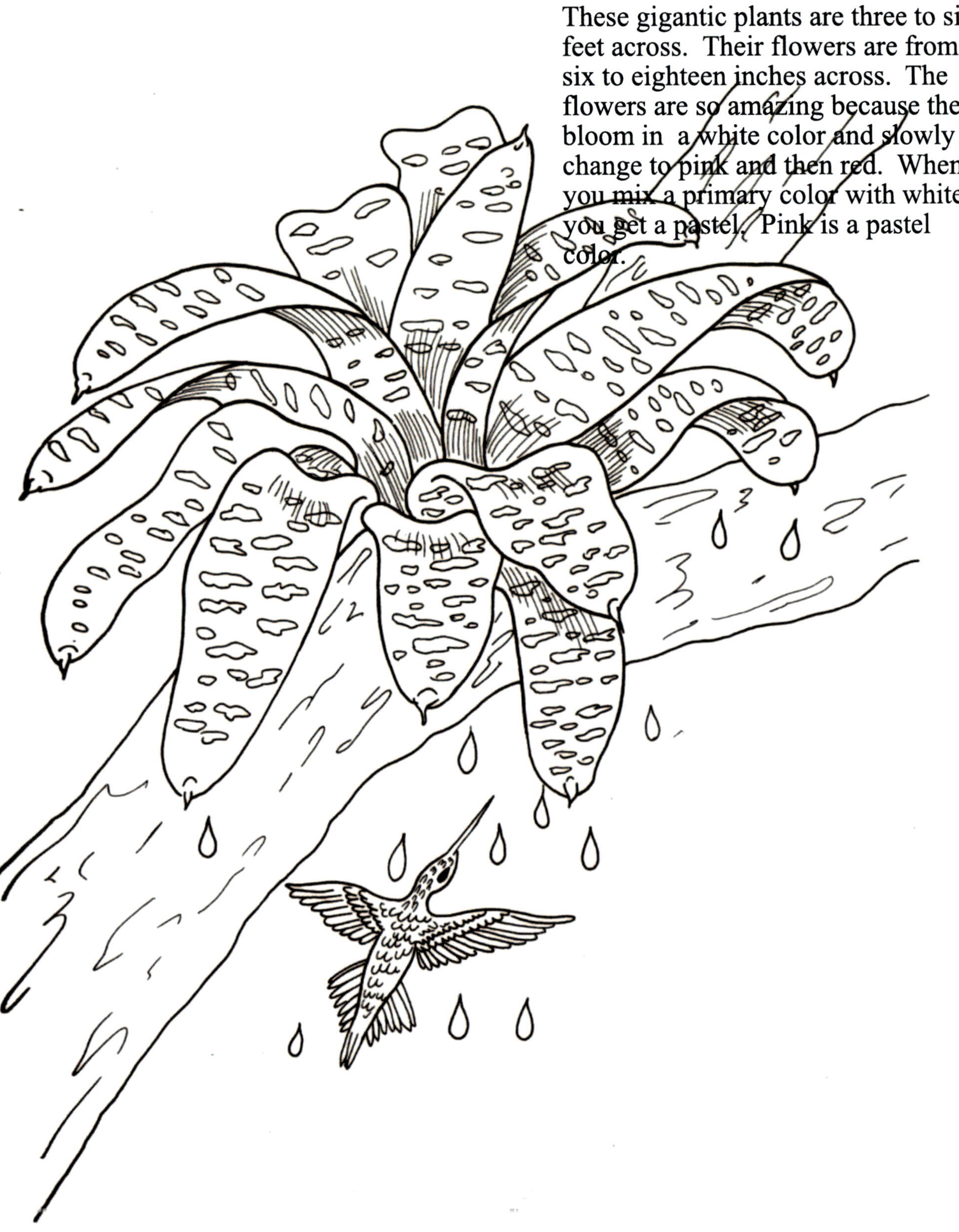

Bromeliad *(Neoregelia punctatissima)*. A native of **al and South** America, the tank bromeliad attaches **to trees by** specialized roots, but only for support—**t parasitic.** The "tank" is the tight rosette formed **leaves, where** water collects and serves as a reser-**r the plant,** since all the water the plant needs is **ed by the leaves.** The tank also supplies needed **es to various** animals. Birds use it for drinking **thing, and tiny** hummingbirds like to take showers **excess water that** drips from the plant on occasion. Mosquitoes and dragonflies lay eggs in the water. In fact, small amphibians spend their entire lives in the tank, feeding on insect eggs and larvae. In return, the bromeliad gains needed food from the organic material left by the animals, after it is broken down by special bacteria that also inhabit the tank. Tank bromeliads tend to show great variety in their coloration and the extent of their markings; the plant illustrated here is golden-green with maroon markings. The hummingbird is iridescent green with a reddish tail.

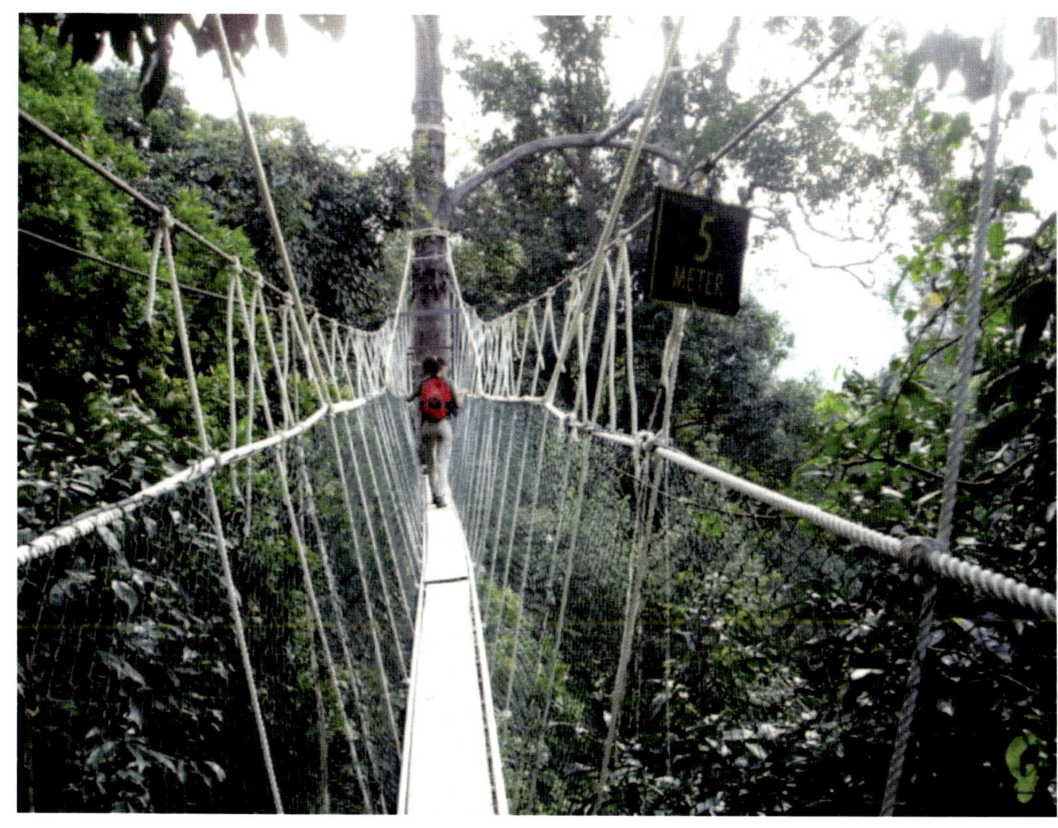

Here is a canopy bridge on top of a rainforest. Can you draw a bridge like this? Is this a one point perspective? Below are the areas you could go if you wanted to go to a rainforest.

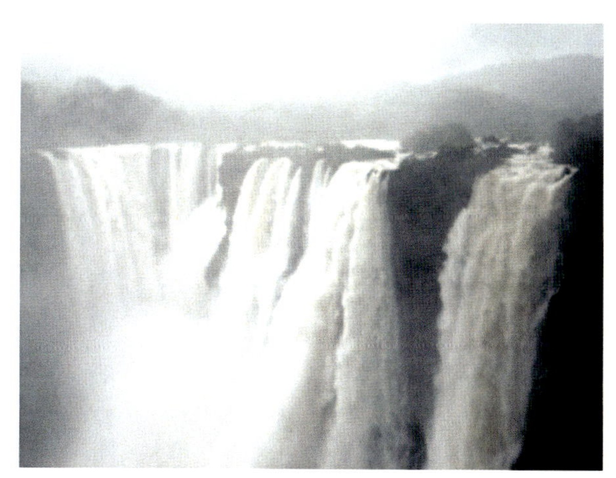

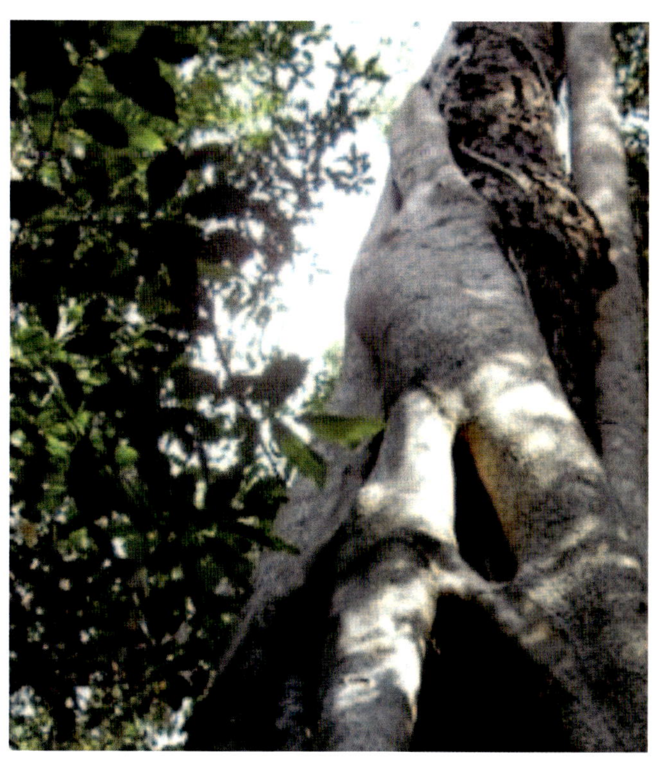

Oceans of the World

To see an animated picture of the oceans of the world go to:http://en.wikipedia.org/wiki/Image:World_ocean_map.gif
Go to this website to hear the sound of the humpback whale:http://en.wikipedia.org/wiki/Portal:Cetaceans
Do you believe Winslow Homer captured the mood of a hurricane in the picture below?y

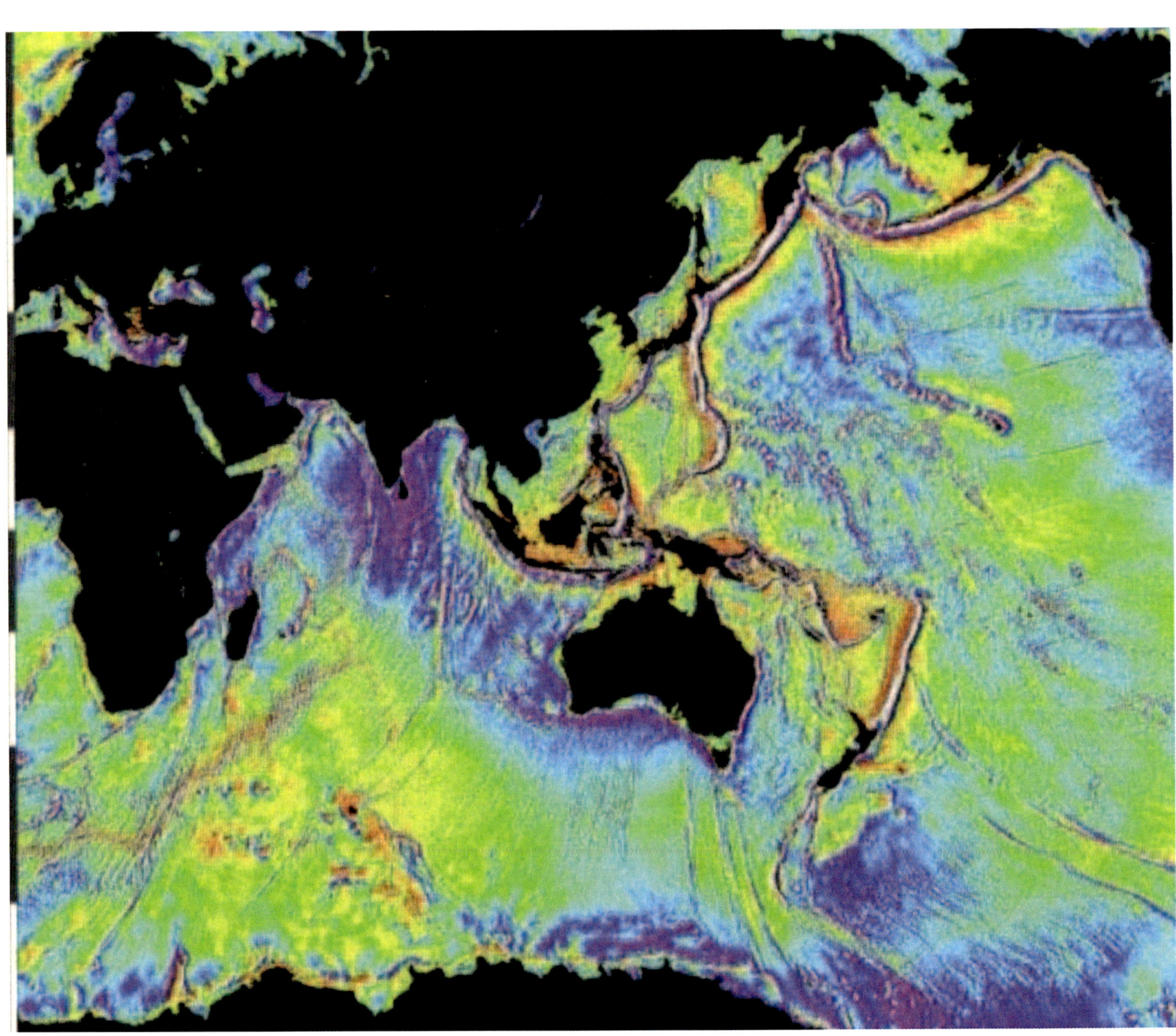

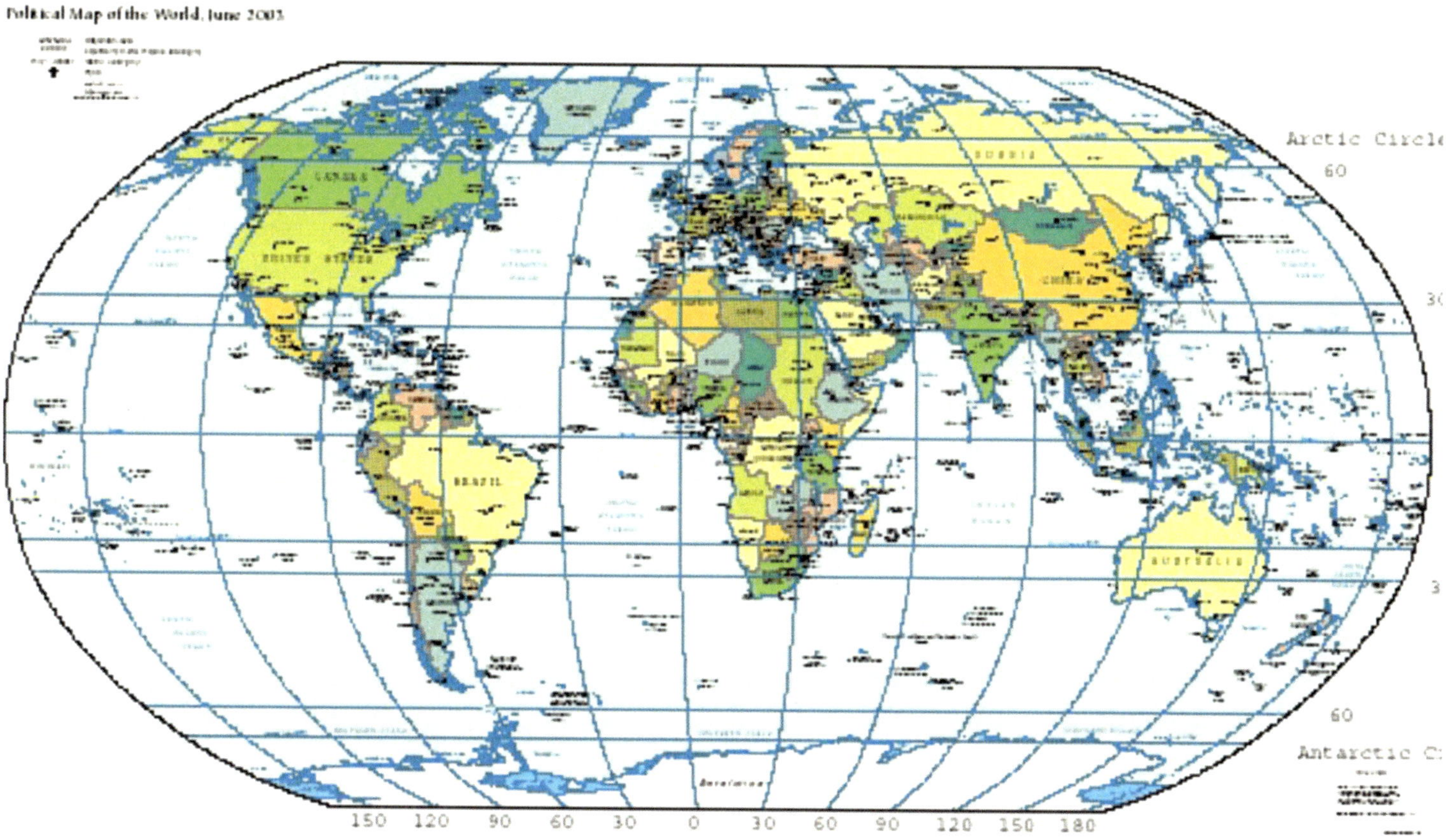

Political Map of the World, June 2003

The major oceanic divisions are (in descending order of size) the Pacific Ocean, the Atlantic Ocean, the Indian Ocean, the Southern Ocean (which is sometimes subsumed as the southern portions of the Pacific, Atlantic, and Indian Oceans), and the Arctic Ocean (which is sometimes considered a sea of the Atlantic). The map above is of the depth of the ocean. Can you tell what oceans are where? Imagine how many treasures are buried under the ocean. Draw a picture of a treasure under the ocean and draw a map of how to get to it.

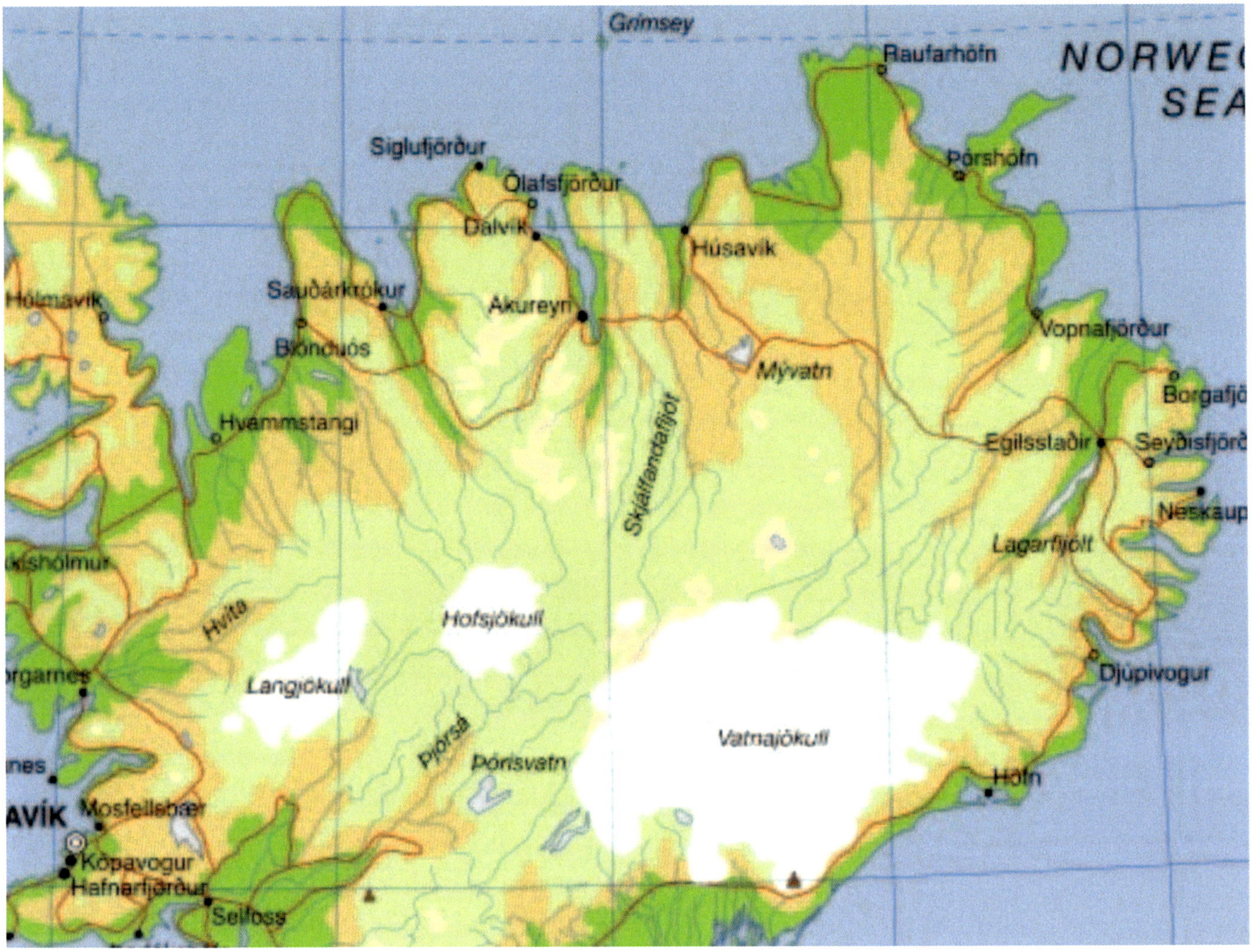

Iceland

Iceland is a very important lone island. It has Islandic Sheep, puffins, and beautiful waterfalls and terrain. **Terrain** is the third or vertical dimension of land surface. For a wonderful website on painting a waterfall: http://www.youtube.com/watch?v=GplVhGkWybo and see and hear a demonstration on painting.

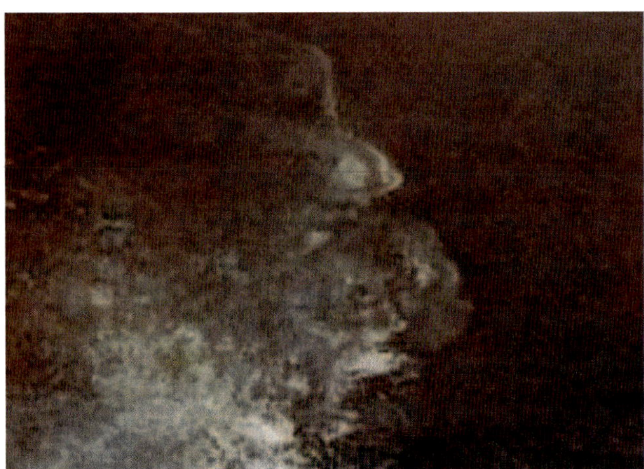

On the left is a geyser in Iceland. A **geyser** is a type of hot spring that erupts periodically, ejecting a column of hot water and steam into the air. Go to this website to see America's most famous geyser:http://en.wikipedia.org/wiki/Image:Old_Faithfull-pdPhoto.jpg

A good art project is to draw the scene on the left. Use a sponge with white paint for they geyser. Some artists even dilute white paint with water and put it in a spray bottle and spray their picture for a watery effect.

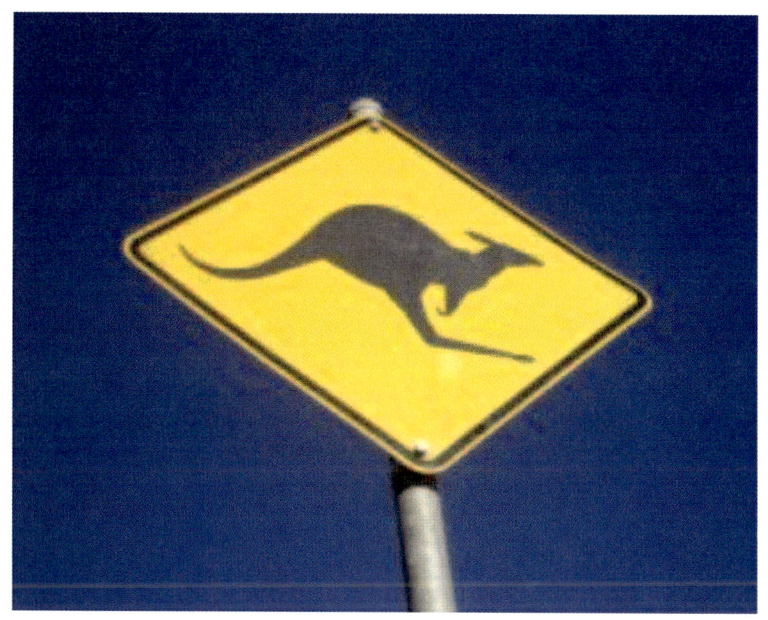

Australia Down Under

Thomas Baines painted the picture below. It is Australian aboriginines at the mouth of the Victoria River. He was an English artist and explorer of British colonial southern Africa and Australia. Born in the United Kingdom, Baines was apprenticed to a coach painter at an early age. When he was 22 he left England for South Africa aboard the "Olivia" and worked for a while in Cape Town as a scenic and portrait artist. He was the official war artist during the so-called Eighth Frontier War for the British Army.

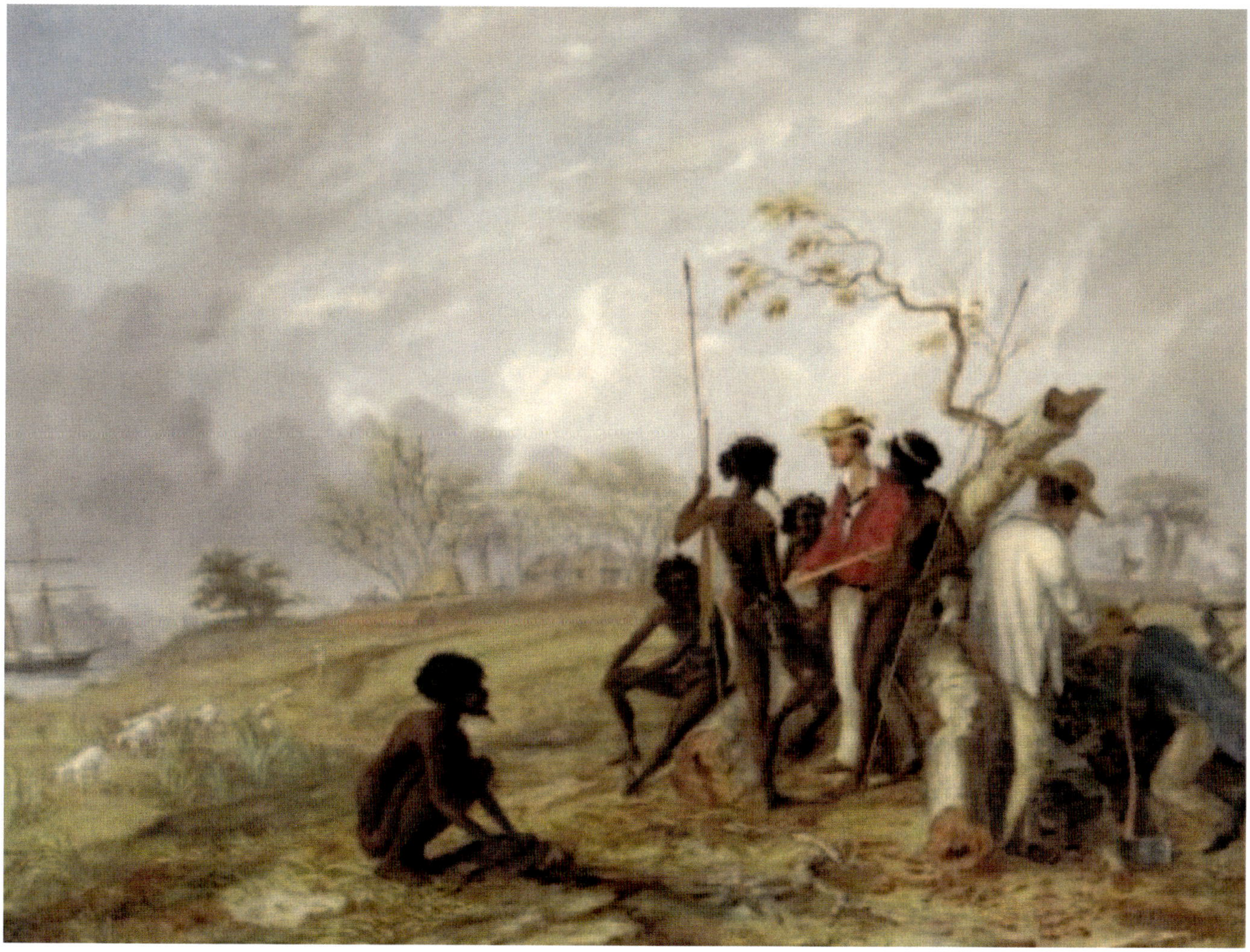

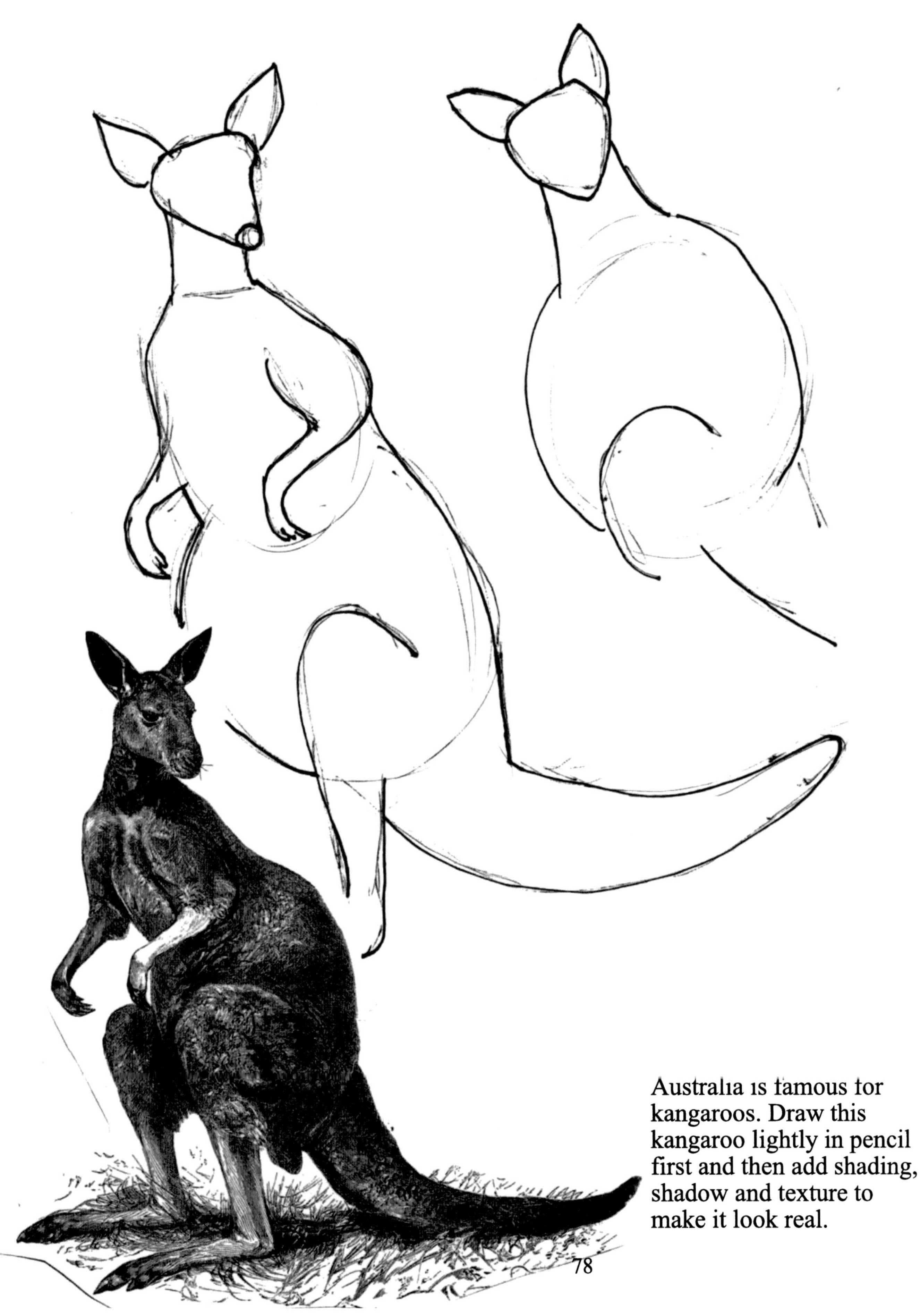

Australia is famous for kangaroos. Draw this kangaroo lightly in pencil first and then add shading, shadow and texture to make it look real.

Antarctia

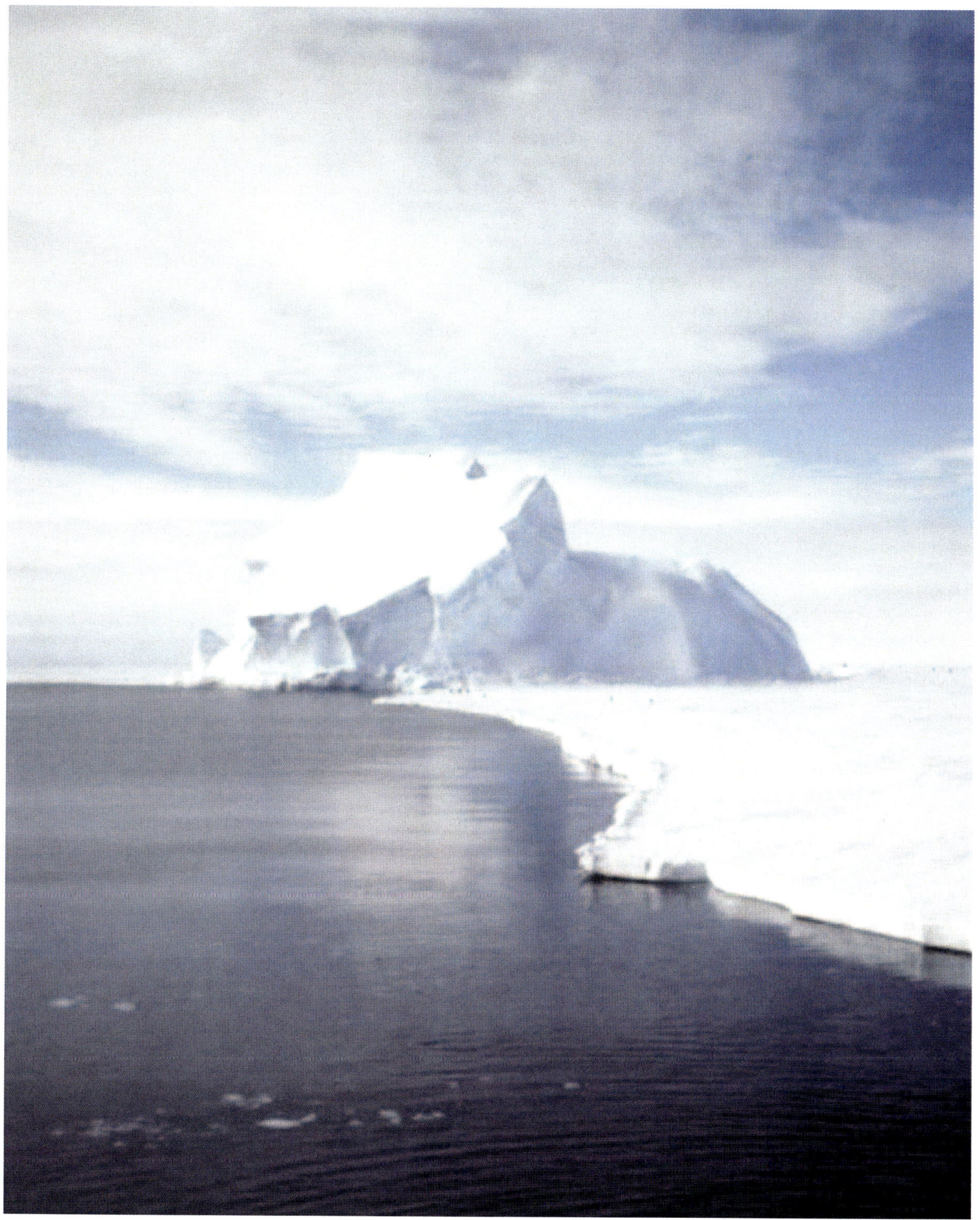

Above is a picture of the beautiful continent of Antarctica. It is a cold desert. When you do a **monochromatic** color scheme, you use one color and shades of that color and black and white. The Antarctic pictures are usually monochromatic. Get newsprint paper and wet it. Use different shades of blue chalk, black and white chalk and color the picture above.

Draw a penguin. Notice how the penguin in the front is larger than the one in the back. Squint your eyes to see the shading on the stomach. Go to this website to see how to draw a penguin: http://www.joysikorski.com/penguin.html With students I have them draw the penquins first and then take wet wipes and different shades of blue and white and use a wet wipe to blend the color.

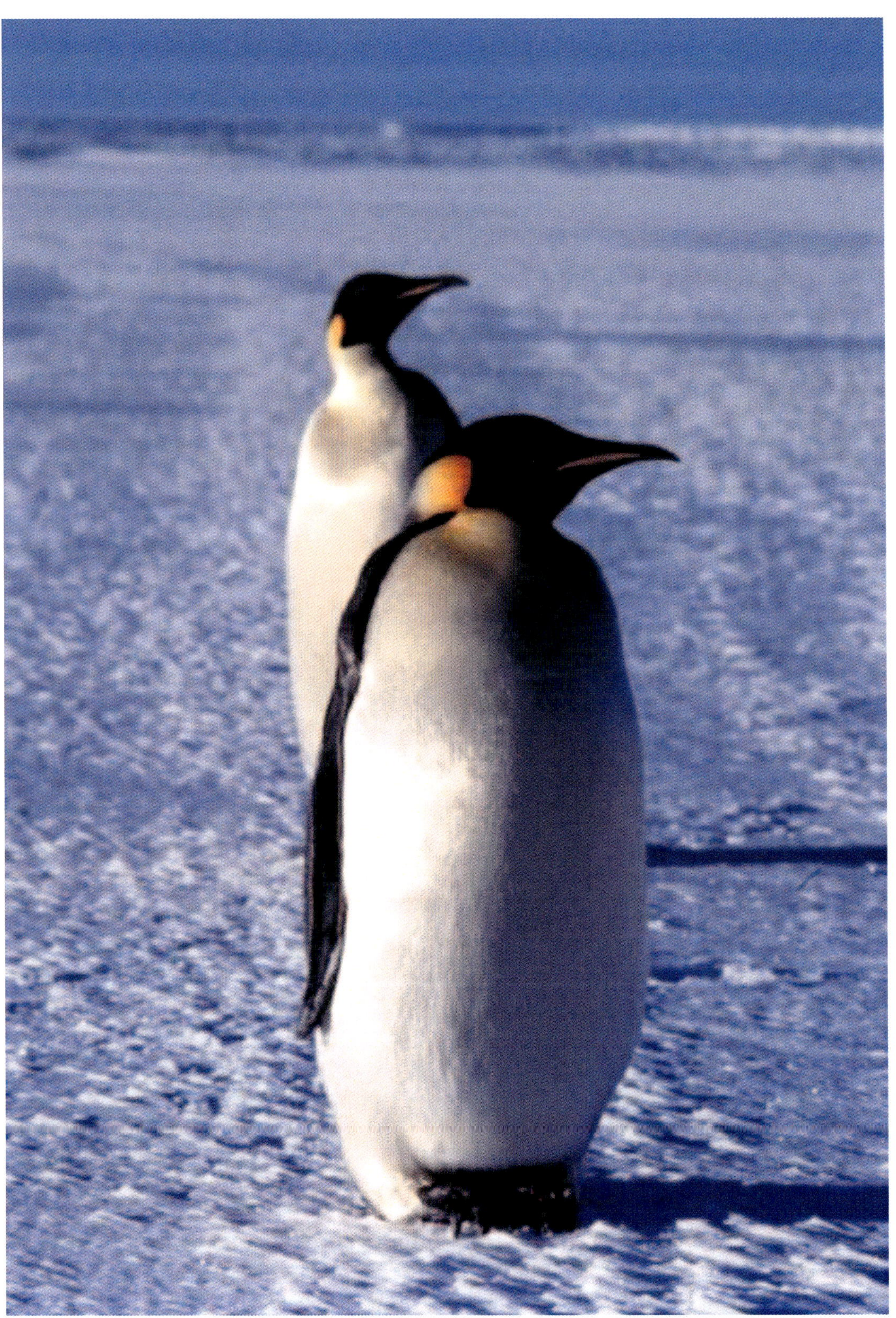

You can see fur seals in Antarctica. Draw the fur seal below. One of my favorite art projects is to have children draw a picture of the North Pole. They draw water, land, a penquin, a fur seal and a cylinder that is striped representing the North Pole. Then I allow them to draw a map from their house to the North Pole. How will they get there? Will they fly part way?

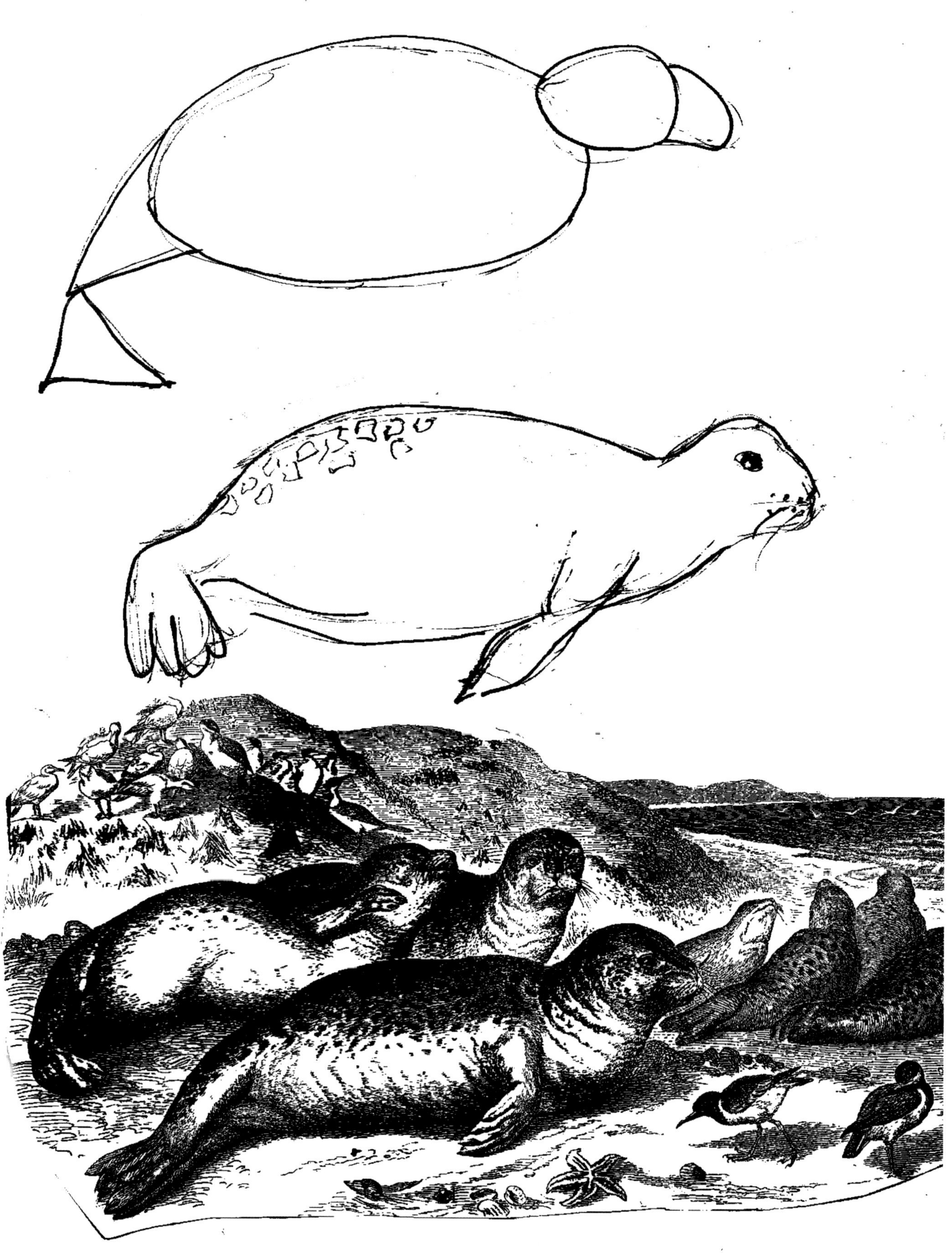

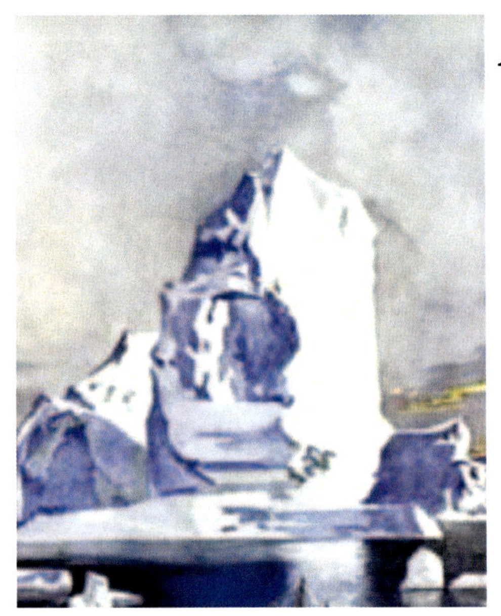

Antarctica

Antarctica is Earth's southernmost continent. It is on top of the South Pole. It is the fifth-largest continent in area after Asia, Africa, North America, and South America. About 98% of Antarctica is covered by ice.
Antarctica is the coldest, driest and windiest continent. Since there is little precipitation, except at the coasts, the interior of the continent is the largest desert in the world. The only plants or animals that survive there are penguins, fur seals, mosses, lichen, and many types of algae. The map below is of Antarctica as seen from space.

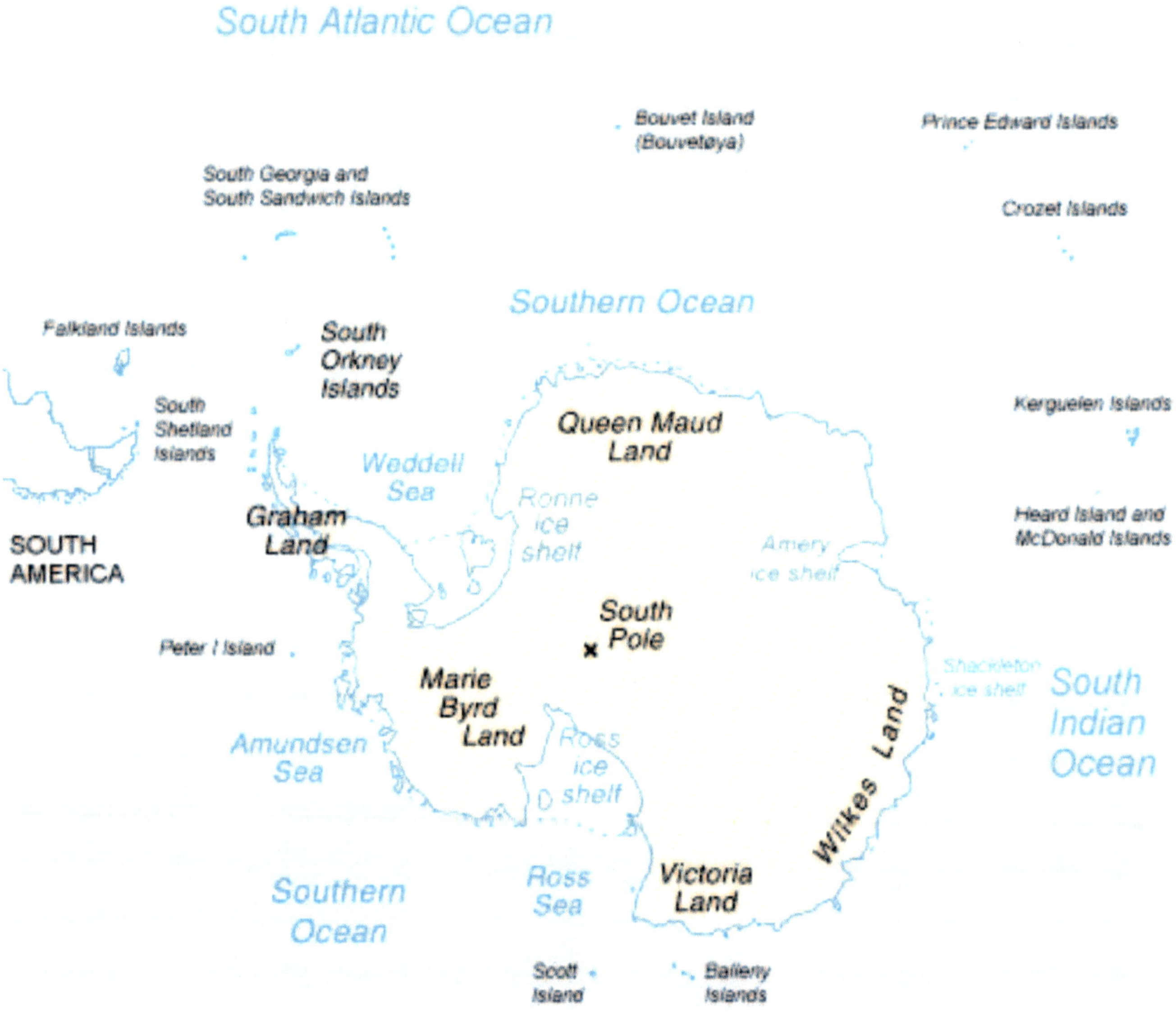

South Atlantic Ocean
Bouvet Island (Bouvetøya)
Prince Edward Islands
South Georgia and South Sandwich Islands
Crozet Islands
Southern Ocean
Falkland Islands
South Orkney Islands
South Shetland Islands
Queen Maud Land
Kerguelen Islands
Weddell Sea
Ronne ice shelf
Graham Land
Heard Island and McDonald Islands
SOUTH AMERICA
Amery ice shelf
South Pole
Peter I Island
Shackleton ice shelf
Marie Byrd Land
South Indian Ocean
Wilkes Land
Amundsen Sea
Ross ice shelf
Southern Ocean
Ross Sea
Victoria Land
Scott Island
Balleny Islands

Have you ever seen one word that expressed something just by the way it looked? Take the word Africa and make the letters look like African animals. You can do this with different countries of the world. How would the continent of Antarctica be written visually?

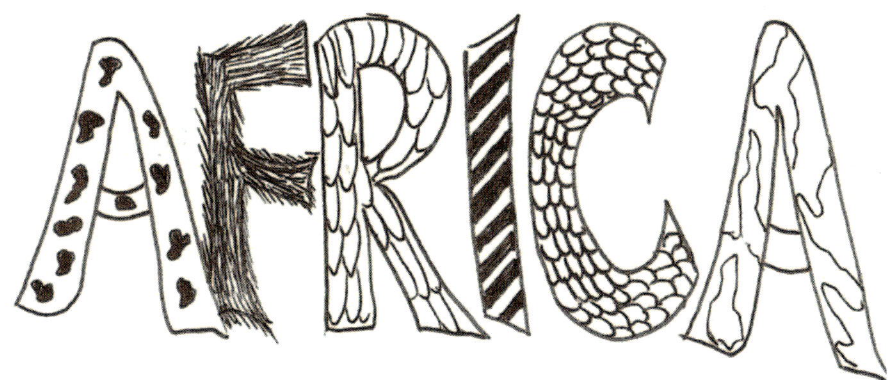

On this page are different pictures of Africa. The one is a map. There are also marks of culture. The fabrics and dishes used are part of Africa's wonderful culture.

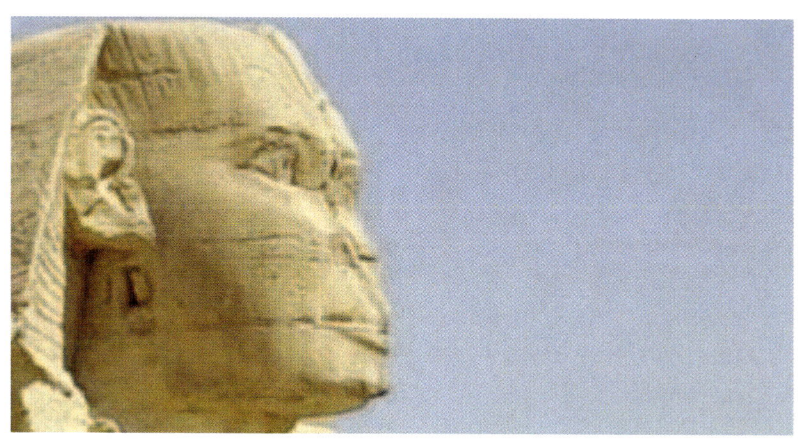

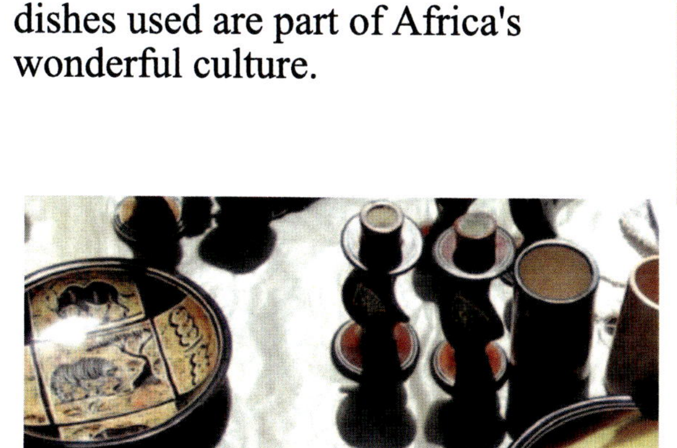

Africa is the world's second-largest and second most-populated continent, after Asia. It covers 6% of the Earth's total surface area, and 20.4% of the total land area. It has more than 900,000,000 people.

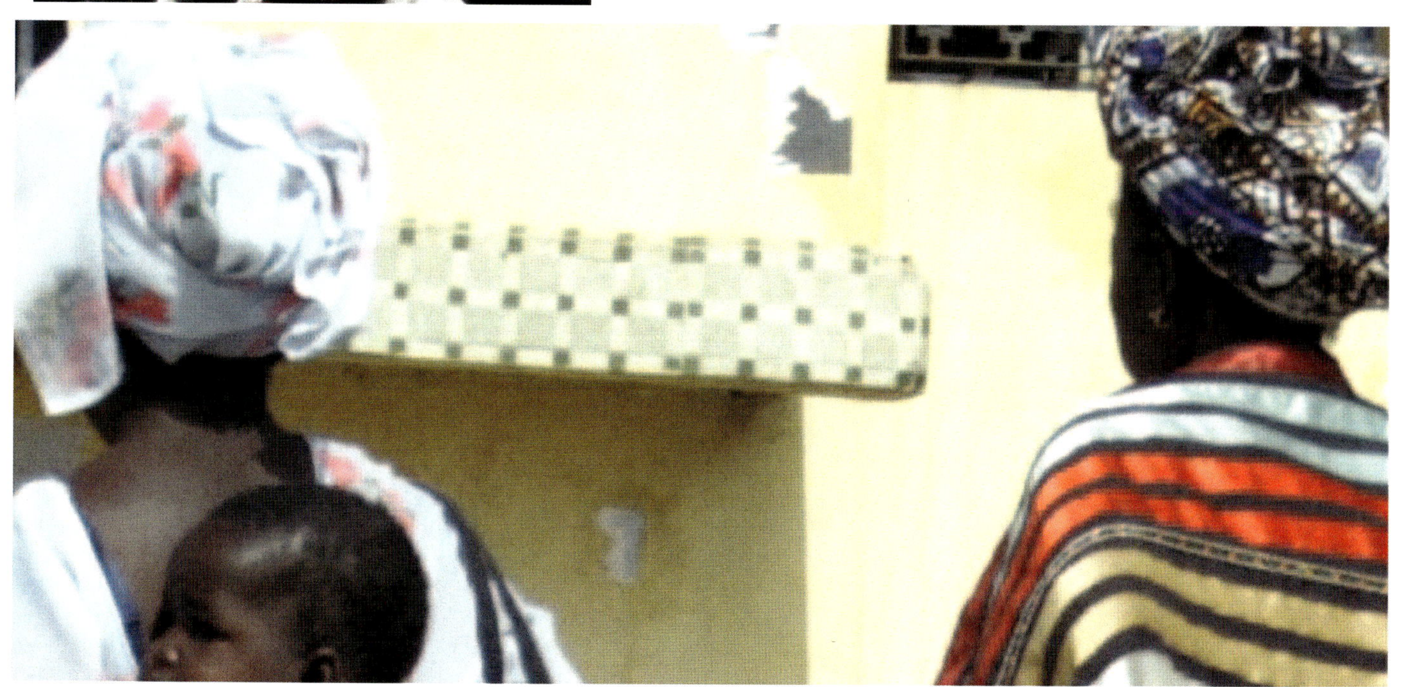

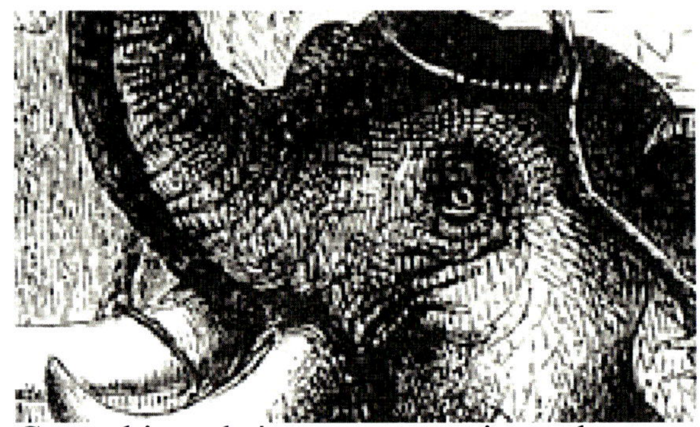

Go to this website to see an animated elephant: http://en.wikipedia.org/wiki/Image:Devi_AsianElephant_SanDiegoZoo_20071230_RockingBehaviour.gif

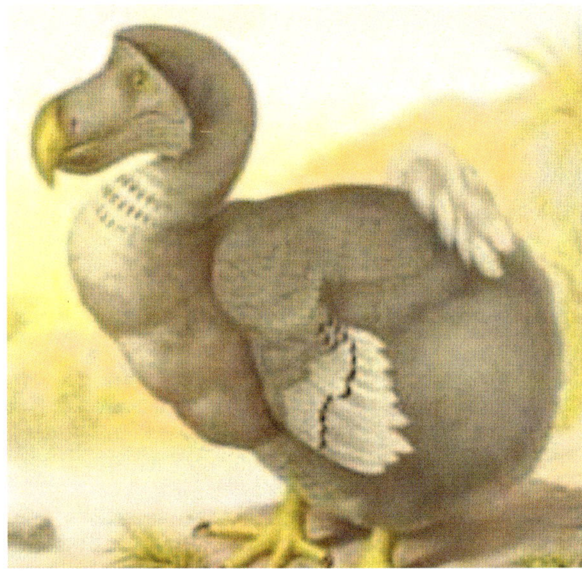

The dodo bird on the left is a famous extinct bird that existed in Africa. This painting is from the 1600's.

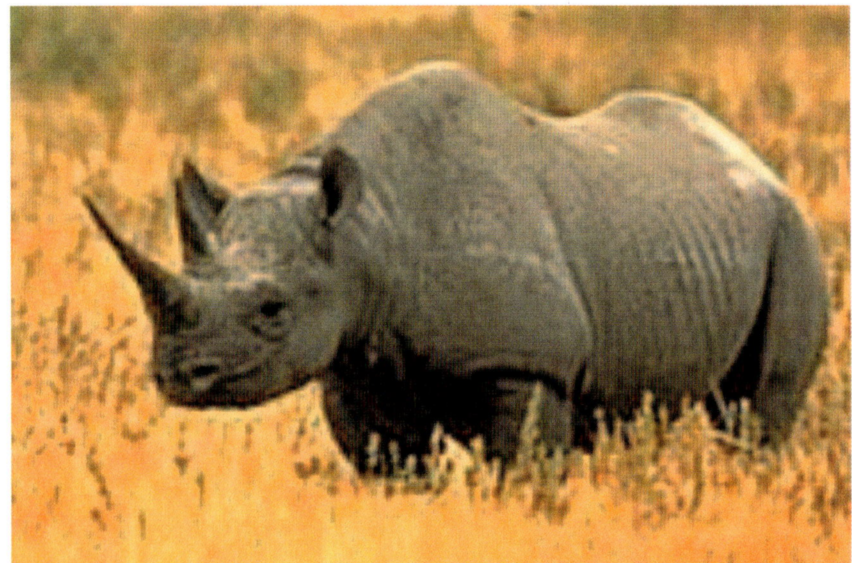

For a wonderful website of these animals, go to: http://www.junglephotos.com/africa/afanimals/afanimals.shtml and stajrt drawing.

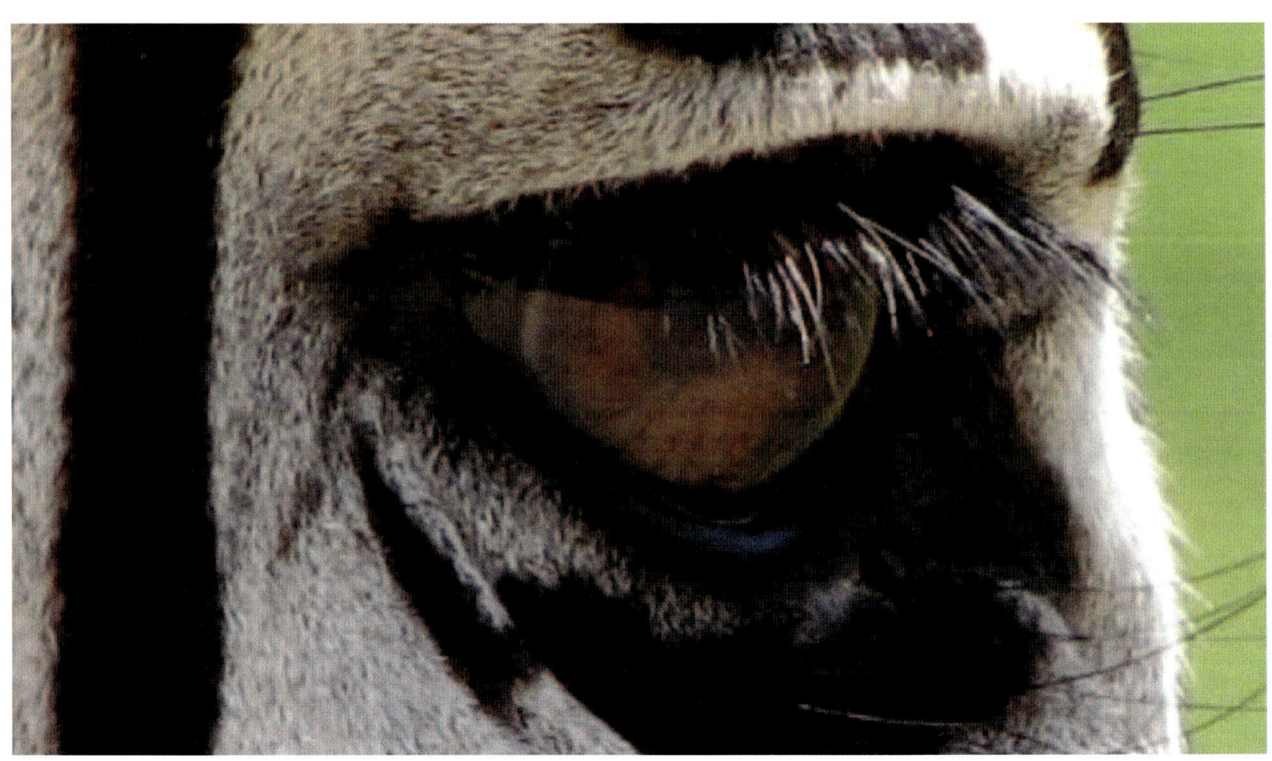

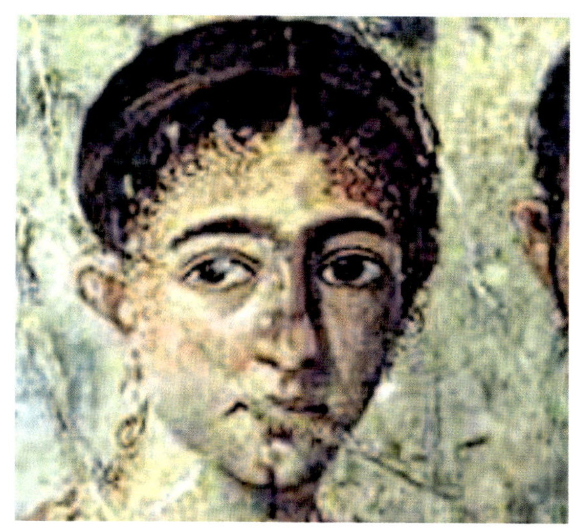

There are many races of people on the earth. Facial structure, however, is the same in all cultures. There are classic Greek proportion of the face, and when drawing a face, you need to follow those proportions. National Geographic Magazine is one of the finest sources for drawing different people from all over the world. Go to one of these websites for a great lesson on portrait art:

http://www.videojug.com/film/how-to-draw-a-face
http://drawsketch.about.com/library/weekly/aa121202a.htm

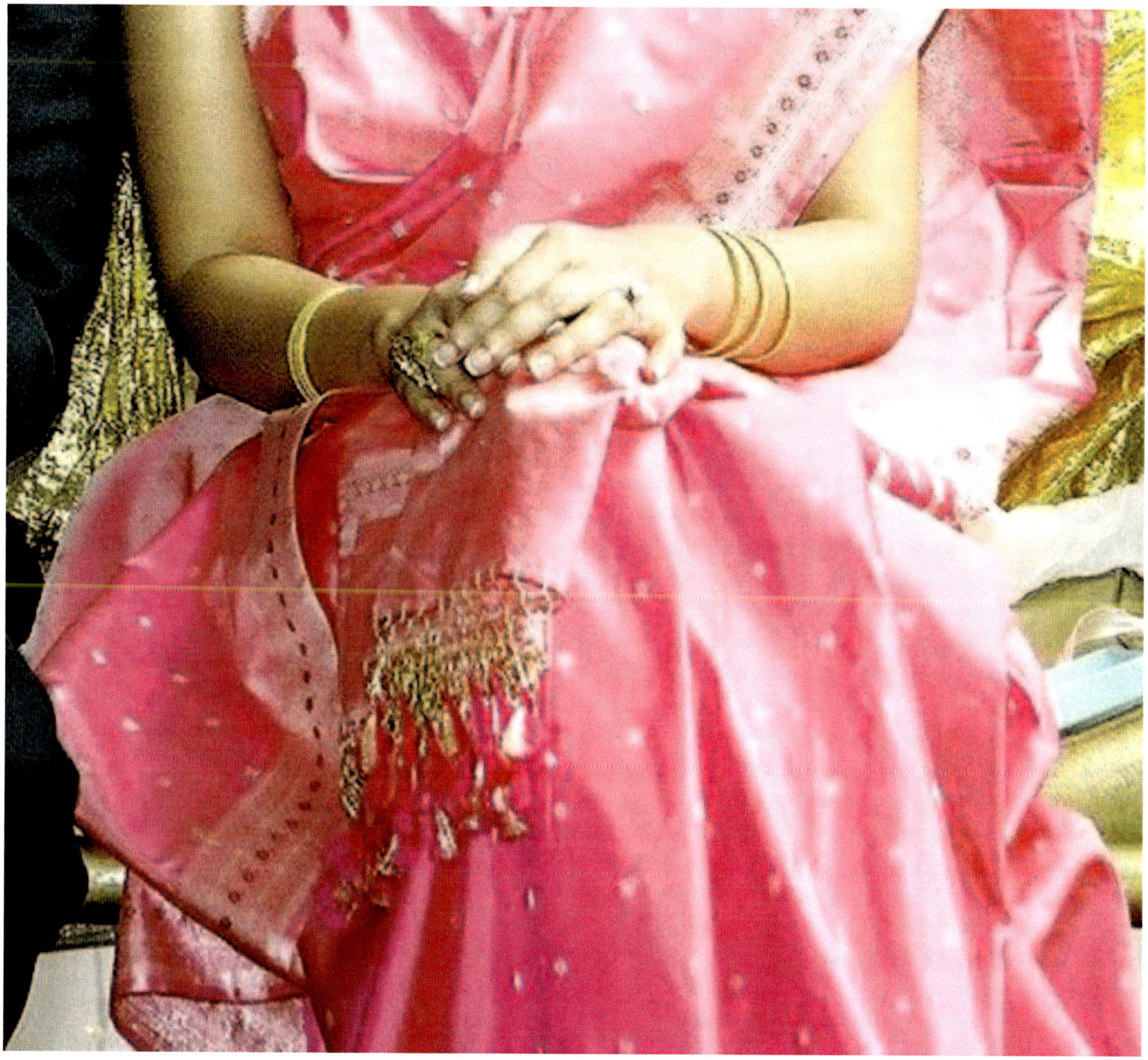

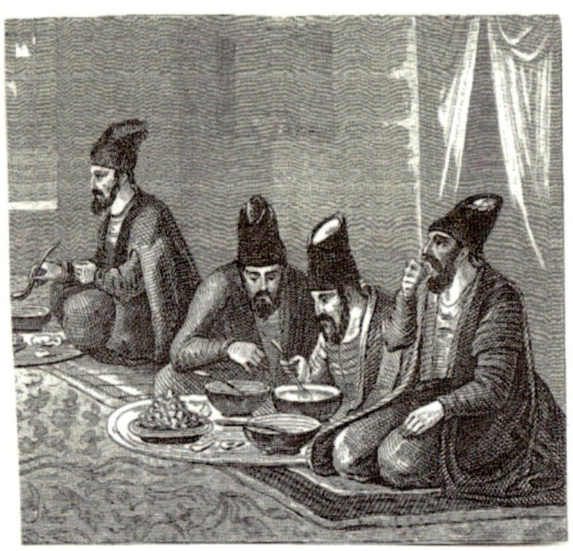

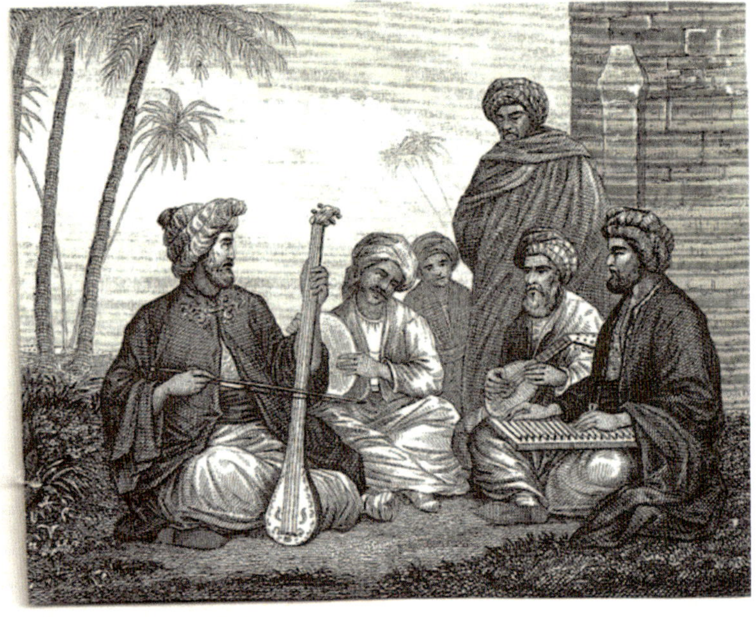

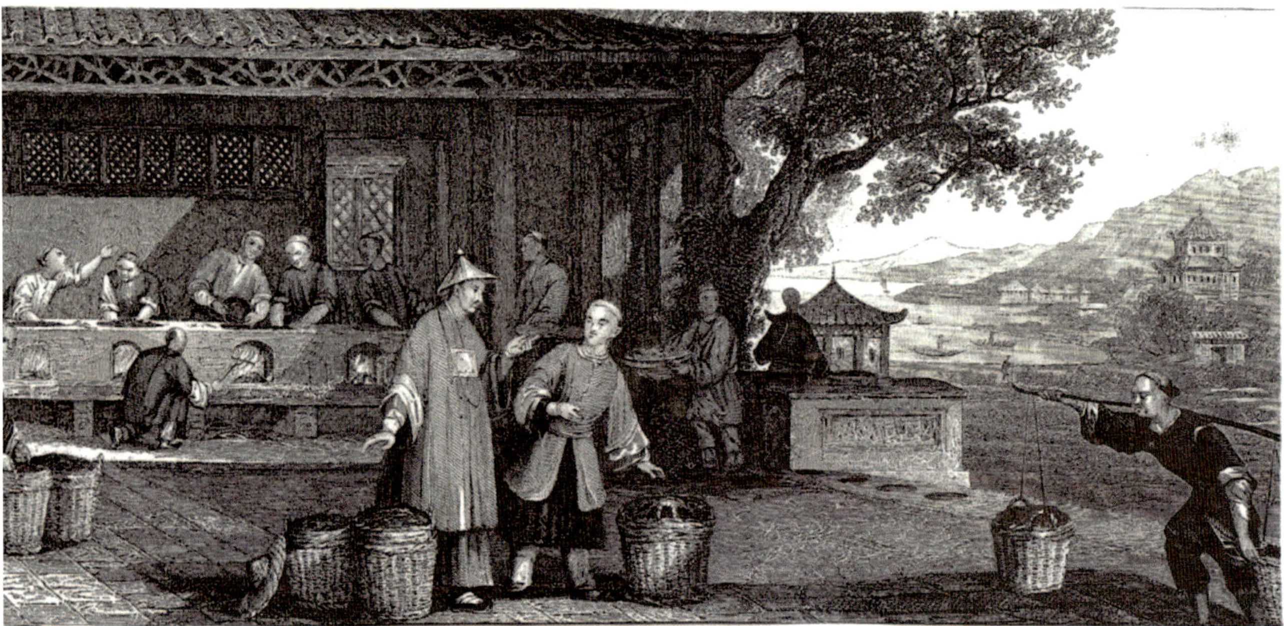

Just looking at the picture above, you can tell where the people might live. In the bottom picture, it is obviously an oriental country such as Japan or China. Look at the hat on the man in the foreground. Look at the pagodas in the background. Above when you see a turbin, you can think India. Draw each of the hats above.

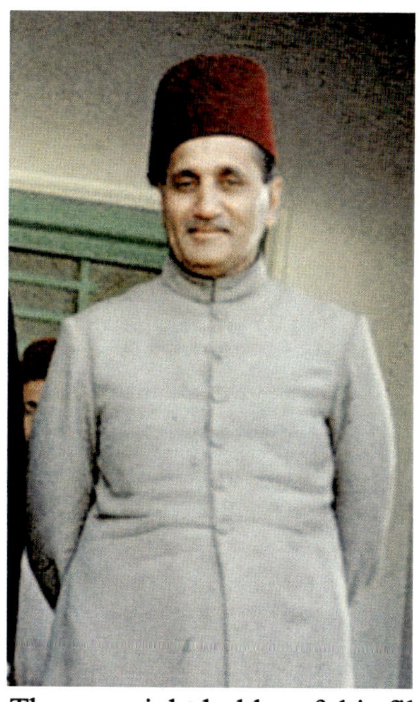

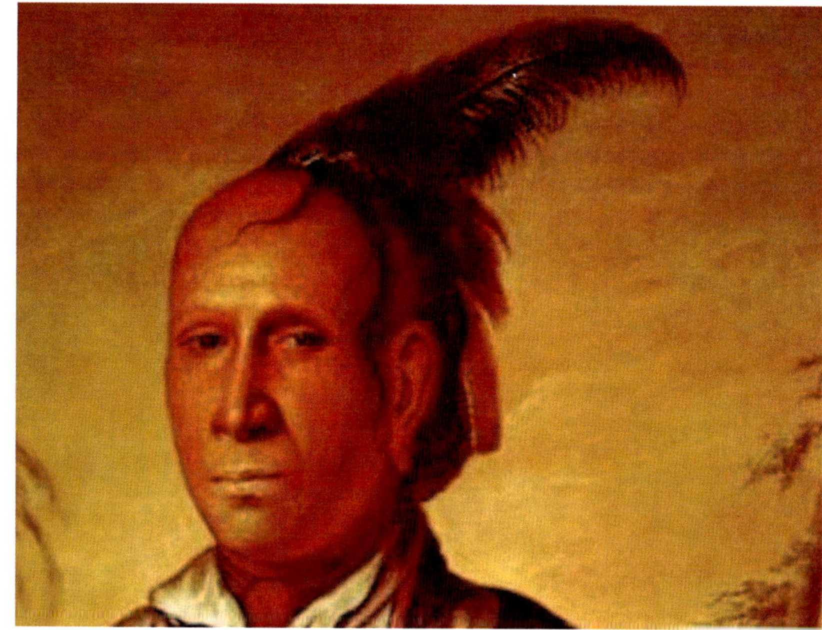

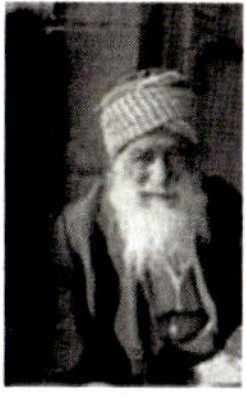

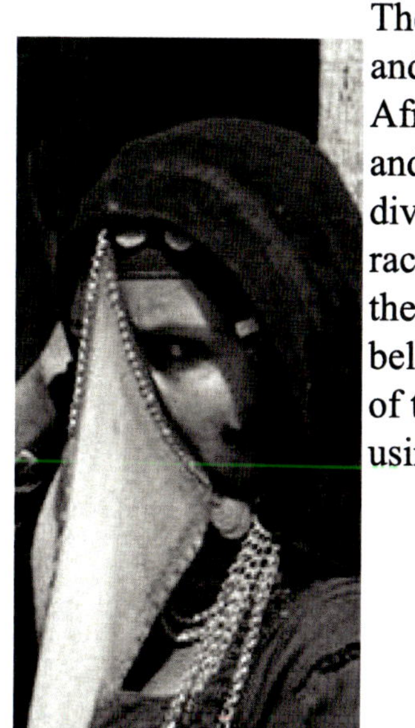

There are many different nationalities and peoples and cultures of the world. Africans, Asians, Native Americans and Europeans are four distinctive race divisions. A member of the Aborigine race of people in Australia is seen on the left. Eskimos are seen in the photo below. Choose a photograph from each of the different races and draw a face using classic Greek proportions.

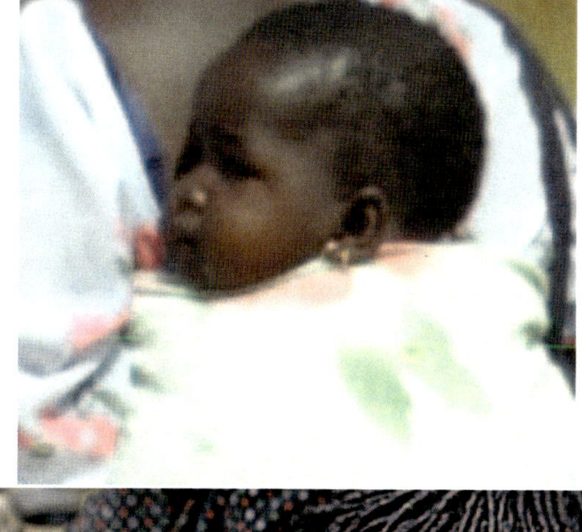

Eyes are from all over the world. See the next page for sample eyes.

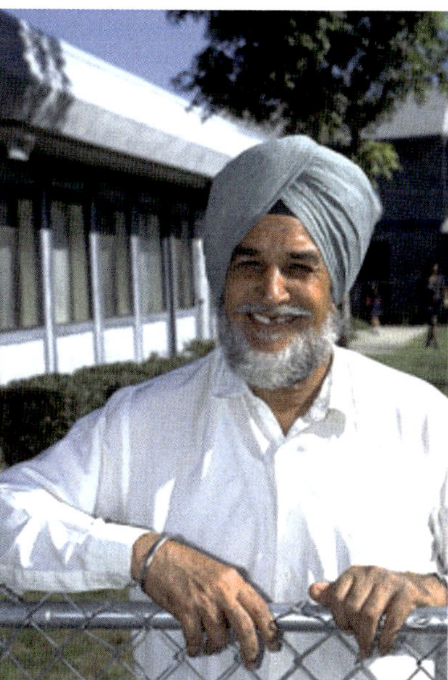

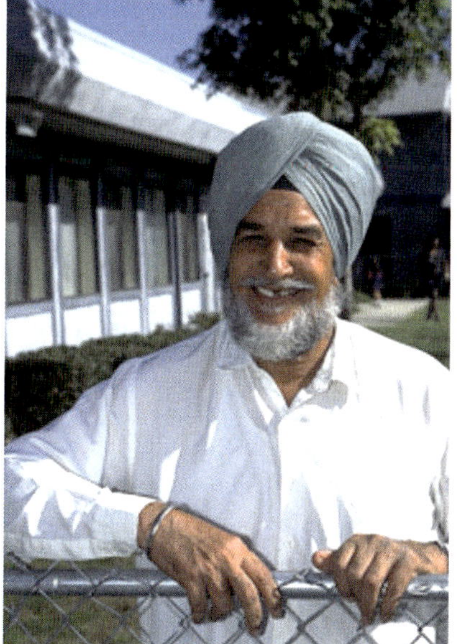

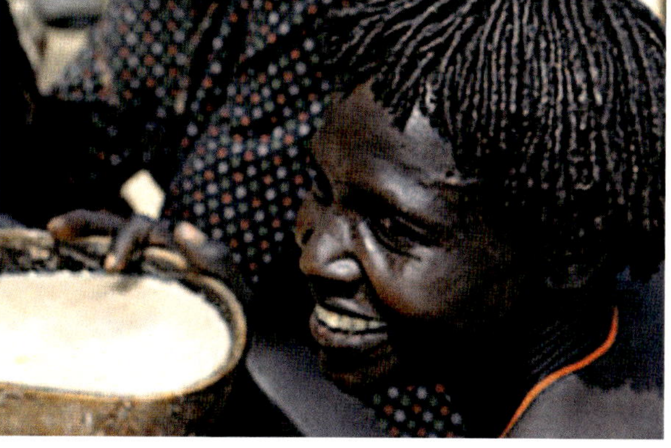

When drawing the eye, remember to always leave a little flick of white in the pupil. This will add life to your drawing. Practice drawing eyes.

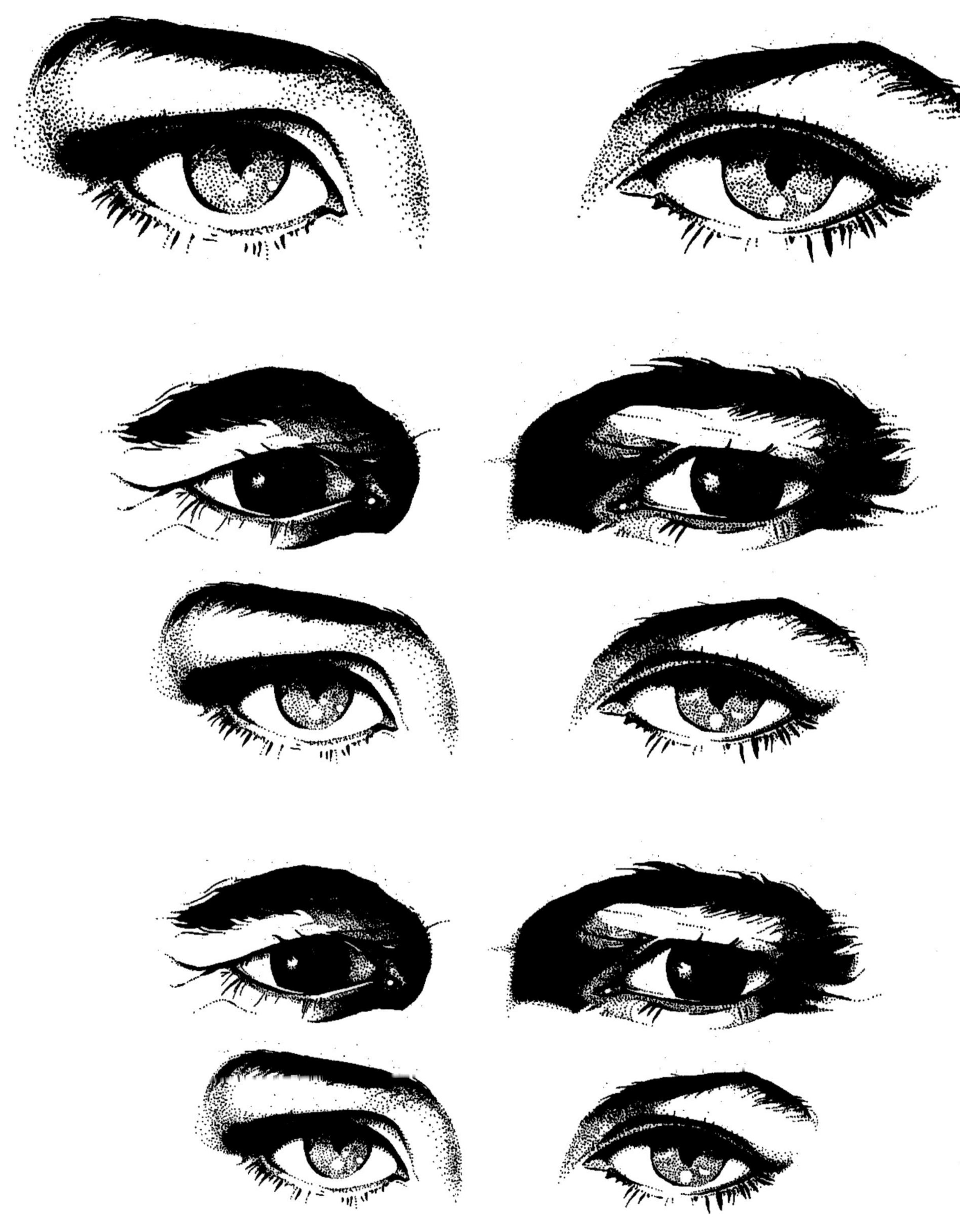

DRAWING THE FACE IN PROPORTION

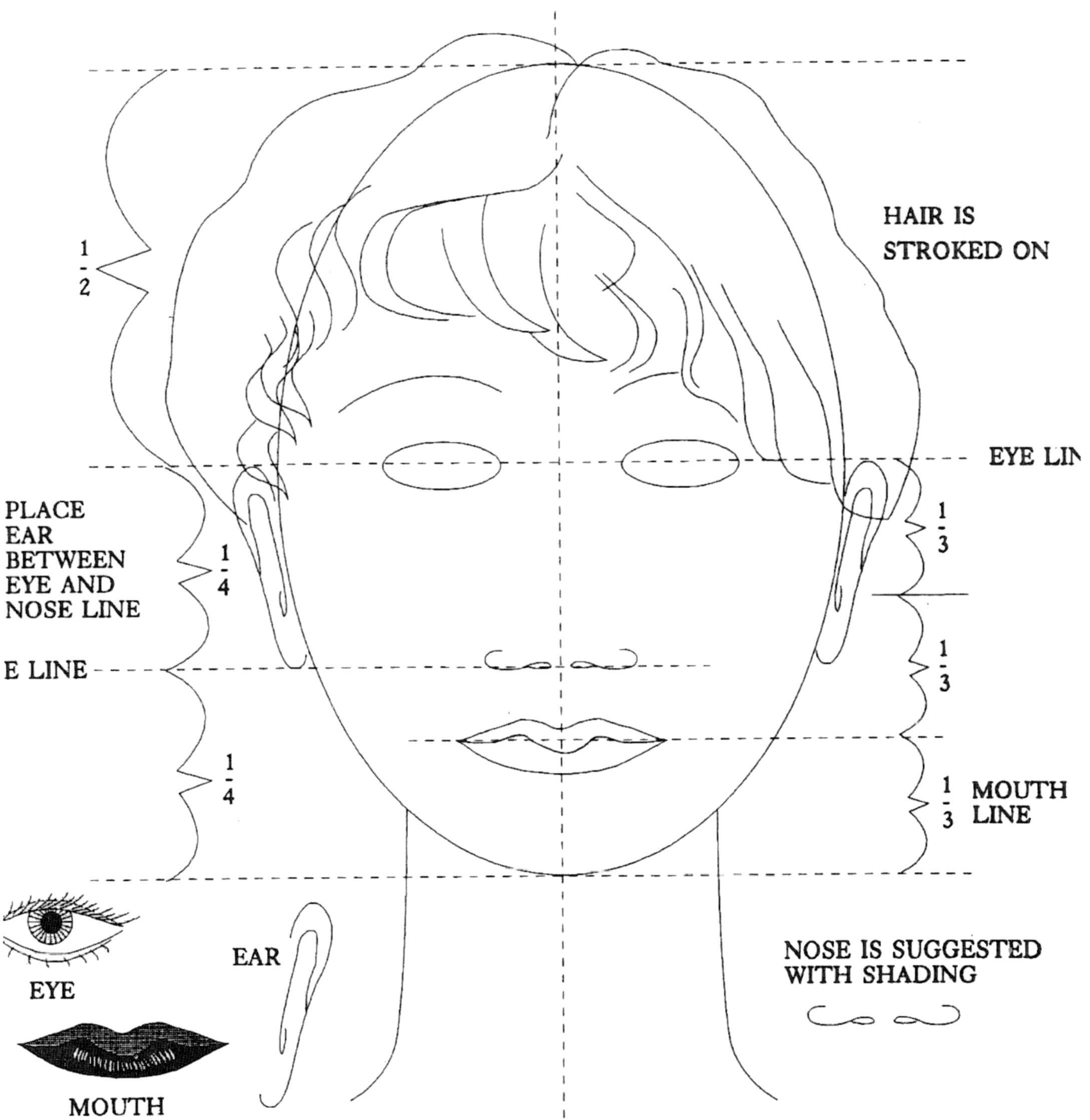

What I would like for you to notice on this young lady is that her head is slightly tilted to your left.

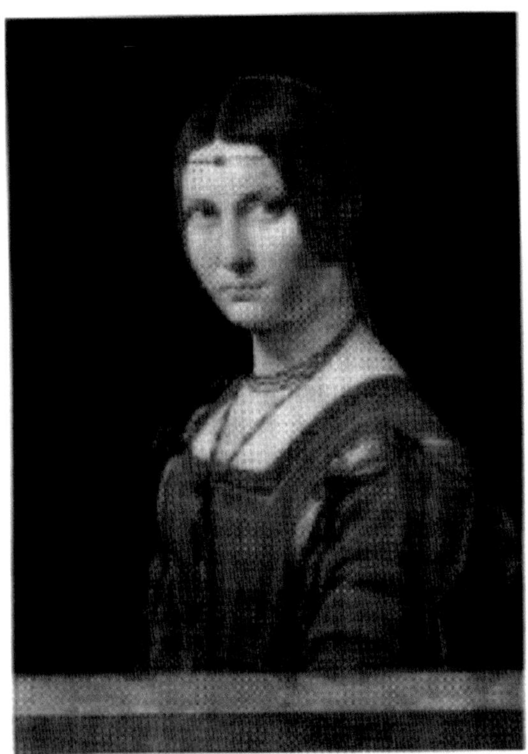

This can only be seen by drawing lines through the center of her eyes and down her nose.

There are two ways to draw a face. The first and most common is to use the classic proportions of the face, (see page 37). (The second method will be discussed later). When you try this first method, the first thing you should do is determine the overall shape of the head. Some people have heads that are round, some oval, some narrower on the top and wider on the chin and visa versa. Some are just plain block headed. You start with this shape, layout the spaces for the eyes, nose, mouth, etc and then look for details that make the differences.

This method of using proportions is only a general outline. You will not often find a person that has all of the average features. They also will have their head turned or tilted as this woman does which makes some of the measurements difficult to determine. Look at this woman. She has an eye's width between her eyes, but doesn't have an eye's width from her right eye to the side of her head. There are two eye's width next to her left eye. All of this is due to the turning of her head. There is an advantage to having a face turned. The picture is sometimes more interesting, and as the head is turned the nose gets more of an edge. This edge makes the nose easier to define and shape.

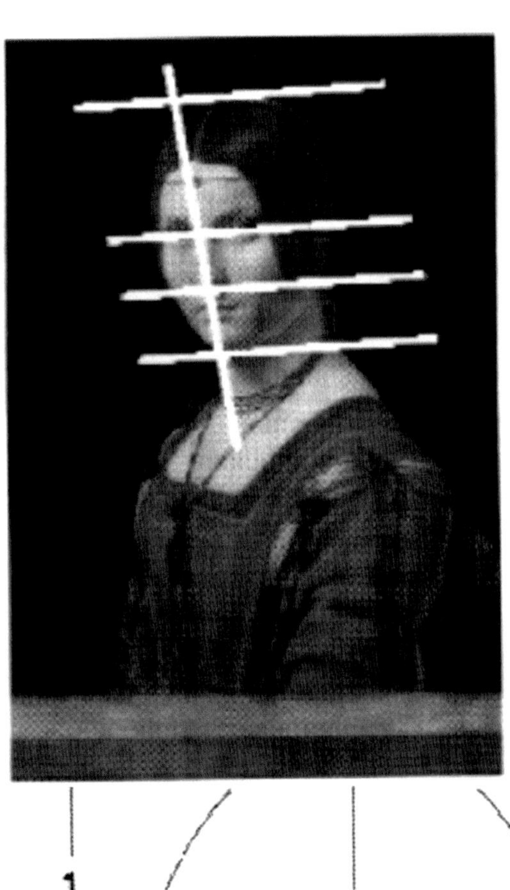

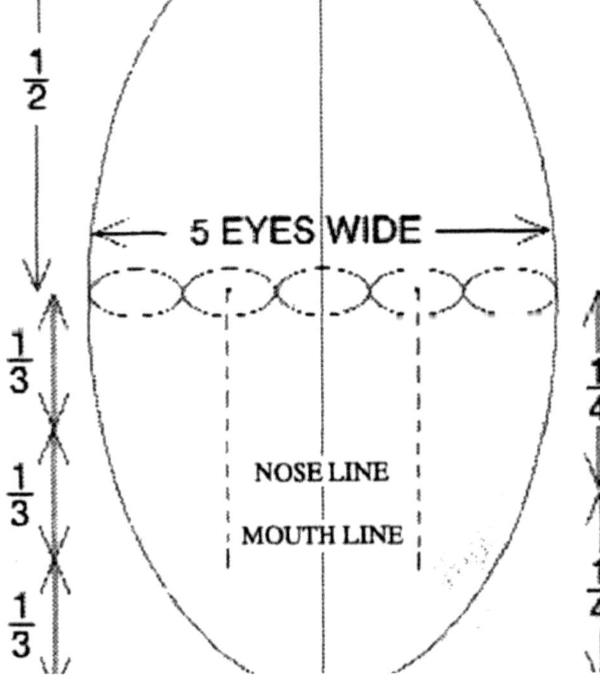

I did this picture of a woman from South America. She is from the mountains of Peru. National Geographic has wonderful portraits of people from all over the world. Practice doing the face in proportion. We are all one race under God, created in his image.

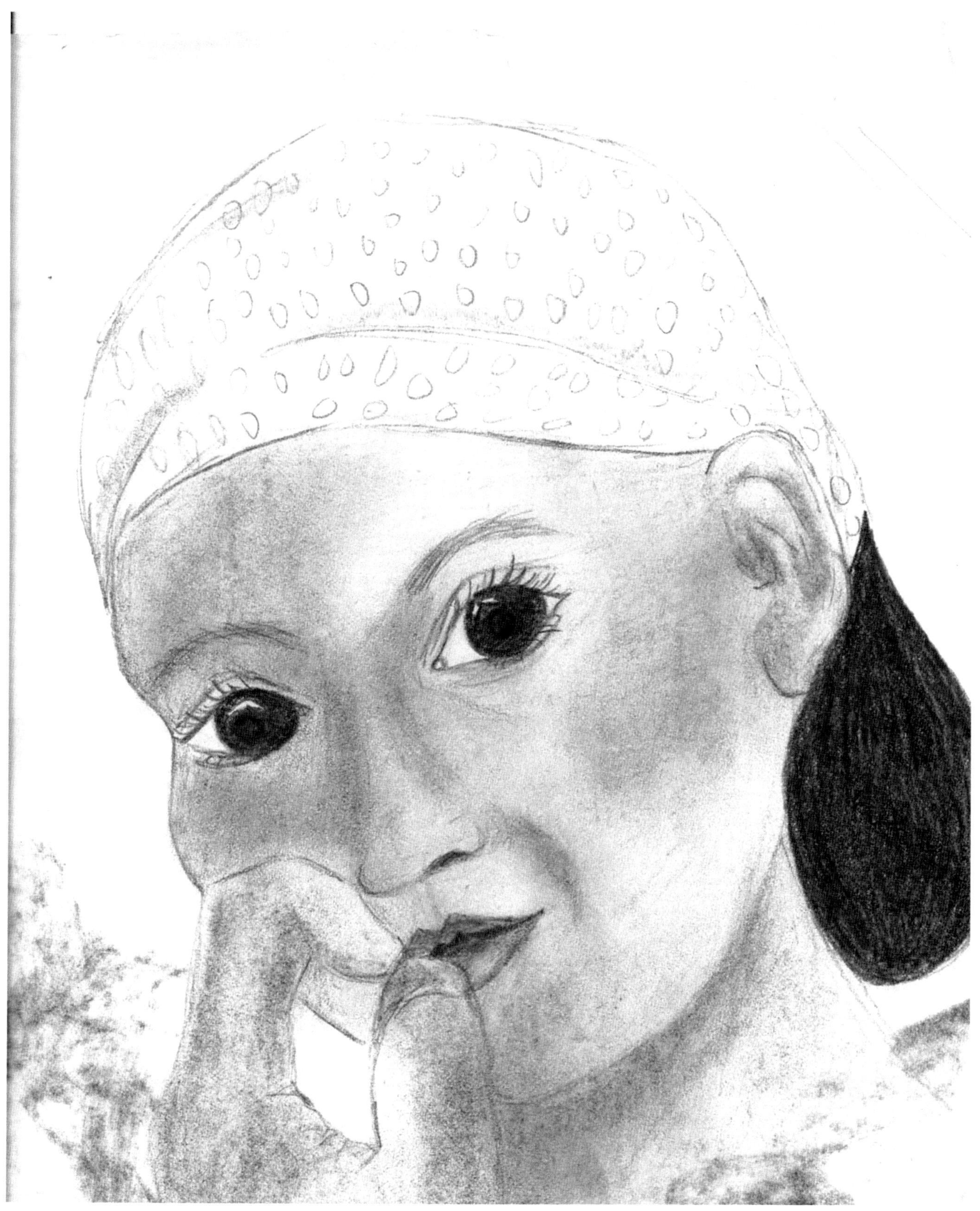

When you do a realistic picture of a person, you want to be sure and sketch it lightly in pencil first and think about your composition.

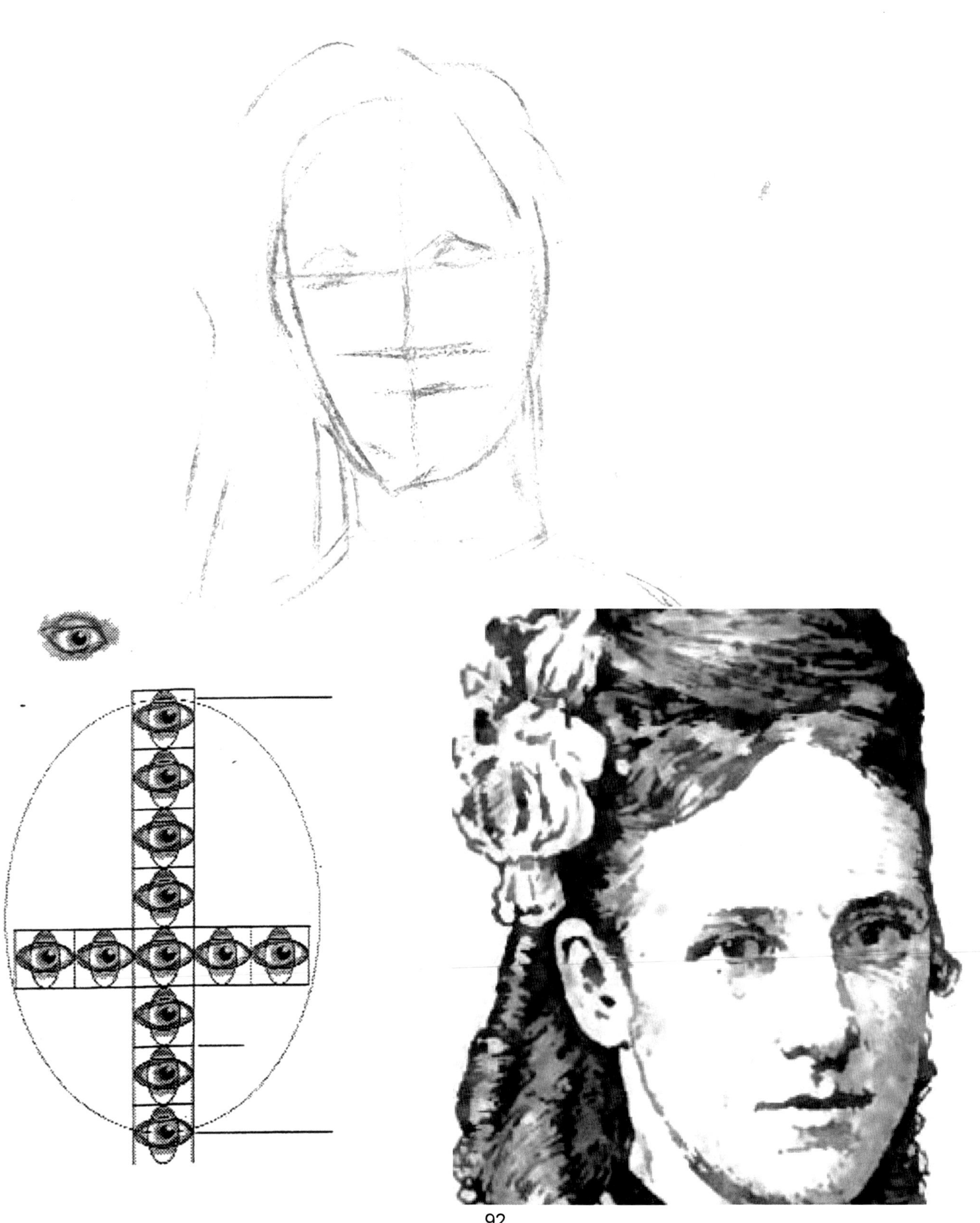

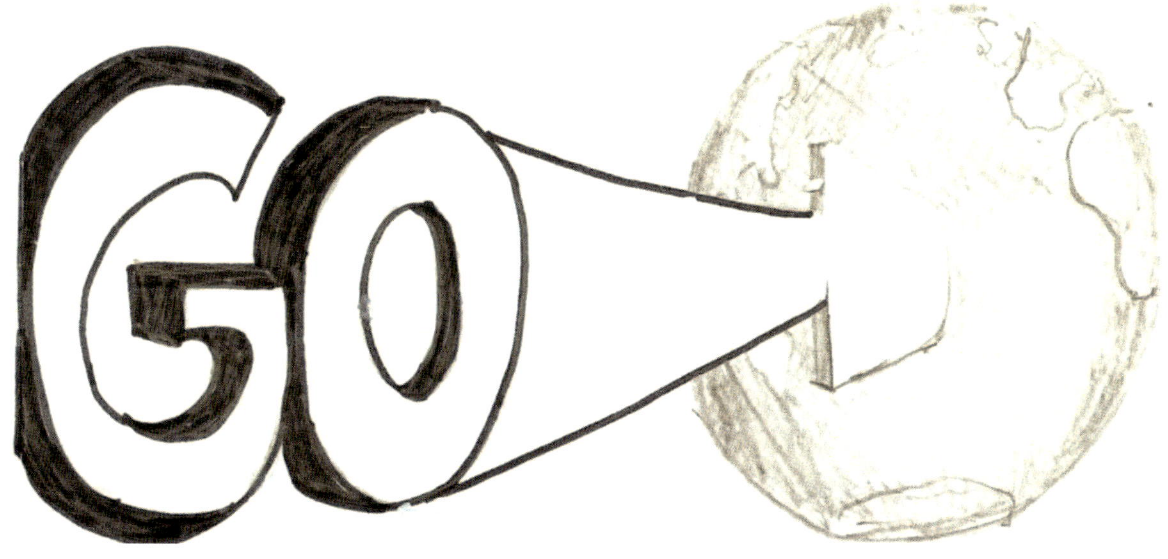

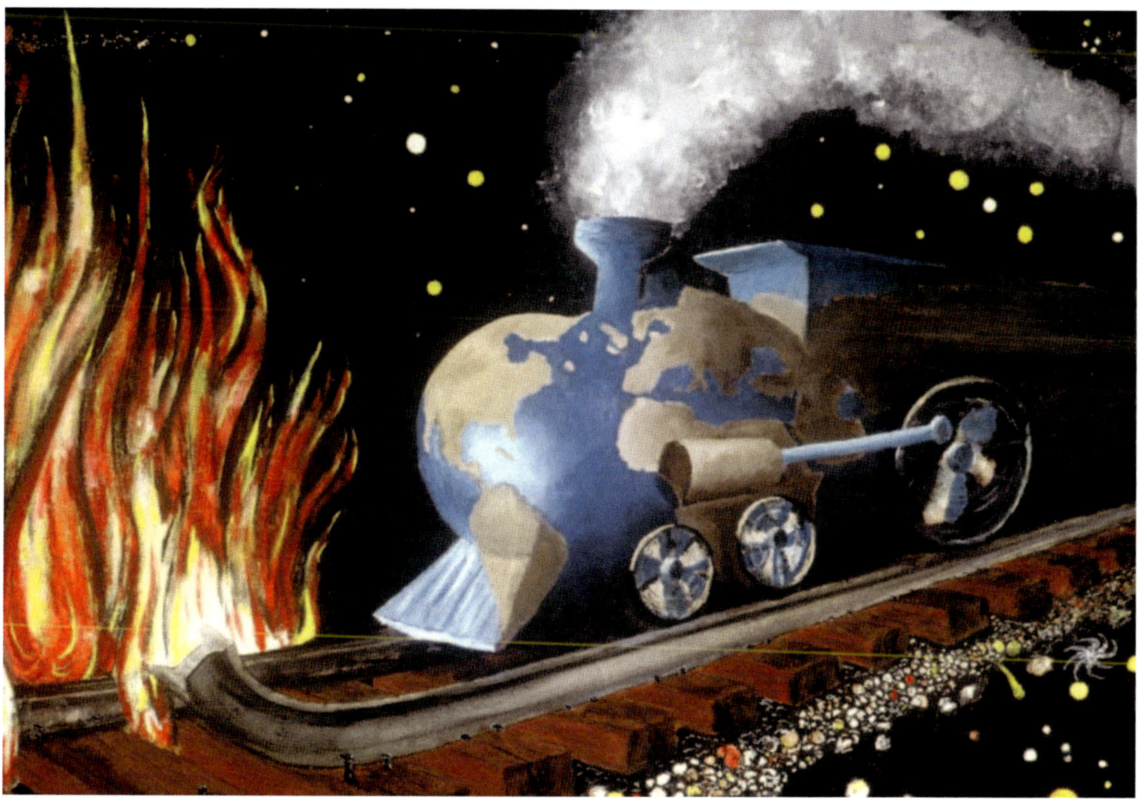

If you enjoyed this book, go to visualmanna.com and order more of our books that use art to support and supplement the core subjects. Email us at visualmanna@gmail.com or call us at 1-573-453-6364 for more information. These two pictures were done by Richard Jeffus. What do you think they mean?

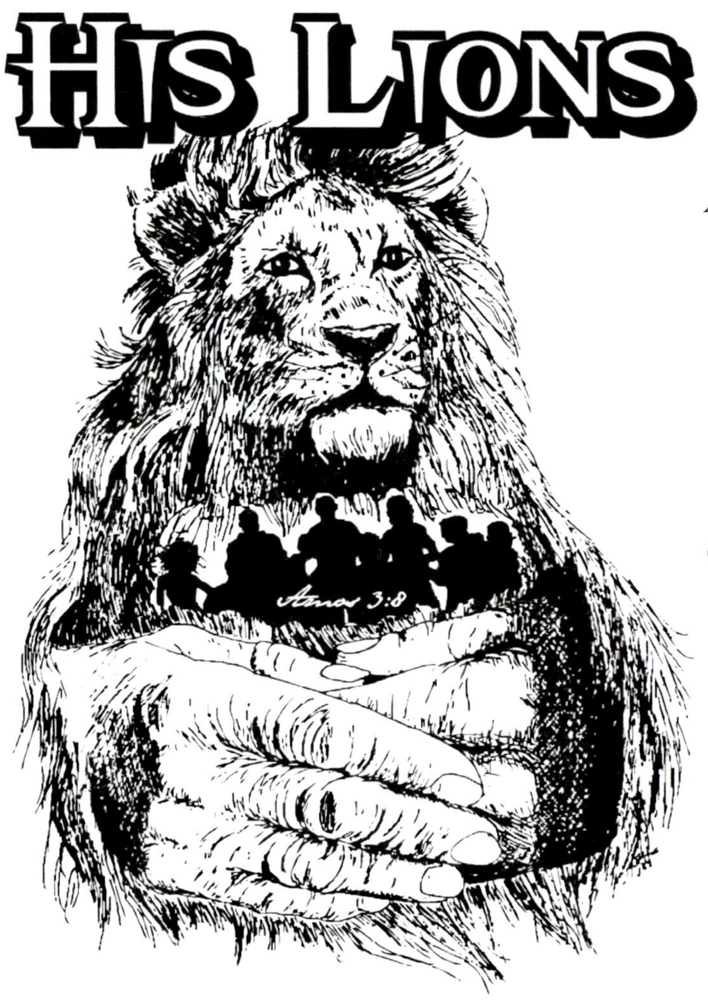

Art Through the Core **series...**

- Teaching American History Through Art
- Teaching Astronomy Through Art
- Teaching English Through Art
- Teaching History Through Art
- Teaching Literature Through Art
- Teaching Math Through Art
- Teaching Science Through Art
- Teaching Social Studies Through Art

Other Books...

- Art Adventures in Narnia
- Art Basics for Children
- Bible Arts & Crafts
- Christian Holiday Arts & Crafts
- Dragons, Dinosaurs, Castles and Knights
- Drawing, Painting and Sculpting Horses
- Expanding Your Horizons Through Words
- Indians In Art
- Master Drawing
- Preschool & Early Elementary Art Basics
- Preschool Bible Lessons
- Visual Manna 1: Complete Art Curriculum
- Visual Manna 2: Advanced Techniques

Contact ***visualmanna@gmail.com*** if you are interested in our Intern program. Students learn how to teach art, do murals for ministry, prepare an excellent portfolio, and much more. Go to **visualmanna.com** for information.

Free art lessons are available at **OurHomeschoolForum.com** and books are available at Rainbow Resource Center (**www.rainbowresource.com**). Try all our "Art Through the Core" series and other books as well! Make learning fun for kids!!! Sharon Jeffus teaches Art Intensives in person for the Landry Academy at **landryacademy.com**.

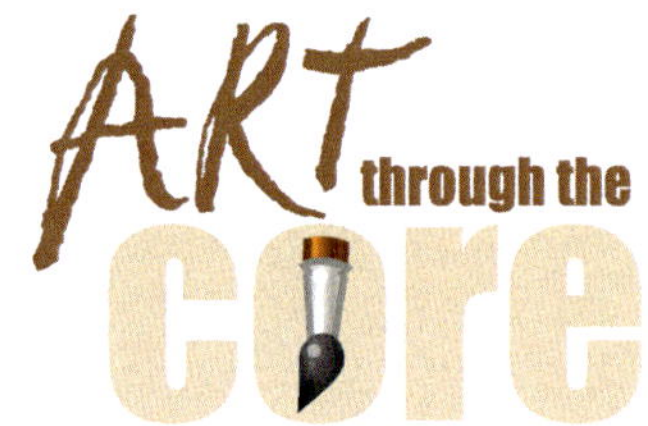

Made in United States
Orlando, FL
02 August 2025

63467882R00059